THE RISE OF REAL-LIFE SUPERHEROES

T0124618

FOR STAN

COPYRIGHT © 2020 PETER NOWAK

1 2 3 4 5 — 24 23 22 21 20

All rights reserved. No part of this publication may be reproduced, stored in
a retrieval system or transmitted, in any form or by any means, without prior
permission of the publisher or, in the case of photocopying or other reprographic
copying, a licence from Access Copyright, www.accesscopyright.ca, 1-800-893-5777,
info@accesscopyright.ca.

DOUGLAS AND MCINTYRE (2013) LTD.
P.O. Box 219, Madeira Park, BC, VON 2HO
www.douglas-mcintyre.com

Edited by Derek Fairbridge
Indexed by Blaine Willick
Cover illustration by Marcus To
Cover and text design by Shed Simas / Onça Design
Printed and bound in Canada
Printed on paper certified by the Forest Stewardship Council

Douglas and McIntyre acknowledges the support of the Canada Council for the
Arts, the Government of Canada, and the Province of British Columbia through the
BC Arts Council.

LIBRARY AND ARCHIVES CANADA CATALOGUING IN PUBLICATION
Title: The rise of real-life superheroes : and the fall of everything else / Peter Nowak.
Names: Nowak, Peter, 1974- author.
Description: Includes index.
Identifiers: Canadiana (print) 20200180649 | Canadiana (ebook) 20200180657 |
    ISBN 9781771622509 (softcover) | ISBN 9781771622516 (HTML)
Subjects: LCSH: Vigilantes. | LCSH: Community activists. | LCSH: Heroes. | LCSH: Crime
    prevention—Citizen participation.
Classification: LCC HV7431 .N69 2020 | DDC 364.4/3—dc23

CONTENTS

AUTHOR'S NOTE

MANY OF THE INDIVIDUALS IN THIS BOOK MAINTAIN SECRET IDENTITIES and spoke with me on condition that I not reveal their real names. In such cases I did my best to verify their identities and the details of what they told me; I note in the text where I may have had my doubts as far as veracity is concerned.

Some individuals are less protective of their alter egos or gave permission to use their real names. Others have been unmasked in other media, court appearances and public documents, in which case I've used their actual identities as well.

INFERNO

MEANWHILE, BACK IN GOTHAM CITY... OR RATHER, DOWNTOWN SAN Diego... our superheroes find themselves in a heap of trouble. It's a sweaty, ninety-degree night and a scowling, shirtless man is bounding around them like a boxer circling his opponent. He's well muscled, over six feet tall, sporting the abs and pecs of a professional wrestler. He is wearing white pants and polished black leather shoes that match his cropped, shiny dark hair. His eyes are glassy, but laser focused—two black, beady pinpoints fixated on the six colorfully costumed individuals who are now backing into a defensive semicircle to meet his imminent attack. The shirtless man isn't the only problem, though. An older and clearly drunken gentleman, with tanned, leathery skin and white hair tucked beneath a baseball cap, is also instigating a fight, threatening on a second front. The air is thick with tension and humidity. You can almost see a collective thought bubble form over the heads of the superheroes, wondering: "How did we get ourselves into this mess?"

The situation arose a few moments earlier, when the shirtless man was still fully clothed. Surprised by the costumed people as they casually walked by him, he swatted at one of them, barely missing. When the superheroes didn't react, he followed them, then again tried to get their attention by attempting to force his way into a closed restaurant. It worked—when they stopped to see what the commotion was, he approached them anew. Using the universal gesture for "I want to fight," the shirted man thus became shirtless. The other man, meanwhile, approached from a different direction, swaying from side to side. Wearing a blue T-shirt and green cargo shorts, he was clad in the telltale uniform of a tourist. Like the shirtless man, he set to glaring at his targets, paying special attention to Grim, the tallest member of the costumed group. With a crooked smirk adorning his face, he began to poke Grim in his blue skull mask. Grim took exception. "Sir, please stop," he said. "I'm going to have to stop you if you don't." The man, undaunted by the menacing skull speaking to him, grinned like a mischievous five-year-old and continued.

A showdown here outside Jolt'n Joe's Gaslamp is now imminent. Two months ago, twenty-seven-year-old Corey Poole and a friend were engaged in a punching game inside the bar, named after New York Yankees slugger Joe DiMaggio, and they went too far—Poole took one hit too many to the chest, then collapsed and died. Eager to prevent something similar from occurring, Grim's teammates—self-styled real-life superheroes who call themselves the Xtreme Justice League (xjl)—maneuver themselves between the poking man and the bouncing man. The xjl members know from years of experience patrolling San Diego's Gaslamp District that bad things tend to happen when such individuals meet. They may have inadvertently created this problem themselves by virtue of their conspicuousness, but it's also possible the two men would have run into each other independently, with a conflagration following. It happens all the time—these sorts of combustible elements have a habit of sparking larger blazes. Just like containing a fire on a submarine, compartmentalization is key.

Mr. Xtreme, wearing a combat helmet and fatigues, ski goggles and a purple cape, tries to defuse the bouncing man. "It's okay, dude, just calm down," he says, his hands up in gentle assurance, like he's trying to soothe an angry bear. "No one wants any trouble, just calm down and let's talk."

Grim, who has had enough of the poking, takes the opposite tack. He grabs the older man's wrist and twists downward. The man buckles like a tree felled by a chainsaw, going with the motion smoothly. "I'm sorry for this," Grim says to the man, now prone on the ground, "but I warned you several times."

The takedown appears to give the shirtless man second thoughts about starting a tussle. He stops bouncing and his demeanor shifts from hostile to curious; he strikes up a conversation with Mr. Xtreme and Fallen Boy, who is wearing a black flak jacket, military fatigues and a domino mask. He says his name is Aaron and he's from Arizona. He and his friend, who had been quietly watching this encounter unfold from the sidelines, had been barhopping in the Gaslamp District. His friend explains that they were waiting for an Uber to pick them up when they spotted the costumed group. They just wanted to say hello.

That's not entirely true. Aaron had indeed swiped an outstretched hand at Light Fist's head as he passed by him a few moments earlier, but no one on the team had paid it any mind. Light Fist, dressed in green sweats, yellow motocross pads and ski goggles, hadn't even noticed.

The older, now-chastened man, meanwhile, needs help. Violet Valkyrie, an African-American woman wearing a purple jacket and sequined bandana across her face, learns his name is Oscar. Marshaling his concentration, Oscar pulls out his phone and dials a number, then hands it to her; his concerned wife answers. The couple are indeed tourists, Violet Valkyrie discovers, and Oscar had ventured into the Gaslamp alone for late-night drinks. Now, he's lost and fall-down drunk. Or, rather, takedown drunk.

A black suv pulls into the intersection. Figuring it's the Uber that Aaron and his friend had been waiting for, Mr. Xtreme and Fallen Boy usher the duo over to it and bid them goodnight. Grim and Violet Valkyrie help Oscar to his feet. His wife tells Violet Valkyrie they're staying three blocks away at the Gaslamp Marriott. Mr. Xtreme and Fallen Boy drape Oscar's arms over their shoulders and help him walk as the suv pulls away. Fallen Boy tries to keep him cogent with chit-chat. "What are your favorite kinds of movies?" he asks as they walk. "Mine are action movies." Oscar mumbles back unintelligibly. The final member of the costumed group, Brick—wearing a black, red and white hockey jersey, camouflage pants and a red skull mask—watches his teammates' backs as they walk.

Oscar's wife is waiting with arms crossed, brow furrowed, at the hotel. She thanks the group and ushers her husband into the lobby. A week later, she will contact the xjl on Facebook and donate a hundred dollars to its registered charity. But for now, the team members col-lectively exhale in relief. The self-proclaimed guardians of downtown San Diego have put out another set of potential fires, dual situations that could have ended much differently—more violently. They may not have stopped a super-villain or even foiled an actual crime, but they served what they see as their purpose anyway. "That's definitely our good deed for the day," Mr. Xtreme chuckles.

CHAPTER 1

FLASHPOINT

BORN IN NEW YORK CITY IN 1916, ALVIN SCHWARTZ BEGAN HIS WRITING career in high school by founding and coediting a literary magazine. He spent his early adulthood watching his dream of becoming a novelist grow increasingly unlikely as the effects of the Great Depression wore on. Like millions of Americans, he and his wife were in dire financial straits as the 1930s drew to a close.

Then, in 1940, Schwartz had a chance encounter with Jack Small, an artist friend who was scraping together a living drawing comic books. Superman had just made his debut and the medium was booming despite the nation's lingering economic malaise. The desperate Schwartz saw Small passing by his apartment building and accosted him in hopes of borrowing some money, but the artist presented him with a potentially better option. Small mentioned that his publisher, Dell, was hiring, which was all the impetus Schwartz needed to give comics writing a try. He later went to the library to do some research. He found a book of Russian fairy tales and adapted one of them into a script. Dell's editors liked it and hired him. His first story appeared in a 1939 issue of *Fairy Tale Parade*.[1]

Several scripts later, Schwartz was at a party hosted by National Allied Publications—the company that would eventually become DC Comics—where a group of editors talked him into writing Batman, another superhero who had recently made a successful debut. Schwartz later described his first effort, an eleven-page story in which Batman and his sidekick, Robin, protect a British dignitary visiting America, as "so-so," but it was enough to earn him further commissions.[2] National's editors liked his work so much that they soon handed him the reins to their golden boy: Superman.

Schwartz was apprehensive at first. He was comfortable writing Batman, who was essentially a glorified detective, but he wasn't sure he could make a hero with superpowers interesting. It was only after considering Superman's alter ego, Clark Kent, that he found the appeal. "There was something necessary about Clark's blandness—that it represented something universal, as though in the ordinariness of each of us there had to be a place of rest, of relief," he later wrote. "I didn't yet grasp all the implications of this, except that Superman seemed to highlight that common condition, because in him the extremes were so much greater—the ultra-powerful Man of Steel alongside the ultra-ordinary Clark Kent. The sharp contrast between the self as non-entity and the self as all-powerful seemed to suggest a secret, private, but universal experience."[3]

Schwartz went on to have a distinguished career writing comics and newspaper strips starring Superman and other DC superheroes, including Green Lantern and Wonder Woman. He also achieved his dream of being a novelist in 1952, with *Sword of Desire*, a psychological detective thriller, followed by two more books. He later moved to Canada, where he wrote documentaries for the National Film Board and lectured on superheroes and their symbolism. His sixteen-year stint with National-DC ultimately garnered him the Bill Finger Award for Excellence in Comic Book Writing in 2006.

Despite his successes, Schwartz himself didn't believe his greatest achievement lay on the printed page, but rather in what he managed to create in real life—the actual, physical manifestation of Superman.

In his 1997 memoir, *An Unlikely Prophet*, Schwartz wrote about how he was first visited three years earlier at his home by a man who identified himself as Thongden, a monk who claimed to be a *tulpa*, a metaphysical avatar of Tibetan mysticism. Thongden revealed that he had been animated into reality through Schwartz's own subconscious will and that the writer had done the same to Superman by devoting so much of his psychic energy to the character over the years. A living, breathing Superman was apparently out there, somewhere in the real world.

Schwartz didn't believe him at first, and he still had his doubts after continued conversations with Thongden, but he eventually changed his mind after a near disaster at a carnival not long after. He was on a ride, inside a cabin resembling a miniature airplane, when the ride malfunctioned:

> I don't know if I can describe it completely. First there was the supreme effort to visualize Superman so that I could see him, at least with my inner eye. I made, you might say, an imaginative pattern of him. ... There was, above all, some greater and more mysterious power that recent events had awakened in me. I do believe that for an instant Superman actually became visible not only to me but to others. ... I felt the fall of our plane being cushioned, then eased slowly down, while at the same time I felt myself bracing the collapsing shaft, all fifty tons of buckling steel, and lower it gently to the ground. Then I found myself standing on the outside of a small crowd that had gathered around. They

were watching people, unhurt, scrambling from the little planes splayed all about. I had apparently left my seat in the plane at some indeterminate point. And I felt as though, magically, I had flown down."[4]

When the excitement died down, Schwartz found himself back in his seat. He reached up to touch his face, but was disappointed to feel his own beard rather than the Man of Steel's immaculately smooth features.

Did it actually happen? Did Schwartz really summon forth Superman to save himself and the other frightened people on the ride that day, or was it an elaborate story dreamed up by a writer who had spent much of his life fascinated by psychological states and religious symbolism?

There's no reason to think that Schwartz, who died in 2011 at the age of ninety-four, didn't believe it. He was deeply interested in metaphysics and saw Superman as more than just a two-dimensional cartoon character. Even if Superman didn't actually exist in the physical world as someone who could be seen and touched, Schwartz had little doubt that he was a spirit that could indeed manifest to some degree. In a note to readers at the conclusion of his memoir, he intimates that his story about Thongden and Superman was one of possibilities, meant to remind us of those moments in our lives that are unknown and unexplainable. "In the face of unbending rationality, we need to be reminded to wipe away the dust that so quickly obscures our second vision," he wrote.[5]

Whichever way the tale is to be interpreted, Schwartz was right. Superman as an alien being with near-omnipotent powers doesn't physically exist—probably—but the idea behind him is real. Superheroes do exist physically by way of spirit. The world is actually lousy with them.

PRELUDES AND NOCTURNES

I'VE BEEN A COMIC BOOK READER FOR MOST OF MY LIFE, STARTING IN earnest at the age of ten with Marvel Comics' *Uncanny X-Men #190* in 1985. I'd read the odd Spider-Man and Superman comic books before then, but that particular issue—in which an evil wizard by the name of Kulan Gath transforms Manhattan into a medieval barbarian kingdom—hooked me on superheroes. It combined all the elements I loved as an adolescent: fantasy, science fiction, adventure, good-ver-sus-evil morality, cool dudes and gals in cool costumes with cooler powers. And, because it was the X-Men—an ongoing saga about a group of genetically advanced mutants struggling to be accepted by the rest of humanity—there was also social commentary. In the first few pages of that issue, a government official suggests that "filthy mutie vermin" are responsible for the whole Manhattan disaster, only to be chewed out by a military commander for his bigotry.[6] The spec-ter of World War II concentration camps is brought up, a continuing theme revolving around racism and oppression that—I'd discover as I kept reading—has defined X-Men comics throughout their publica-tion history. It was weighty stuff for an impressionable ten-year-old, to be sure, but I was old enough for challenging educational matter and the suggestion of deeper substance intrigued me. This wasn't just fan-tasy, where colorful, costume-clad super people fought off alien and other-dimensional threats—there were direct links to the real world.

Over the next few issues, the heroic X-Men, including the weather-controlling Storm, steel-skinned Colossus and teleporting Nightcrawler, join the likes of Captain America, Doctor Strange and Spider-Man in combating Kulan Gath. The heroes eventually restore fictional New York to its glory, but the effects on me were tangible. I couldn't help but snap up every issue thereafter for the next ten years or so. The X-Men proved to be the gateway that led me to become one of Marvel's best customers. Before long, I was riding my bicycle to the comic book store every Saturday morning, eagerly spending my allowance on every issue of *The Amazing Spider-Man*, *Captain America*, *The Avengers* and anything else I could get my hands on. I'd pedal home furiously and have those comics devoured by dinnertime.

Like many children of the eighties, I strayed from comics in the nineties. The hormonal changes of late teenage-hood and early adulthood, combined with the fact that the comic-book industry lost its collective mind by catering to speculative investors—more on that in the next chapter—meant I had little time for superheroes. Rock concerts, action movies and trying to impress girls took over as my preferred interests.

But like so many lapsed readers of the era, the recent wave of movies brought me back. They were a trickle at first that quickly turned into a tsunami. Tim Burton's *Batman* in 1989 paved the way, followed by Bryan Singer's *X-Men* in 2000 and Sam Raimi's *Spider-Man* in 2002. This trio of films proved to Hollywood that there was plenty of money in costumed characters.[7] *Iron Man* kicked off the bonanza in earnest in 2008, and now superheroes dominate pop culture. In 2019, no fewer than eleven superhero movies hit theatres, a new record. *Avengers: Endgame* became the first film in history to reap more than a billion dollars at the global box office in just its opening weekend, making it the biggest movie of all time. On TV, at least thirty-nine comic-book properties were in various stages of production or development. You'd best believe I've been watching all of it.

I've also been reading again since 2013, when Marvel Unlimited launched for smartphones and tablets. The app, offering millions of digitized comic books in exchange for a monthly subscription fee, is effectively the Netflix of superheroes. It has allowed me to go back and frolic in the nostalgia of eighties-era X-Men comics, but also to appreciate the deeper history of how those titles and characters have evolved since their origins in the sixties. More contemporarily, I've been able to see how comics have changed and matured in recent decades to cater to an older audience—those readers, like myself, who are coming back.

All of this is to say that I've got comic books on the brain, which is where this book germinated one fateful night.

For as long as I can remember, I've used a special technique for getting to sleep in those instances when it doesn't happen quickly and naturally. Here's the secret: try not to think about anything real. No school or work thoughts, no musings on what you might have to do tomorrow or next week, no tangents on what you're going to have for breakfast. The real world keeps the conscious mind working and a busy brain is anathema to sleep.

It's better to think about unreality—those things that don't exist or actually impact one's life. For some people, simply counting sheep does the trick (although sheep do exist, they may as well not for most of us city dwellers). For me, it's figuratively counting superheroes. Sometimes I picture them fighting villains, or each other. Sometimes I mentally list Avengers members by the order in which they joined the team, a trick that works unfailingly (I'm usually asleep by Ms. Marvel or so). It may sound dumb to some, but it's relaxing and gets my mind off the day-to-day, replacing it with a healthy dose of nonsense.

This was all working nicely until one evening when these two mental states came crashing together, with Batman at the overlapping center of this reality/fantasy Venn diagram. It started with me imagining the Dark Knight patrolling the streets of Gotham City, looking for criminals to thwart. Inevitably, the fateful question percolated in my semiconscious mind: why hasn't anyone actually tried this in real life? Batman is, after all, supposedly the most realistic of superheroes; sure, he has tons of money, but otherwise he doesn't have superpowers, just a bunch of training and gadgets. Surely someone could pull it off, so why has no one attempted *being* Batman?

The question gnawed at me, to the point where the nonsensical fantastical thinking that was supposed to lull me to sleep turned into a real, conscious, driving curiosity that could not be quieted. I got up, turned on the computer and typed "real-life superhero" into Google. The screen spat back thousands of results, a real eye-opener. Forget sleep, this was too fascinating.

A SUBCULTURE UNFOLDS

SURFING AROUND ON THE WEB TURNS UP HUNDREDS OF REAL-LIFE wannabe Batmans—Batmen?—all over the world. Some dress up like the fictional Dark Knight himself, but the majority have created their own personas. Like comic-book characters, they range dramatically in look and demeanor—from grim-and-gritty types in military gear and black masks, such as Oregon-based Arachnight and Virginia-based Deaths Head Moth, to colorful individuals in spandex and capes like Red Ranger in Seattle and Captain Caregiver in Toronto. Many call themselves real-life superheroes, or RLSH for short, while others prefer to be known as "costumed activists" or "extreme altruists." Some actively try to fight crime while others patrol the streets and hand out food and supplies to the homeless. Some pick up used needles in parks, remove graffiti and even help little old ladies cross the street. Most are inspired by comic books, though I'd later learn that's not a prerequisite.[8]

Defining these individuals collectively, as I would spend the next two years trying to do, is more easily done by underlining what they are not. For one thing, they don't actually believe they have superpowers. Or rather, most don't, with the odd exception (we'll get to that in later chapters). Many real-life superheroes stress that they are just everyday people—that it could be you or me under the mask. The only thing required to be a real-life superhero is the performance of good deeds.

That's their main delineation from "cosplayers," people who dress up as existing fictional superheroes like, say, Spider-Man or Deadpool. Some cosplayers do indeed raise money for charity, but they don't usually patrol the streets—they tend to stick to attending comic-book conventions and parties. Real-life superheroes endeavor to help people in person, face-to-mask.

Real-life superheroes have received a good amount of media attention over the years, appearing in newspaper articles, television reports and an HBO documentary. One of them, Seattle's Phoenix Jones, was even mocked on an episode of *Saturday Night Live* for getting his nose broken in a fight. Amazon Prime Video ordered a pilot episode based on Orlando's Master Legend, though the streaming service didn't end up going ahead with the series.

Many real-life superheroes team up, creating functional equivalents of the Avengers or the X-Men that regularly patrol the streets of their home cities. There's the Xtreme Justice League in San Diego, who deftly avoided a melee in the prologue; the Bay Coast Guardians in St. Petersburg, Florida; the Emerald City Heroes Organization in Seattle; the London chapter of the United Kingdom Initiative in England; the Trillium Guard in Ontario, Canada; and many more. The community has also developed its own support structures. Facebook and the internet in general are replete with groups and websites such as the World Superhero Registry, the Real Life Superheroes Forum and the Heroes 101 Radio podcast, where fledgling do-gooders can get advice on everything from protecting one's secret identity to whether it is appropriate to carry a sword on patrol.[9] Rock N Roll, a real-life superheroine in San Francisco, has written an instructional manual, *A True Origin Story: How to Be a Real-Life Superhero in 12 Steps*, available on Amazon. A number of real-life superheroes, such as RazorHawk in Minneapolis, create and sell custom costumes, masks and assorted paraphernalia for their fellow adventurers. Zachary Levine, a lawyer in Glendale, California, has advised some members of the community on legal matters, such as being cited for wearing a mask in public, which is illegal in some jurisdictions. For a few years, there was even a school in Las Vegas, the Superhero Foundry, where aspiring superheroes could study the criminal code while learning martial arts and weapons use.

This subculture I had discovered appealed to me on several levels. I was initially fascinated to learn that a large number of people were bringing comic books to life. But the further I dug into it, the more I realized it's also a movement whose members are trying to effect positive change in their communities and within themselves. More so than other nerdish subcultures like, say, Trekkies or Bronies, I found this to be a group with something to say about the state of the world, and that was reflective of how society may be failing its members.[10]

On the other hand, I also had the same reaction that many people do when they first learn of real-life superheroes—I wondered what was wrong with them. Are they crazy, or just naive? Are they the quintessentially stereotypical basement-dwelling virgins who just want attention?

It's an easy line of thought to subscribe to, especially given comicdom's long history of being considered escapist kids' stuff at best, or a juvenile, unintellectual rot on society at worst. Comedian Bill Maher offered perhaps the most concisely reductive summary of this view on his blog after comics legend Stan Lee died in 2018: "The problem is, we're using our smarts on stupid stuff," he wrote. "I don't think it's a huge stretch to suggest that Donald Trump could only get elected in a country that thinks comic books are important."[11]

OUT OF THE BASEMENT

THE BASEMENT-VIRGIN STEREOTYPE IS EASY ENOUGH TO DISPEL. REAL-life superheroes, it turns out, come from all walks of life. Exact demographics are hard to come by, given the relative anonymity many try to maintain, as well as the overall paucity of quantitative studies on the subject, but one such report—a 2016 study by researchers at the University of Sydney in Australia—found the real-life superhero phenomenon to be global, with cross-cultural appeal. Participants identified with a broad range of nationalities and ethnicities, including Irish, Scottish and Asian, though most said they were American. Of the forty-two real-life superheroes surveyed, three-quarters were located in the United States. Thirty-two were male, three were female and the rest didn't indicate. Ages ranged from eighteen to fifty-two. Other findings concluded that the average length of a real-life superhero's "career" was about seven years, which I found to be accurate; it's likely that some of the characters quoted in this book have decided to hang up their masks and costumes by the time you read this. The study also found that about three-quarters acted as part of a team and respondents spent an average of nineteen hours per week on their activities, involving both online communications and on-the-street patrols. Just over half said they hid their real identities. A quarter also said they had first-aid skills, while a similar number said they had martial arts or combat training.[12]

The community does count a good number of young, white men among its members, but it's also surprisingly diverse. Nyghtingale, Violet Valkyrie and Hawt Flash of the Xtreme Justice League in San Diego, Miss Fit in Los Angeles, Nyx and TSAF in New York, Spirit Fox in Seattle and T.O. Ronin in Toronto are just a few of the active or retired women who have taken up the mask. Grim in San Diego, Phoenix Jones in Seattle, Captain Black in New Orleans and Dark Defender in

Harrisonburg, Virginia, are African American, while Mr. Xtreme and Light Fist in San Diego and Samael in Iowa City are of Asian descent. Freedom Fighter and Fallen Boy in San Diego are Hispanic.

Age isn't a barrier, either. Jaguar and Master Legend, both active in Orlando, are in their fifties, as is Lord Mole in Birmingham, England. Vancouver's Thanatos was active into his sixties before reportedly retiring. Conversely, Seattle's Red Ranger and Liverpool's Black Mercer are both in their twenties and representative of the younger wave of real-life superheroes who are just starting out.

San Francisco's Aaron Almanza, also known as Shadarko, identifies as gay and Zimmer, formerly of New York and now in Austin, Texas, is transgender. Many real-life superheroes consider themselves liberals, but several, including New York's Dark Guardian and San Diego's Mr. Xtreme and Urban Avenger, seem more conservative judging by their social media posts. Temper, of the Washington Initiative group, serves as a council member in the town of Burien, near Seattle, in her civilian identity of Krystal Marx. Some real-life superheroes, such as Orlando's Master Legend or Seattle's Skyman, are day laborers or students who frequently complain on Facebook about their underemployment. Others are firmly middle-class, like Ikon in St. Petersburg, Florida, who is a systems engineer; Nyght in San Diego, who is a teacher; and Urban Knight, who is an automation technician for a car parts company in Windsor, Ontario. Miss Fit of Los Angeles is both a body builder and a porn actress.

"It's a perfect cross-section of our society," says Peter Tangen, the Los Angeles photographer behind the Real Life Superhero Project, a website devoted to the community. Tangen befriended a number of real-life superheroes from around North America in 2010 when he brought them together for a photo shoot. He mentions one secretive individual he got to know who claimed to hold a position high up in the us government. "When something bad happens in the world, his phone rings," he says. "He's in the situation room advising presidents of the United States. I've got as good a verification of that as I can possibly get."[13]

Many real-life superheroes themselves had preconceptions of the community before they got involved, only to be proven wrong. "None of these guys were the basement virgins I pictured them as," says James Marx, also known as Evocatus, husband of Temper. "I was surprised to learn that they had mortgages, cars, kids and families, and that they didn't play World of Warcraft all day long. Most of them were everyday citizens who wanted to do some good on the side."[14] Nyght, in San Diego, agrees that this is the case, at least among his Xtreme Justice League teammates: "Everyone is a functioning human."[15]

APATHY AND THE PUNCH CLOCK

SO... WHAT'S UP WITH THE COSTUMES? IF THESE PEOPLE WANT TO FIGHT crime, why not become police officers? If they want to help the homeless, why not volunteer in a soup kitchen or work with an outreach organization?

The answers here aren't that simple, because real-life superhero motivations are as varied as those of their fictional counterparts. Batman, for one, wages war on criminals because he is haunted by the murder of his parents. At the other extreme, Superman is a high-powered boy scout from another planet who seeks to spread truth, justice and morality. Real-life superheroes tend to fall between these two poles, or, rather, somewhere on that spectrum. As we'll learn in later chapters, some indeed do it for the attention.

Many take action independently because they distrust the status quo, or are uninterested in following established protocols, or both. They prefer to operate on their own and eschew the bureaucracy and long hours of training that working within an organization can entail. A real-life superhero from New York City known simply as Life, for example, tells of how city officials called him and Dark Guardian in for a conversation after they noticed their homeless-aid activities. The officials praised the duo at first, but then asked the self-styled heroes to stop because they were supposedly encouraging homeless people to stay out of shelters and therefore the overall social system. "We looked at each other and said, 'Fuck those guys,'" he says. "We're going to keep doing what we're doing because we're not beholden to anyone or anything. As long as we're not breaking the law, we can do whatever the heck we want."[16]

Some real-life superheroes simply don't want to work to specific schedules, which they would have to do as police officers or soup kitchen volunteers. "I want to do my own thing, so I can go out when I want to," says Seattle's El Caballero.[17] Blackhat, in Ottawa, agrees: "Being able to do it on my own lets me see if there are any gaps and if I can fill any of those gaps."[18]

Grim explains that race also comes into play. For African Americans like himself, dealing with police is best avoided whenever possible, which is why he tries to stop altercations before law enforcement gets involved. "I would like to resolve issues without violence, without death," he says. "I'm not trying to replace the police, but there are situations where they do not need to be involved. If you can resolve that without having the police involved, you save yourself time and money, you save yourself the headache of getting involved with the legal system."[19]

The costumes, meanwhile, have an express purpose, where the point is indeed all about getting attention. A typical homeless outreach worker, many real-life superheroes say, ends up much like the people he or she is trying to help—they blend in with the scenery, becoming an invisible part of the street furniture. A colorful costume, however, demands to be noticed. "You have a chance to cross a barrier where the average person doesn't," Nyghtingale says. "The uniform allows people to come up and be curious and then it gives you a chance to inspire them and hopefully awaken something in them that they didn't know was there."[20]

This apathy is the super-villain many say they're fighting. "We're flooded with things we can't change," says Crimson Canuck of Windsor, Ontario. "There's too much to be empathic about, so we turn it off."[21] Urban Avenger offers a more direct assessment: "People are really self-absorbed and in their own little world. They wouldn't piss on you if you were on fire."[22]

"I've seen such a disconnect," Rock N Roll says. "There's no face-to-face and that leads to a lack of empathy and the normalizing of anything heinous. You see a horrifying crime, you don't even have time to mourn about it or get over it and you're hit with the next one. People just say, 'I don't give a crap, why should I? I'm just going to get hit with the next thing in ten minutes.'"[23]

Skyman suggests superheroes are the answer—they're conspicuous reminders to people that positive forces still exist in the world: "Superheroes and comic books present hope to people and that's our image. We use the comic book's colorful persona to instill the belief that there are people out there who care."[24]

The image of the superhero is currency in the attention economy, a visible method of attracting eyeballs to a cause. Given the prevalence of superheroes in pop culture, it's no surprise that hundreds of people thought to try this. "They intelligently recognize there's a great deal of power in the costume," Tangen says. "It's smart using that kind of imagery if your goal is to inspire people. Many are doing it for that reason."

Despite that, some real-life superheroes admit their getup is simply a way of injecting fun into charity work and safety patrols. The attention gives them an ego boost, but so what? It's a small reward in exchange for good deeds. It's also a method for escaping mundanity, or "edgework," as a 2015 study by researchers at the Western Sydney University terms it. "'Edgework' incorporates elements of voluntary risk taking and involves exciting, emotionally challenging and often dangerous activities," the study says. "The RLSH persona is engaged in a more colourful, interesting 'second life' than that of the 'first life' or what RLSHs refer to as the 'citizen world.'"[25] Patrolling the streets at night looking for crimes to stop or even handing out supplies to homeless people in the sketchy part of town can offer an escape—the potential for a thrill, dangerous as it may be, that disrupts and enlivens an otherwise boring existence.

There's something to this point. Whether they consciously articulate it or not, real-life superheroes may themselves be the biggest beneficiaries of their activities. Besides having a bit of fun or shaking up the monotony of the daily routine, for some it's also a form of self-help therapy—a way to feel better about oneself. Helping others is a proven method for helping oneself; charitable actions can be a way to atone for past wrongs. Just ask Spider-Man—he only became a do-gooder after he apathetically ignored a criminal, who then went on to murder his uncle Ben. Hence his motto: With great power comes great responsibility.

AMERICAN GODS

INEVITABLY, ALL ELEMENTS OF POPULAR CULTURE—MOVIES, MUSIC, sports and so on—evolve to some degree from being merely something to consume to being something to participate in. They get to a point where passively watching or listening isn't enough anymore for some consumers, which means that some small portion ultimately *do* it. Some people can only watch baseball or listen to music for so long, for example, before they feel the urge to pick up a bat and ball or a guitar and try doing it themselves. Comic books have arrived at this inflection point; for some superhero fans, reading about them or seeing them on screens no longer cuts it. For a growing number of comic readers and movie watchers, it's time to start *being* superheroes. Some who seek to participate keep it in the realm of the fictitious by writing their own fan-fiction stories involving, say, Spider-Man or Batman. Others choose to emulate the characters through cosplay—by dressing up as them and attending comic-book conventions. Creating and adopting a unique superhero persona and fighting crime or helping the helpless, however, is the ultimate participatory conclusion of this strand of pop culture. In a way, it's a manifestation of Alvin Schwartz's *tulpa*—that which previously existed only in people's minds is now becoming reality.

What's especially fascinating about this phenomenon is how *American* it is. Comic-book superheroes are popular everywhere in the world, judging by the staggering box office numbers taken in by every new film, but they are a uniquely American invention that reflects American sensibilities and challenges. They find their origins not so much in ancient mythology, but rather in the fiber of Americanism— the entrepreneurial spirit that has, for good or for ill, driven many aspects of American society since the days of the Wild West. The very founding and expansion of the country depended on individuals stepping up to maintain law and order in the absence of official oversight. American superheroes operate on the same principles—that police forces and the military aren't sufficient to do the job at hand, so they must rise to the occasion. In that sense, superheroes owe more of their ancestry to the likes of Wild Bill Hickok or Davy Crockett than to Thor and Hercules, unless of course they happen to be the actual Thor and Hercules characters found in comic books.

Comic-book superheroes were born in the 1930s and '40s as simple escapist fantasies, but they have evolved since into vehicles for commentary on a wide range of social issues, from crime and racism to sexism and mental health. For the most part, these commentaries have been filtered through a distinctly American lens. The same goes for real-life superheroes. As the few studies on the subject show, some real-life superheroes do operate in other countries but the overwhelming majority are in the US, where they are, again, the product of societal needs combined with cultural manifestation. As New York's Life puts it, "Superheroes are American and real-life superheroes are really American. That's all part of the American story, this entrepreneurial free spirit thing. The real-life superhero is a realization of the American superhero myth."

If so, are real-life superheroes a reflection of American problems—and an Americanized solution to those problems—exported to the rest of the world? Or are they, as Schwartz observed about Clark Kent when he first took on the job of writing Superman comics, a private but universal experience? The answer to these questions, as we'll learn in the chapters ahead that explore all of these issues, is yes.

CHAPTER 2

KINGDOM COME

FORDHAM COMICS ISN'T EASY TO FIND. TO GET THERE, YOU HAVE TO trundle up three flights of rickety stairs, past a generic electronics shop, up over Red Dragon Tattoos. There are no signs at street level or in the store's windows. You have to hope that Google Maps has delivered you to the right place and that you're not going to stumble into a backroom drug deal or gambling den.

The fear of possibly being mugged—or worse—is worth it if it's a truly old-school, dyed-in-four-colors comic-book store experience you're looking for. Fordham Comics spreads across the third floor of this building on the corner of East Fordham Road and Webster Avenue. At street level, honking gridlock, throngs of quickly moving shoppers and hawkers punctuate this as the bustling heart of an increasingly trendy area in a rapidly gentrifying Bronx. Best Buy is across the street, Old Navy is a few doors down.

The comic shop's organization, or lack thereof, is controlled chaos at its best. A pile of boxes marked *Diamond Distributors* sits stacked to the right of the entrance. Shelves crammed with Dragon Ball Z action figures and Magic: The Gathering cards line the wall on the left. A clothesline draped with Joker, Spider-Man and Wolverine

T-shirts hangs just in front of the doorway. Beyond it, a metal rack props up an assortment of random Marvel action figures in plastic boxes: Doctor Strange, Lady Deadpool and, for some reason, Thor's sometime sweetheart, Jane Foster. A shelf with the week's latest comics faces the door; back-issue bins form a perimeter around the store. Several tables sit farther in, closer to the windows looking down upon the busy shopping frenzy below. A foursome of pimply teenagers is there playing Magic: The Gathering. There's an odor to the place that's hard to place—like wet cardboard, but with a hint of cat pee. As one customer puts it in his Google review, the place smells like the nineties.

At the center of it all sits Phil Hui, the proprietor who has been running Fordham Comics since Ronald Reagan was president. Hui is in his fifties, but we should all be as lucky to age so well. He's not your stereotypical comic-shop owner: He has all his hair, which falls a little past his ears with only a trace of grey. There's also no paunch on him— he's trim, wearing a pristine white T-shirt under a black hoodie. His desk, however, is another story: hand sanitizer, a calculator, a stack of Magic cards, a jar of rubber bands and, oddly, a rice cooker. Piles of comic books are strewn everywhere in between.

Hui greets customers with a thick Bronx accent. A *Goodfellas*-esque "How ya doin'?" gives him an air of toughness that you don't generally associate with comic-shop owners. Still, he is genuinely welcoming to everyone who makes the effort to find his out-of-the-way shop. We sit down to chat about the state of the comics industry and he gets right to the point. "Business isn't that great, you know what I mean?" he says matter-of-factly. "It used to be a lot better. But it could be worse." As if on cue, a young man in his twenties enters and asks where the Venom comics are. The movie opened in theatres a few days ago, so the Spider-Man villain-cum-antihero is the superhero property du jour. Hui directs the customer then gets back to explaining his store's status. "The movies definitely help, you know what I mean?" (He says that last part a lot.) "But it's not like it was."[1]

Indeed, it isn't, at least not compared to the early nineties when Hui's shop smelled, well, current. Fueled by the mega-success of the 1989 *Batman* movie and a corresponding wave of exciting new artists, the comic-book business was scorching at the time. Top titles were selling millions of copies each. Stores were packed, the unofficial gathering places for fans of the medium, a far cry from the small handful of patrons at Fordham Comics right now. But, like Hui says, it could be worse. According to conventional wisdom, comic-book shops should have followed their record shop and bookstore cousins into some degree of obsolescence. An explosion of entertainment options, the fragmenting of consumer attention across many different media and the encroachment of digitalization should have meant the end, or at least the significant decline, of comic shops.

They've held out longer and better than expected. The number of brick-and-mortar stores in North America held steady or even grew slightly over the second decade of the new millennium to around three thousand.[2] Comic-book sales in the United States, meanwhile, hit a billion dollars in 2016, up dramatically from just two hundred million in 2000. Comic retailers purchased nearly nine million comics in June 2016, the best monthly result since December 1997.[3] That was on top of digital sales, which also continued to grow. Downloaded comics hit ninety million dollars in revenue in 2017, taking a bite out of physical sales with them. Still, that represented just a small chunk of the overall total. It's a growing segment that could prove problematic to Fordham Comics and other old-school physical retailers. Gentrification and rising property prices aren't helping. As we head into the 2020s, the storm clouds are growing more ominous with dozens of store closings reported in the United States, the United Kingdom and other English-speaking countries. There's no question comic-book stores, such as they are, have been held aloft by the multibillion-dollar superhero movie cultural juggernaut, which raked in more than eight billion dollars at the global box office in 2018 alone. The movies have held the line by spurring some degree of new readers into the fold and bringing lapsed ones back, maintaining sales and therefore livelihoods for old-timers like Hui, even in the face of diminishing prospects.

The movies are also one of the two main factors behind why superheroes are becoming a participatory phenomenon rather than just a consumer one. Hui played an integral role in the latter, but we'll get back to him shortly. First, it's important to understand how superheroes—through comic book shops—came to dominate pop culture and, in doing so, how they came to inspire real people to don costumes and fight crime.

SECRET ORIGINS

PINPOINTING THE ORIGIN OF COMICS DEPENDS LARGELY ON HOW THE medium is defined. If comics are considered to be merely a sequence of pictures that tell a story, then cave paintings or Egyptian hieroglyphs can be considered the first comics. The first superheroes, meanwhile, could be mythological figures such as the ancient Sumerian king Gilgamesh, who battled monsters thousands of years ago, or Achilles and Theseus, those muscled he-men who engaged in similar epic action in Greek poems, the ancient world's version of the summer blockbuster.

Modern comics properly originated in New York at the turn of the twentieth century as an outgrowth of periodicals experimenting with color printing. The *World* was the first newspaper to successfully print in color, with yellow ink coloring a nightgown worn by a child in a cartoon drawn by Richard Outcault. Appearing in February 1896, this "Yellow Kid" was immediately popular with readers, leading to a collection of reprinted strips in *The Yellow Kid* magazine. Other publishers followed suit with cartoon reprints bound in hardcover format, giving them the appearance of proper books. In 1917, the Saalfield Publishing Company released a collection of humor strips with a title that reflected precisely what the new phenomenon had come to be known as: *Comic Book*.

It wasn't until 1933 that the comic book, as we know it, was born. Publishers had by this point figured how to print in four colors and had learned through trial and error that readers preferred thinner, smaller books with soft covers. *Funnies on Parade*, published by the Eastern Color Printing Company in the spring of 1933, was an eight-page newsprint tabloid offered by Procter & Gamble as a promotion: customers could receive it in exchange for mailing in a coupon found on the back of the company's soap products. The initial print run of ten thousand copies was gone in a week, which suggested there might be a market for the medium. It was soon followed by the thirty-six-page one-shot *Famous Funnies: A Carnival of Comics*, considered by historians to be the first true American comic book. Seven more publications followed in 1934, then nineteen in 1935. When publishers began experimenting with genres beyond humor, the boom began.

Detective Comics #1, an anthology of private-eye stories, hit newsstands in March 1937, sparking a movement that would see more than 170 titles published by year's end, more than twice as many as the previous year. Among the stories in that first issue was "The Streets of Chinatown," starring Slam Bradley, a hard-boiled detective assigned with the task of guarding a prize dog named Mimi. Bradley sprang from the minds of Jerry Siegel and Joe Shuster, a pair of aspiring writers in their early twenties who a year earlier had created Doctor Occult, a detective with supernatural powers who is considered to be

the first comic-book superhero. Doctor Occult was soon to be wildly
overshadowed by another Siegel and Shuster creation.

Siegel had come up with the idea for Superman one summer night
back in 1933 while he was trying to fall asleep. He was picturing the
moonlit clouds over his home in Cleveland, wondering what it might
be like to fly among them.[4] Piece by piece, a superpowered character
emerged in his mind. "I hop right out of bed and write this down, and
then I go back and think some more and get up again and write that
down," he later recalled. "This goes on all night at two-hour intervals,
until in the morning I have a complete script."[5] As soon as the sun was
up, he raced to Shuster's house where he breathlessly explained his
idea to his friend. Shuster loved it and the two teenagers—both just
seventeen years old—spent the day bouncing ideas and sketches off
each other. They came up with the now-familiar basics: Superman was
strong, he could fly and he came from another planet.

Their initial pitches to comic-strip syndicates landed with a thud.
"We are in the market only for strips likely to have the most extraordinary appeal and we do not feel Superman gets into that category," read
the Bell syndicate's rejection. Superman was "a rather immature piece
of work," United Features told them. "Pay a little attention to actual
drawing... Yours seems crude and hurried," said Esquire Features.[6]
The character sat on the shelf for five years until Harry Donnenfield,
recently minted publisher of Detective Comics, decided to try him
out. For 130 dollars he commissioned thirteen pages from Siegel and
Shuster, which he released in spring 1938 as part of *Action Comics #1*.
The cover featured Superman in redesigned threads, his now-iconic
red-and-blue costume with a flowing cape, lifting a car over his head
as criminals fled in terror.

It wasn't an immediate, obvious success, which made Donnenfield second-guess his initial enthusiasm. He took Superman
off the cover for the next five issues, but sales rose anyway. Most

contemporary comics were selling around two hundred thousand copies, but Action Comics was heading toward half a million. Unable to explain the bump, the publisher ordered a newsstand survey. The results were surprising—kids weren't asking for Action Comics, but rather the book "with Superman."[7] From then on, the Man of Steel was permanently affixed to the cover and every issue sold out. Superman got a second, eponymously titled book the next year and that sold out too. By the end of 1939, Superman had inspired dozens of clones and other superpowered characters, including the Arrow, the Crimson Avenger, Sandman, the Fantom of the Fair, the Masked Marvel, the Flame and Wonder Man. The superhero phenomenon was officially underway.

Superman's quick success was the product of the medium's novelty and the universality his creators brought to the character. Siegel and Shuster were both sons of Jewish immigrants from Europe who faced anti-Semitism in their previous and adopted homes. To them, Superman represented their experiences—that of an alien in a new land, hopeful of the promise offered by America. He also provided an escapist fantasy and a means of revenge. Siegel and Shuster made the Man of Steel everything they weren't: big, strong, confident and handsome. "They were, in their own way, striking back at a world of bullies that had threatened, bruised and beaten them," wrote comic artist and historian Jim Steranko. "No small measure of Superman's success can be attributed to their explicit tenacity for acting out their juvenile fantasies of swift justice against their persecutors."[8]

While Superman himself was the escapist draw, Steranko saw—like Alvin Schwartz did—that his mild-mannered alter ego, Clark Kent, was the real-world attraction that readers truly identified with. Superman was the representation of a childhood fantasy but Clark Kent "existed so that we might lock into that part of him in our own fantasies, hoping that a superman lived inside us until the right moment came for him to emerge." Comics writer Grant Morrison, in his book *Supergods*, suggests that in the relatable Clark Kent, Siegel and Shuster "had struck a primal mother lode."[9] The world didn't have to wait long for an even more primal mother lode to arrive.

THE DARK KNIGHT RISES

A FIVE-MINUTE WALK NORTH FROM FORDHAM COMICS IN THE BRONX, ON the corner of East Kingsbridge Road and the Grand Concourse, a quaint white cottage sits at the head of a small park. The building, believed to have been built in 1797, is notable as the final home of legendary American writer Edgar Allan Poe. Known for his macabre mystery stories and poems, Poe moved into the cottage in 1846 with his wife, Virginia, and mother, Maria. During his time there, he wrote spooky poetry while caring for his wife as she battled tuberculosis. Virginia died in the cottage in 1847, while Poe himself passed away on a trip to Baltimore two years later. Maria moved out shortly thereafter. In 1913 New York City officials designated the building and its environs as Poe Cottage and Poe Park, respectively. Today, the cottage is open to the public as a museum dedicated to the writer's life and works.

In 1939, Poe Park became the location for a different type of dark creation: it's where Bob Kane and Bill Finger met to brainstorm ideas for a new superhero they were developing—a character intended to be the opposite of Superman. Whereas the Man of Steel had fantastical powers and lived in a bright, modern Metropolis, this new hero was to be a real-world creature of darkness operating in a corrupt, crime-ridden city, relying only on his wits and physical aptitude to foil bad guys. While Superman inspired hope, this character would live to induce fear. He sounded very much like something out of a Poe story, which was why Kane and Finger chose this particular spot to meet. They were hoping to channel some of the writer's dark mojo into their creation. Their character, of course, was Batman.

Donnenfield and his editor Vin Sullivan knew they were onto something with the growing success of Superman. Sullivan told Kane, one of his artists, to think up ideas for new superheroes. Kane went home and spent the weekend sketching, coming up with a character that looked a lot like the Man of Steel, albeit with a few differences. He wore a red-and-blue costume with a black domino mask and a pair of outstretched bat wings affixed to his back. Kane figured he needed help fleshing out the concept, so he rushed over to Finger's apartment. Kane had recently met Finger—a voracious reader of literature and pulp detective novels—at a party, and the two had already collaborated on several comic-book stories. He thought his writer friend might have some suggestions on how to improve the character he had dubbed "The Bat-Man." Boy, did he.

Finger pointed out the obvious—that the character was too much like Superman. To solve that problem, he recommended darkening his costume to make him more menacing. He also suggested replacing the domino mask with a cowl, complete with pointy ears, to cover most of his face. The bat wings had to go as well, substituted with a scalloped cape instead. "It would flow out behind him when he runs and *look* like bat wings," he told Kane. Perhaps most importantly, Finger thought Bat-Man should be a human being without powers. He would be a detective who outwitted criminals with his deduction abilities and who could throw down physically when necessary. Finger put it all together into a kind of character readers hadn't seen before—a hero who resembled a villain, but also a vigilante-slash-detective.[10]

Sullivan loved Bat-Man and made him the lead story in *Detective Comics* #27, published in April 1939. In "The Case of the Chemical Syndicate," Bat-Man investigates the murder of a prominent industrialist. He's a hard-boiled vigilante at this point—he pushes a villain over a railing into a tank of acid, then coldly remarks that it's "a fitting end for his kind." Indeed, in Bat-Man's first year of stories he routinely wielded a gun, and racked up a body count of two dozen men. It wasn't till he got his own eponymously named series in 1940 (and dropped the hyphen from his name) that editors banned him from using lethal weaponry. The addition of young sidekick Robin also took some of the edge off, but still, Batman was darker and grittier than any other comic-book character yet—and he was a huge success as a result. By 1943, he was starring in three comic series, selling a collective three million copies each month. An estimated twenty-four million Americans read his stories monthly, enough to prompt interest from other media—Columbia Pictures got the ball rolling with a fifteen-part Batman movie serial complete with fight scenes, bad guys and cliff-hangers.

With Superman and Batman as its twin engines, the newly christened National Comics Publications charged headlong into superheroes. The Flash, Hawkman, Green Lantern and the Atom all made their debuts in 1940, making it the most auspicious year yet for comics—approximately 150 new titles were published, sixteen new publishers entered the field and total revenue hit twenty million dollars.[11] The following year was big, too, with Timely Comics—the company that would eventually become Marvel—launching Captain America to join its other superheroes, the Sub-Mariner and the Human Torch. National Comics, meanwhile, debuted Wonder Woman—but, contrary to popular belief, she wasn't the first female superhero. That distinction goes to Ma Hunkel, a regular, powerless working mother in New York who dons long johns and puts a cooking pot on her head to become the Red Tornado. Debuting in *All-American Comics #3* in 1939, the meta-character might technically be considered the first real-life superhero.

With rapidly multiplying superheroes fueling a sales boom, the Golden Age of Comics was in full swing.

THE BRAVE AND THE BOLD

FICTIONAL SUPERHEROES OBVIOUSLY WEREN'T ABLE TO SOLVE REAL-world problems, but their collective genesis was certainly a response to one. Many of the superheroes who dominate pop culture today never would have existed were it not for widespread anti-Semitism in Europe and especially in the United States in the thirties.

Virtually every major character, starting with Siegel and Shuster's Superman, was created by Jewish writers and artists. As was often the case with Jewish immigrants and their children, many had to change or anglicize their names to avoid persecution: Bob Kane (Robert Kahn), Bill Finger (Milton Finger), Captain America creators Jack Kirby (Jacob Kurtzberg) and Joe Simon (Hymie Simon), and later, Marvel impresario Stan Lee (Stanley Lieber), among many others. Rejected by "serious" media because of rampant anti-Semitism at the time, these creators had little choice but to manufacture their own creative outlets. "I don't think that the central role played by Jews in film and comics from the outset was due to special abilities or talents in these areas," Dr. Ben Baruch Blich, a senior lecturer in the department of history and theory at the Bezalel Academy of Arts and Design, told *Haaretz* in 2016. "What caused it was the open and latent anti-Semitism that prevailed in the United States at the time. Since daily newspapers refused to accept illustrations or comic books made by Jews, they had no other choice.... The same was true for cinema. This was a restriction that forced Jews to develop a new approach."[12]

Some of the characters and stories were transparent revenge fantasies. Captain America, for example, is depicted punching Hitler on the cover of his 1941 debut. Superman, Siegel and Shuster's allegorical attempt to fight back against both low-level and geopolitical bullies, was banned in Germany after he smashed the country's defenses on the French border in a 1940 story. "Superman is Jewish," Nazi propaganda minister Joseph Goebbels declared.[13]

Danny Fingeroth, an editor at Marvel in the eighties and nineties, saw a great deal of the Jewish experience reflected in superheroes:

> I think the idea of a being who wields great power wisely and justly would be very appealing to people whose history involves frequently being the victim of power wielded brutally and unjustly. In retrospect, we can see coded, disguised content that could be interpreted as Jewish in the stories of the superheroes. For instance, Superman, Batman and Spider-Man's origins are about sudden, traumatic, violent loss—which could be seen to echo the loss of stability that Eastern European Jews had regularly experienced.... These are major themes, as is the secret (or dual) identity—also of interest to all immigrants, but especially attractive to Jews who, in that era, felt that they could succeed in America only if they disguised their identities as Jews. One might speak Yiddish at home, but that was the language of your embarrassing immigrant parents and grandparents. You speak English in public so you can fit in with your friends at school. But which is the real you? So just as Superman would disguise himself as Clark Kent in order to fit in with non-super people, so would Jews change their names or "fix" their noses to assimilate.[14]

Superheroes also appealed to a broader, non-Jewish audience on several levels. They represented fantastical escapism, but also universally aspirational virtues: hope, charity, the triumph of good over evil, an incorruptible spirit. Steranko summarized Captain America, a superhero created during World War II for the singular purpose of fighting Nazis, as a "pure" idea: "He was not a man, but all men; not a being, but a cumulative god that symbolized the inner reality of man. He was the American truth. [His] shield was a visual metaphor for two hundred years of democratic freedom." The character was an American manifestation of an American art form.[15] He represented everything that everyone hoped America would and should be.

Captain America, like Superman and Batman before him, was a hit with both Jews and Gentiles as a result. (That Hitler-punching issue sold a million copies and has a minimum value today of fourteen thousand dollars.) Over all, 143 monthly comic-book titles were read by fifty million Americans in 1942—no small feat, given the population of the country at the time was only about 130 million.[16] Superheroes continued to migrate into other media as a result, including the Superman cartoons of the early forties and the Captain America serial films from Republic Pictures in 1944. By the end of World War II, superheroes were an established part of Americana.

BLACKEST NIGHT

LIKE MOST PHENOMENA THAT SUDDENLY EXPLODE OUT OF NOWHERE, superheroes' immense popularity eventually began to wane. Despite the lofty heights attained during the Golden Age, it would take several more decades to achieve cultural domination, with fits and starts along the way.

Readers began showing superhero fatigue soon after World War II ended. In response, publishers diversified into other genres, including western, crime, teen, humor and war comics. EC Comics emerged to serve up horror stories that pushed the envelope in terms of how much blood and gore could be depicted in the medium. Television's arrival also fragmented readers' attention. By 1953, the craze was over. Superman, Batman and Wonder Woman were the only superheroes left standing with their own titles.[17]

EC Comics' horror stories also became the figurative lightning rod for the wrong kind of attention, mainly from psychiatrist and long-time industry critic Dr. Fredric Wertham. In his 1954 book, *Seduction of the Innocent*, Wertham posited that comic-book publishers were perverting children's minds with a constant flood of images depicting crime, sex and violence. The US government was listening and charged the Senate Subcommittee to Investigate Juvenile Delinquency with finding answers. In response, publishers established a self-regulating Comics Code Authority, which instituted a strict set of rules for what could and could not be depicted in their pages. By today's standards, the rules were unabashedly draconian. A sampling: "Crimes shall never be presented in such a way as to create sympathy for the criminal, to promote distrust of the forces of law and justice or to inspire others with a desire to imitate criminals.... No comic magazine shall use the word horror or terror in its title.... All characters shall be depicted in dress reasonably acceptable to society.... The treatment of live-romance stories shall emphasize the value of the home and the sanctity of marriage."

Not surprisingly, the industry tanked. Publishers closed down as creators fled for different occupations. By the end of 1955, there were only 250 comic titles left—a precipitous drop from 650 a year earlier.[18] Those publishers who were still afloat had to get creative to stay within the rules, so they pivoted into science-fiction and humor comics. Titles starring talking animals became a thing.

The remaining superheroes got pretty silly. Batman spent much of the fifties battling super apes and aliens or being transformed into a robot, genie, mummy or any other inoffensive goofiness writers could dream up. A mischievous baby-like imp named Bat-Mite showed up. Superman, meanwhile, got a dog named Krypto and spent his time concocting elaborate ruses to avoid marrying Lois Lane. The once exciting Man of Tomorrow became the über-dull Man of Mundanity.

At about the same time, the US government was on a science kick. The space race with the Soviet Union was heating up and politicians wanted more kids studying science, which they felt was the best weapon to counter the growing communist threat. They entreated comics publishers to get on board, and the industry complied.

National got it rolling in 1956 by dusting off one of its old heroes, the Flash, and recasting him as Barry Allen, a scientist working for the police who gained super speed after being splashed with chemicals and hit by lightning. Opposing him was a horde of science-based villains, from Captain Cold to Doctor Alchemy. The Flash was a hit, leading National to reimagine a number of its Golden Age heroes with science-based origins and stories, including Green Lantern, Aquaman and the Atom. It worked—public interest in superheroes rekindled into what became known as the Silver Age of Comics. Then Marvel Comics joined the party in a big way.

HEROES REBORN

LIKE MANY OF HIS CONTEMPORARIES, STANLEY LIEBER WAS A JEWISH KID who grew up in New York. He was a strong writer in high school who dreamed of penning the Great American Novel. His uncle Robbie thought he might benefit from being around professional writers, so he used his connections to finagle young Stan a job as an assistant at Timely Comics in 1939. Lieber was stuck with lowly tasks at first, such as refilling inkwells and getting lunch for the artists. If he was lucky, he got to erase pencil lines from finished pages. His writing debut came two years later in *Captain America Comics #3*, in which he wrote text filler under the pseudonym "Stan Lee." He later explained in his autobiography that he was too embarrassed to use his real name because comics were seen as lowbrow entertainment and he didn't want to hurt his chances of becoming a respectable novelist later on.

His life plans took a detour later that year when Captain America creators Joe Simon and Jack Kirby left Timely. Publisher Martin Goodman installed Lieber, who later legally changed his name to Lee, as interim editor. He was only nineteen, but he had quickly graduated to writing full stories. He had also impressed Goodman with his business acumen and his ability to direct artists. Lee was named permanent editor before long, though a stint in the army forced him to take a break. He returned to Timely after the war and continued writing and editing, but by the late fifties he was considering leaving the comics field to get back to his plan of writing novels. National's launch of the Silver Age, however, got him thinking.

Lee had an affinity for superheroes, but he felt they were out of touch with their audience. Many of the kids who had read comics in the thirties, forties and fifties were by now teenagers or adults who wanted more sophisticated stories. If superheroes were to survive over the long term, he believed they had to grow up along with their readers and become more real. The Fantastic Four was his first effort in that vein.

Published in 1961, *Fantastic Four #1* starred a family of superheroes who fought amongst themselves almost more than they did with the bad guys. In keeping with the zeitgeist, the foursome came by their powers through scientific means: they boarded a rocket to "beat the commies" into space, only to be bombarded by mysterious cosmic rays that ultimately gave them powers. Reed Richards; Susan Storm; her brother, Johnny; and Ben Grimm were unlike anything seen in comics before: they could be arrogant, hotheaded and outright mean, and they didn't even wear costumes for the first few issues of the series. Their instant success confirmed the direction Lee was taking with Timely, which rebranded itself as Marvel Comics. The Hulk, Thor, Ant-Man and Spider-Man followed in 1962, each marked by some sort of relatable internal conflict: Bruce Banner was as frightened of his monstrous Hulk alter ego as the military forces that hunted him; Thor was struggling with the loss of his godhood, a punishment for his arrogance from his father Odin; Ant-Man was on a mission of redemption to atone for allowing his wife to be murdered; Spider-Man was similarly trying to make amends for indirectly causing the death of his uncle Ben. By infusing anxiety, doubt and self-loathing into the characters, Lee and his staff of artists and writers made them more real. It was a direct appeal to readers to invest in superheroes emotionally and to see them as distinctly human, rather than as the mythological god types they resembled during the Golden Age.

Spider-Man in particular resonated with people. In his Peter Parker alter ego, he was badly bullied by jocks at school on top of being plagued with guilt over his uncle's demise. He also had girl problems and had to deal with an overbearing boss at work. Unlike other superheroes at the time, he also sported a mask that fully covered his face— an intentional touch that allowed readers to imagine themselves in the role. His first appearance, in *Amazing Fantasy #15*, ended with the words "He could be you."

Lee took the keeping-it-real approach even further with an editorial at the back of each comic. Under the title of "Stan's Soapbox," he opined on the issues of the day and how he and his staff were approaching them. In one notable missive, published in *Avengers #74* in 1970, Lee addressed criticisms from some readers that there was too much moralizing in Marvel comics. His response:

It seems to me that a story without a message, however sub-
liminal, is like a man without a soul. In fact, even the most
escapist literature of all—old-time fairy tales and heroic leg-
ends—contained moral and philosophical points of view. At
every college campus where I may speak, there's as much
discussion of war and peace, civil rights, and the so-called
youth rebellion as there is of our Marvel mags *per se*. None of
us lives in a vacuum—none of us is untouched by the everyday events about us—events which shape our stories just as
they shape our lives. Sure our tales can be called escapist—
but just because something's for fun, doesn't mean we have
to blanket our brains while we read it!

Marvel kept pumping out new angsty characters, including the
X-Men in 1963 and Daredevil the following year. Along with a revi-
talized National, the company pushed the Silver Age to respectable
results. Of the hundred titles published in 1967, a third starred superheroes, many of which pulled in per-issue sales of a couple hundred
thousand copies each.[19] The results were again good enough to draw
attention from other media. Spider-Man got his own television cartoon in 1967. National's Batman, meanwhile, got his own live-action
television show on ABC in 1966. Premiering on January 12, it was a phenomenon right out of the gate. Half of all American households tuned
in to the first episode, climbing to a now inconceivable 60 per cent
the next night to see whether Batman could save Robin from a
seemingly inescapable death trap set by the Riddler. (Holy spoilers,
Batman: he did!)[20]

Reinventing the Dark Knight as colorful sixties camp, the show
kicked off a veritable Batmania. Ratings in the first season were huge,
prompting monthly sales of Batman comics to surge into million-
copy territory, a level not seen since the forties. ABC and National,

meanwhile, soaked up the spoils of seventy million dollars in Bat-merchandise sold. Not bad, considering Marvel's more grounded direction. The *Batman* TV show—with its "Zap!" and "Pow!" visualized sound effects, cheesy dialogue and disco-dancing Caped Crusader—was as unrealistic as you could get, a point of consternation among old-school fans who remembered him as a pulp noir vigilante. But its success was key in bringing superheroes further into the mainstream. Comic books had arrived at a point where they could successfully parody and satirize themselves, which broadened the medium's appeal. It was simultaneously okay to take superheroes seriously, but also not seriously at all.

This first wave of Batmania was ultimately short-lived, as was the Silver Age of Comics. Ratings fell in the second and third seasons and took comic-book sales with them. ABC canceled the show in 1968 and supermarkets stopped stocking low–profit margin comic books before the decade was through. The future looked bleak as the industry headed back in the direction of the dark Wertham era.

It wasn't all gloom, though, as the Silver Age and the *Batman* TV show both sowed seeds that would ultimately bear fruit. The TV show tantalized the entertainment industry with a taste of what these characters could do when transposed from the printed page into larger visual media. Meanwhile, by shifting the superhero genre toward realism, Marvel encouraged readers to put themselves in characters' shoes.

AGE OF APOCALYPSE

THE SEVENTIES SAW THE COMICS INDUSTRY SHRINK INWARD. WITH overall circulation and the number of titles contracting, publishers reoriented their efforts toward pleasing hard-core fans—those who fondly remembered Batman throwing villains into tubs of acid.

Seeing Marvel's characters succeeding on the basis of their individual personality disorders, DC's editors—the company formerly known as National Allied Publications finally officially became DC Comics in 1977—followed suit.[21] Batman, they decided, wasn't motivated by altruism, but rather by obsession. His stories and opponents grew more psychologically complex to reflect the new approach. Robin, that element of upbeat color introduced in 1940 to soften Batman's harder edges, was shipped off to college and banished from the newer, darker Dark Knight's pages.

Society had also changed. The sixties had washed the country with a wave of sex, drugs and rock 'n' roll, loosening up pop culture in the process. Publishers increasingly looked at the Wertham-inspired Comics Code as an anachronism at best, or censorship at worst. As it had done the previous decade with its anti-communism efforts, the US government again wanted to enlist publishers' pipelines to young readers for its nascent war on drugs. Lee relayed a request from the Nixon administration to publish an anti-drug story in one of his books to the lawyers running the Comics Code Authority, but got a rejection in response. The request sparked debate among the organization's members, who ultimately decided to update the code later in 1971. Lee didn't want to wait, so in May 1971 he published *Amazing Spider-Man #96* without the authority's seal of approval. The issue saw Spider-Man save a teenager, who was high on drugs, from killing himself. The next instalment had Peter Parker's friend Harry Osborn overdose on illegal pills. DC followed a few months later with *Green Lantern/Green Arrow #85*, where it was revealed that Green Arrow's sidekick, Speedy, was a heroin addict. In both cases, the storylines treated drugs as a villainous scourge: "DC attacks youth's greatest problem... drugs!" read the cover of *Green Lantern/Green Arrow*. The Comics Code Authority finally lifted many of the more restrictive terms later that year: criminals could again be depicted sympathetically on occasion and drugs could be incorporated into storylines as long as they weren't glorified. The code would continue to be loosened over the years, mirroring the larger growing tolerance in pop culture, until it was essentially abandoned in the 2000s.

With supermarkets ditching comic books, a wave of stores dedicated to the medium sprung up and took over as the primary mode of distribution. These were stores much like Fordham Comics in the Bronx—hidden away from the mainstream public or unwelcoming to it, where hard-core fans could gather to buy their weekly stash and discuss the finer points of characters and stories: Was the Silver Age Flash superior to the Golden Age version, and how did Superman shave, anyway? Superheroes subsisted in mainstream media through the seventies and early eighties largely through Saturday morning cartoons such as DC's *Super Friends* and Marvel's *Spider-Man and His Amazing Friends*, and decently received but not blockbuster shows such as *Wonder Woman* and *The Incredible Hulk*. During this era, superheroes were either nerd stuff or kids' stuff. They were far away from pop-culture domination.

Warner Bros., which had acquired DC in 1967, wasn't content with that fact. In 1978, *Superman* became the first live-action blockbuster superhero movie of the modern age. Directed by Richard Donner and starring Christopher Reeve, the film grossed three hundred million dollars worldwide and netted a trio of Oscar nominations. Its tagline was "You'll believe a man can fly," but it also proved that superhero movies could too. As critic Roger Ebert later wrote, the movie succeeded on the basis of the filmmakers pulling off a fine balance of satire, action and rom-com: "The film came in an era of Disaster Movies that took themselves with dreadful earnestness, and they knew the essential element of Superman was fun."[22]

As with the genesis of superhero comic books forty years earlier, Batman followed Superman into the film pipeline. The Caped

Crusader got caught in development limbo, however, as internal debate raged over how to portray the character. Some executives within Warner wanted a continuation of the campy approach of the sixties TV show while another faction pulled for the darker tone reestablished in the comics of the time. The latter won out, but not before Warner pumped out another trio of Superman movies, to diminishing returns. The long-awaited *Batman* movie finally hit theatres in 1989, launching a second wave of Batmania.

THE DARK KNIGHT RETURNS

DIRECTED BY TIM BURTON AND STARRING MICHAEL KEATON, *BATMAN* became something of a *Star Wars*–level phenomenon. Critics praised Burton's dark tone and visuals and gushed over Jack Nicholson's over-the-top performance as the maniacal Joker. The film dominated the box office, with more than four hundred million dollars grossed globally, and won an Oscar for art direction. Perhaps more importantly, it moved more than 1.5 billion dollars in merchandise: toys, games, memorabilia, lunch boxes and anything else you could slap a Batman logo on. The simple black T-shirt with said logo became trendy. Prince's soundtrack for the movie sat at number one on the Billboard charts for six weeks; MTV played that god-awful "Batdance" video in heavy rotation. *Batman: The Animated Series* followed in 1992 and became the top-rated cartoon in America. Warner also churned out a trio of sequels, with the four movies grossing an overall 1.2 billion dollars in global box office.[23] All told, the 1989 film kickstarted what would become one of the richest pop culture franchises in history, with an estimated value of twenty-five billion dollars as of 2019.

Batman's post-1989 popularity and ubiquity was as much a reflection of the times as anything else. The end of the Cold War, the beginning of the Gulf War and the corresponding economic recession injected uncertainty and turmoil into the public zeitgeist, at least as far as American audiences were concerned. The color and excesses of eighties pop culture gave way to darker sensibilities; hence the rise of grunge and alternative music. Movie theaters, meanwhile, said goodbye to the Goonies and Marty McFly and hello to the Terminator and Hannibal Lecter. Batman was the perfect, well-timed tonic for the average movie-goer—his problems, such as the Joker, could be solved through the simple application of technology, scowling and fisticuffs. There were no patriotic chants of "U-S-A!" in that first *Batman* movie, but there might as well have been. The bat logo that everyone was wearing on their T-shirts and lunch boxes bore no aesthetic resemblance to the American flag, but symbolically they were one and the same.

Marvel tried to get in on Batman's runaway success with its own films, but lacking the heft and expertise of a major film studio parent, its attempts were... less successful. *The Punisher* and *Captain America* were bad enough to warrant straight-to-video releases in 1989 and 1992, respectively, which was more than can be said for *The Fantastic Four*, an awful 1994 effort that never even saw the light of day. Mismanagement and questionable creative decisions were partly responsible, but there was also the inescapable fact that special effects were not yet good enough to convincingly translate some of the more fantastical superheroes to the screen. Marvel did have better luck with kids' TV, though, with X-Men and Spider-Man cartoons both delivering solid ratings.

The *Batman* movie was a big factor in the doubling of comic-book stores in the US, pushing the total from just four thousand in 1986 to ten thousand by 1993, which by that point were collectively selling forty-eight million comics a month.[24] DC pumped out new Batman titles to take advantage of these heightened sales. Marvel jumped in with a wave of hot new artists including Todd McFarlane, Jim Lee and Rob Liefeld. Taking the reins of Spider-Man, the X-Men and New Mutants, the newcomers transformed the brooding, introspective stories of the seventies and eighties into eye-popping action-packed spectacles. Male characters wore costumes sporting dozens of pouches of questionable usefulness and toted implausibly giant guns. The women, meanwhile, thrust their impossibly large breasts toward readers in ridiculous cheesecake poses. But hey, sales exploded. *Spider-Man #1*, written and drawn by McFarlane and published in 1991, sold 2.6 million copies, followed a few months later by Liefeld's *X-Force #1*, which sold 3.9 million. They were both left in the dust by Lee's *X-Men #1*, released in August, which sold eight million copies, making it the best selling comic book of all time.

There was just one problem: many of those sales weren't exactly organic. Unlike the massive results they had posted in the Golden Age, publishers were depending on gimmicks to pad the numbers, including number-one issues and multiple covers embossed with metallic foil and holograms. *X-Men #1*, for example, was released with five different covers, which encouraged buyers to snap up multiple copies. It was all geared toward speculators, who saw that older comics from previous decades were worth lots of money. Figuring that all these special issues would eventually become similar gold mines because of their supposed rarity, they piled in. Buyers and publishers didn't reckon with the obvious paradox of plentiful rarity: when there is too much of anything, its value drops precipitously.

That's exactly what happened to the comic-book business as the Batman sequels ran out of steam. Speculators drifted away and hard-core readers were put off by the gimmicks and the focus on style over substance. Sales plummeted and stores went out of business at a brisk pace—a thousand closed in January 1994 alone.[25] Marvel, the worst offender of the speculator-driven frenzy, filed for Chapter 11 bankruptcy protection in December 1996. DC's sales also nosedived as Warner's film efforts fell into disarray.

The road to domination had to wait until both companies got their houses in order. That started to happen with *Blade*, a 1998 film starring Wesley Snipes as Marvel's half-vampire vampire hunter, and then accelerated in earnest in 2000 and 2002 with the *X-Men* and *Spider-Man* movies, respectively. Both were box-office hits, thanks in no small part to advances in special effects that finally allowed for convincing translations. Like Batman before them, both became tentpole franchises that compiled massive value through sequels, merchandizing and promotional partnerships. Marvel, which had been rescued from bankruptcy in 1997 by toy maker Toy Biz, was acquired by Disney in 2009 for 4.2 billion dollars. Disney, seeing mega-value in the comic publisher's intellectual property, set to reacquiring many of the character rights that Marvel had previously doled out in an effort to stave off bankruptcy. The so-called Marvel Cinematic Universe, a reality shared by characters across different films that mirrored the comic books, kicked off with *Iron Man* and *The Incredible Hulk* in 2008, accelerated with *Thor* and *Captain America: The First Avenger* in 2011, and culminated with *The Avengers* mega–team up in 2012. Broadcast television shows including *Agents of S.H.I.E.L.D.*, *Runaways*, *Legion* and *The Gifted* followed, as did a host of Netflix series such as *Daredevil*, *Jessica Jones*, *Iron Fist* and others. All told, Disney's Marvel Cinematic Universe had grossed more than twenty-two billion dollars by 2019; the Spider-Man franchise, largely controlled by Sony, had grossed seven billion dollars; and the X-Men franchise, held by 20th Century Fox, had grossed just under six billion dollars.[26]

Warner also powered ahead, led by a Dark Knight reboot that started with Christopher Nolan's *Batman Begins* in 2005. More so than any other superhero films, Nolan's trilogy proved to be hugely influential to real-life superheroes, depicting Bruce Wayne's transformation into Batman in gritty, realistic detail. Out with Bat-Mite, disco dancing and bright colors; in with military gadgets and vehicles, scars and injuries, and righteous, angry vengeance. If any series of films can be pointed to as the blueprint for how an ordinary person might become a vigilante crime fighter, the Dark Knight Trilogy is surely it. Following Batman's reestablishment, Warner also launched its own shared universe with new movies starring Superman, Wonder Woman, Aquaman and others. DC's TV shows—*Arrow*, *The Flash*, *Supergirl* and more—multiplied, all posting solid ratings.

Superheroes accounted for six of the top twenty-five grossing movies in 2016, seven in 2017 and eight in 2018. They also became moneymakers in video games, with successful franchises from Batman and Spider-Man. Spidey even hit Broadway as a musical in 2011, complete with songs composed by Bono and Edge of U2. In 2019, *Black Panther*—starring the king of the fictional African country Wakanda who gets superpowers by taking mystical herbs, and created by Lee and Kirby in 1966—marked a new milestone as the first superhero movie nominated for a best picture Oscar. The same year, *Avengers: Endgame* topped *Avatar* to become the highest grossing movie of all time. Superheroes' domination of pop culture was now complete. At the conclusion of the second decade of the new millennium, there was no shortage of superhero content supply and no evidence of public demand for it waning.

We now know how this happened, but why did it happen?

Nostalgia is one big factor. Superheroes are escapist fantasy at the best of times, but they become even more so when the real world darkens or becomes more complex. For many people who flock to theaters and watch the TV shows, superheroes evoke the simpler times of youth, a time when rising political tensions and worsening economic situations weren't daily concerns.

Superheroes aren't just pure escapism, though, because they also have their own problems, conflicts and drama. As Stan Lee intended, audiences identify with them. Readers and viewers recognize that a superhero's tribulations might provide new perspectives with which to deal with their own issues. Perhaps Bruce Banner's recognition of the monster who lives within him, for example, can help the viewer face his own inner demons. Maybe the choices Captain America makes in coping with his alienation from modern society can help a reader adjust to her own aging.

Superheroes are also aspirational, because they generally convey positive messages of good triumphing over evil. They inspire audiences to want to do good, or to imagine that they can. At the very least, they can make viewers feel bad about not doing more good.

The makers of the best of the films also implicitly understand that audiences don't necessarily want to take superheroes too seriously—that, true to their origins as *comic* books, they also represent levity, humor and color. Joel Schumacher, the much-maligned director of the last two nineties-era Batman movies, was at least partially right when he said, "They're called comic books, not *tragic* books."[27] Amidst all the seriousness, angst and reality, superheroes are supposed to be fun and entertaining.

For good or for ill, these factors add up to a formula that is likely to keep the superhero phenomenon powering ahead for the foreseeable future. Although their popularity has waxed and waned over the decades, there's no reason to believe they aren't here to stay.

CHILDREN OF THE ATOM

A MERE THREE HUNDRED PEOPLE ATTENDED THE FIRST GOLDEN STATE Comic Book Convention in San Diego in 1970. Since then, like the industry it was founded to celebrate, the event has mushroomed. A few name changes later, it's now known as Comic-Con International, an entertainment mega-event that draws more than 160 thousand people each year. Comic-Con's success, which grew in lockstep with the multimedia superhero phenomenon, has spurred similar conventions across the country. The top five US events by attendance—New York, San Diego, Denver, Phoenix and Seattle—collectively draw nearly seven hundred thousand visitors annually. Similar conventions have popped up and are experiencing growth in virtually every major city around the world, from London and Toronto to Paris and Sydney. Shanghai's comic convention grew to thirty thousand attendees in 2018 from just fourteen thousand three years earlier. Comic Con Africa, in Johannesburg, had forty-five thousand attendees in 2018.

The phenomenon is closely related to box-office figures. Superhero fans clearly like to congregate—whether it's in theatres or at conventions, they want to experience their preferred form of entertainment collectively and socially. They're not unlike sports fans in that way; they aren't the basement-dwelling loners they've been made out to be in other popular media. Convention buildings are like sports arenas; the events held in them are like the Super Bowl or the World Series.

A big part of convention-going is cosplay—a portmanteau from "costume" and "play." Originating in Japan in the eighties, where attendees of science-fiction conventions dressed up as anime and manga characters, cosplay is a form of role-playing. Attention to detail and fidelity to one's chosen costume is vital, but cosplayers also score points by staying in character. Cracking jokes as Deadpool, for example, is a plus, as is brooding and looking cranky when dressed as Batman. One survey of frequent convention-goers conducted in 2014 found that about a quarter of men and half of women considered cosplay as one of the top three reasons for their attendance.[28]

Some commentators see the rise of cosplay and so-called nerd culture, much of it spurred by the superhero phenomenon, as a negative development. A few have pointed out that the rise of cosplay in Japan coincided with that country's prolonged economic recession. Young people ended up "escaping to virtual worlds of games, animation, and costume play," said Masahiro Yamada, a sociology professor at Chuo University in Tokyo, to the *Financial Times* in 2014. "Here, even the young and poor can feel as though they are a hero." The same might be happening in the United States. "When you're disillusioned with the reality of your early adult life, dressing up like Doctor Who starts looking better and better," writes James Pethokoukis, a commentator for the conservative American Enterprise Institute. "It's not to say that all or even most cosplay aficionados are struggling to find work. It's only to say that any rise in people fleeing reality for fantasy suggests problems with our reality."[29]

The flip side of the argument, put forward by American economist Adam Ozimek, is that a cultural shift is underway, especially with young people, whom polls say are less likely to follow sports than people of previous generations. Sports, in their way, were just an early form of nerd culture where people obsessed over key plot points (also known as statistics) and wore costumes (also known as jerseys). "I bet that being a fan of cosplay is less correlated with unemployment than being a fan of hockey," Ozimek wrote. "I bet being a fan of cosplay is more correlated with higher wages than being a fan of football. I bet that the post-manufacturing towns that have high levels of blue-collar unemployment have way less Final Fantasy cosplaying than fantasy sports playing."[30] Ozimek didn't back up his assertions with data, and hard numbers comparing employment and income levels between cosplayers and sports fans don't exist, but his point is valid nonetheless— these are just different flavors of leisure that are unlikely to reflect measurable swings in the greater economy. And to further his point, it's also worth noting that Japan—at least for all of this century so far—has had a much lower unemployment rate than the United States.

Back at Fordham Comics in the Bronx, where the smell of mildew and cat pee prevents the mind from delving too deeply into economic analysis, Phil Hui has decided he's hungry. He enlists one of the Magic-playing teens to fetch him a slice of pizza from a shop around the corner. In return, Hui offers to buy the kid a slice for himself.

The conversation in the shop turns to New York Comic Con, which concluded the day before. Hui is a veteran of the event, having been both an exhibitor and an attendee many times. His reasons for going these days are different than they were in the eighties and nineties, though. "You used to be able to sell some comics there, but things have changed, you know what I mean?" he says. "These days it's more about the cosplay, and there are some fantastic cosplayers there." He pulls out his phone and shows me pictures of him posing with attendees dressed as Spider-Man, Deadpool and other characters.

The teenager returns bearing limp pizza slices on paper plates almost soaked through with grease. Hui thanks him and digs in. He gets excited as the conversation turns to the real reason I've sought him out here in his archaic comic shop. He's keen to talk about that other pillar of the real-life superhero movement, the one that spurred some small portion of comic-book fans into transposing what they saw on the screen or printed page into the real world. He wants to talk about how he became a vigilante.

CHAPTER 3

DAWN OF JUSTICE

VISITORS ARRIVING AT NEW YORK CITY AIRPORTS IN 1975 WERE GREETED by men distributing an unsettling tourist orientation pamphlet. "Welcome to Fear City," read the headline above a picture of a large, glaring skull. Inside the four-page brochure was a series of tips on how to survive a city that was quickly falling apart. Visitors were urged to stay off the streets after six o'clock in the evening, not to walk anywhere if they absolutely had to go out, and never to take the subway under any circumstances. They were also cautioned against venturing out of midtown Manhattan or leaving valuables in their rooms' safes, because "hotel robberies have become virtually uncontrollable, and there have been some spectacular recent cases in which thieves have broken into hotel vaults." Even scarier was who was passing out the pamphlets—the distributors were mainly plainclothes police officers.

New York City was indeed a terrifying place in the mid-seventies, thanks to an unprecedented and out-of-control fiscal crisis. Budget shortfalls had led to virtually all public services being cut to the bone, especially police and firefighters. This was happening at a time when a heroin epidemic was killing scores of residents and sparking violence across the city. Crimes of all sorts were skyrocketing—1975 saw almost seventeen hundred murders, more than doubled from a decade before; car thefts and assaults had also more than doubled in the same period; rapes and burglaries had more than tripled; robberies had risen tenfold. Urban blight was also in full effect—subways were filthy and dangerous, roads and buildings were rotting, low-rent porn theaters and sex shops were multiplying like cockroaches. As historian Kevin Baker wrote, it was hard to overerstate just how precarious and paranoid life in New York felt around that time: "Signs everywhere warned you to mind your valuables and to keep neck chains or other jewellery tucked away while on the subway. You became alert to where anyone else might be in relation to you, augmented by quick looks over your shoulder that came to seem entirely natural."[1] Some police officers, as beleaguered and despondent as everyone else in the city, felt their only recourse was to shame politicians into action. The Fear City pamphlet campaign at airports was their attempt at doing so.

Up in the Bronx, citizens were fed up with the constant paranoia and fear. Among them was Curtis Sliwa, the twenty-four-year-old son of Polish and Italian immigrants and night manager of the McDonald's restaurant on Fordham Road, just a few doors away from where Fordham Comics would eventually be established. In 1978, Sliwa recruited some of his employees to help him clean up the neighborhood. Armed with brooms, the group—whom he dubbed the Rock Brigade—spent long hours sweeping trash off the streets. Sliwa forced politicians to take notice of the group's activities with shrewd publicity stunts, like when he had his workers camp out at city hall until Mayor Ed Koch publicly complimented them. Sliwa also convinced local business organizations to acknowledge the Rock Brigade with community service awards.

In 1979, the city announced that police would no longer patrol subways between seven o'clock at night and five o'clock in the morning. The move worsened the situation on the already-dangerous trains, leading Sliwa to refer to them as "mugger movers." He decided to reorient his volunteer crew toward a new mission: rather than cleaning garbage off the streets, they would sweep the human trash off the subways. Sliwa felt his team's patrols would be more effective if both citizens and criminals could easily see them coming, so he put together a uniform. He found a box of red Boy Scout berets at a surplus store, removed the badges from them, then emblazoned T-shirts with an image of the number 4 subway train. He handed the gear out to his McDonald's employees and rechristened them the Magnificent 13.

As with the Rock Brigade, the group's activities attracted newspaper and television attention, spurred by its increasingly media-savvy founder. This, in turn, drew new recruits from around the city who were fed up with the festering crime. By September 1979, the Magnificent 13 had swelled to a magnificent hundred, which necessitated another name change. Sliwa's volunteer crime patrol finally became the Guardian Angels, a group that would grow to seven hundred members within a year.[2] Growth led to institutionalization, meaning that the group developed policies, background checks and training procedures for every new member. Angels members were schooled in street-level laws—as in how to make citizens' arrests—as well as in self-defense techniques.

Official reactions were mixed. Still stinging from feeling forced into praising the Rock Brigade, Koch was no fan. He was wary of Sliwa's slick media manipulation, so he labeled the group with a loaded term that would stick to them no matter what they did: vigilante. "Good Samaritans don't ask for rewards," the mayor said at a press conference in 1980. "I suggest they join the police force if they want to continue their efforts to increase public safety. I don't know everything about the Guardian Angels, but I do know they love publicity." Captain Gerald McClaughin, commander of the Central Park police precinct, had similar thoughts: "We don't need 'em and we don't want 'em. Historically, these groups have always turned bad. I think they'll probably assault somebody."[3]

Other officials, including New York Lieutenant Governor Mario Cuomo, became fans. "These are not vigilantes," he said. "They have decided, without compensation and at great risk to themselves, to perform a major public service. They are the best society has to offer. We should be encouraging their kind of strength and their kind of courage."[4]

To the beleaguered public, the Guardian Angels were often a welcome sight because they intimidated the right kind of people. In a 1980 *New York* magazine article, author Nicholas Pileggi reported on a typical Angels patrol on a Brooklyn-bound train:

> It was after midnight, and as the young men in their red berets and Guardian Angel T-shirts boarded the train, the passengers smiled.... Their faces were hard and it was apparent that they would tolerate very little from a group of feisty adolescents surprised by their sudden appearance. The youngsters slouched in their seats, pulled in their legs and began giving the Angels furtive, sullen looks.[5]

Whether officials liked it or not, the Angels were accomplishing what they had set out to do. They were making the subway—at least the cars they happened to be on—feel safer. Sliwa claimed the Angels made ninety-two citizens' arrests in their first year, though officials and media observers disputed the figures. Their modus operandi involved group patrols in uniform, with teams acting as visual deterrents to would-be criminals. When they encountered crimes in progress, they physically intervened in attempts to stop and apprehend the perpetrators. They were like a street militia, but operating without any sort of official license—and they made a specific point of not carrying weapons.

Before he became a comic-shop owner, Phil Hui was there for all of it. He was attending college in New York at the time while his younger brother, Robert, was still in high school. They were both gym rats who spent hours each day working out and training in martial arts. They also both happened to work at Sliwa's McDonald's. "Unfortunately, Curtis found out that me and my brother could fight," Hui recalls between bites of pizza. Sliwa drafted the brothers into the Rock Brigade, the Magnificent 13 and the Guardian Angels, luring them—as Hui tells it—with promises of television and movie deals. One of those actually materialized in 1981, with the film *We're Fighting Back*, an action-drama loosely based on the Angels. Sliwa also surreptitiously counted their volunteer hours as part of their work shifts, so, ultimately, McDonald's picked up the tab for their subway patrols. "We got swindled into doing it," Hui says. "But we got paid for doing what we did. It was on the clock, so that was pretty cool."

The Hui brothers were also avid comic-book readers—evidently, given Phil's future profession—but that didn't come into play at the time. They weren't interested in playing superhero, nor were they particularly civic minded or interested in fame and fortune. It was a far more basic concern that kept them on board for the few years they participated. "Honestly, we were looking for bad guys to beat up," Hui says. "We just wanted to see if our martial arts worked."

The Guardian Angels have since expanded and established chapters in more than a hundred cities and thirteen countries. In each case, local authorities, media and citizens have struggled with how to define them. Some, like Koch, have considered them dangerous vigilantes. Others have accepted them as well-meaning community activists. Whichever the case, the Guardian Angels are an example of a uniquely American manifestation of entrepreneurial law enforcement, where everyday citizens step up to augment or replace police work in the fight against criminals. They're also the connective tissue that joins real-life superheroes to the very beginnings of the United States.

A HISTORY OF VIOLENCE

ENTREPRENEURIAL LAW ENFORCEMENT EXISTS ON SOME LEVEL IN EVERY country. Whether it's community patrols or private security, no government in the world has a complete monopoly over keeping crime in check. The phenomenon in the United States, however, goes further and deeper than anywhere else.

Take private investigation, for instance. The profession has a long history in the United States, the United Kingdom and France, where the first detective agencies were all established in the nineteenth century. But the industry's development in America has been far more robust since. The state of Colorado first instituted detective licenses in 1877, with nearly every state now requiring them. Meanwhile, the United Kingdom—birthplace of Sherlock Holmes—didn't require licensing and therefore any recognized skills or training until 2001. The United States has an estimated forty-one thousand private investigators and detectives—forty-one thousand and one if you count Batman—while Britain has somewhere between one and five thousand.[6] Licenses are also required in France, but stringent privacy laws there have kept the industry small. Only a thousand or so private detectives are estimated to be operating.[7]

Bounty hunting is also a profession that is almost entirely unique to the United States. Most jurisdictions consider the hunting and capturing of fugitives in exchange for money to be immoral and discriminatory, not to mention illegal. But in America, not only is it allowed, it can get you your own reality TV show. Indeed, Duane

Chapman—otherwise known as Dog—of television's *Dog the Bounty Hunter* was arrested in Puerto Vallarta, Mexico, in 2003 for illegally detaining convicted rapist Andrew Luster, heir to the Max Factor cosmetics empire. Ironically, Chapman jumped bail and fled back to the US after serving two weeks in a Mexican jail.

Private security is another area in which the US leads. A 2017 investigation by the *Guardian* found that at least half the world's population lives in countries where there are more private security workers than public police officers. That's to be expected in developing nations where police forces are underfunded, overwhelmed or corrupt, but it's a little surprising in so-called advanced economies. Among G7 countries, Japan, Britain, Germany and Canada employ more private security—which includes security guards, surveillance and armed transport—than police. The US ratio, however, tops them all, with 1.1 million private security employees compared to 660,000 police.[8]

A 2016 story in *Town & Country* magazine explains the phenomenon as a side effect of growing inequality in the US, where bodyguards aren't just for celebrities anymore. The article also suggests that perhaps New York City is still quite frightening for many residents, despite a massive drop in crime since the seventies. "Now it's like everyone has bodyguards," says one resident, adding that one of her neighbors has a housekeeper who accessorizes her maid uniform with a holster.[9]

This assessment of the modern climate may be accurate, but private security is far from a recent phenomenon in the United States. The idea of entrepreneurial law enforcement is indeed baked into the fabric of the country, starting with its founding and romantically enshrined since as an integral part of its evolution. Vigilantism, while not exclusively American, is well associated with the United States. The country's origin, historical rebelliousness and later glorification of vigilantism in pop culture has inextricably linked the phenomenon with Americanism despite its occurrence elsewhere.

As Ray Abrahams defines the phenomenon in his book *Vigilant Citizens*, vigilantism exists in the absence of law; it is found in places where official authorities either have little power or have otherwise abdicated responsibility. Abrahams writes, "Its emergence is often a vote of no confidence in state efficiency rather than in the concept of the state itself.... Vigilantism is a social movement giving rise to pre-meditated acts of force or threatened force by autonomous citizens... it often constitutes a criticism of the failure of state machinery to meet the felt needs of those who resort to it."[10]

Vigilantes are often associated with the American Wild West, where they arose in force starting in the eighteenth century as the frontier expanded. Hundreds of groups of "regulators" enforced their own form of law on transgressors, tracking down trespassers, horse thieves, murderers and rapists. Punishments ranged from imprison-ment to execution. The mid-nineteenth-century San Francisco gold rush, which saw the city's population boom from several hundred people to tens of thousands in just a few years, especially height-ened the need for civilian law enforcement. The city's Committee of Vigilance, formed in 1851, attracted hundreds of volunteer members who, in secret courts, tried, imprisoned and executed people they deemed criminals. Similar committees formed and operated through-out California and Montana.[11]

For the most part, such organizations had the approval of their communities. The public was generally in favor of the order these groups helped maintain, despite the apprehension about the lack of proper due process. As in New York many years later, the lawless alternative was less appealing.

US vigilantism took on an uglier mien with the growth of the Ku Klux Klan in the mid-nineteenth century. The first version of the

Klan was formed around 1866 in Pulaski, Tennessee, by six young Confederate officers as a kind of fraternal order with occult under-tones. It began as a club where members gave each other grandiose titles and pulled relatively innocent pranks, such as showing up unan-nounced at social functions dressed in odd costumes.

They quickly lost control of their creation, however. As Albert C. Stevens wrote in *The Cyclopædia of Fraternities*, the Klan founders saw their group gradually transformed into something of a Frankenstein's monster. "They had played with an engine of power and mystery, though organized on entirely innocent lines, and found themselves overcome by a belief that something must lie behind it all—that there was, after all, a serious purpose, a work for the Klan to do."[12] The tenor morphed away from pranks, and toward promoting white suprem-acy. Membership grew as Klan vigilante groups sprung up around the South. Their targets, who they threatened and sometimes murdered, were mainly Republicans, both white and black.

Historians believe a lack of central organization led to the dis-parate groups fizzling during the latter part of the nineteenth cen-tury. The Klan found new life, however, following the 1915 release of the wildly successful film *The Birth of a Nation*, directed by D.W. Griffith, which portrayed its members as heroes and black men as unintelligent and sexually aggressive toward white women. The Klan's second iteration, formed in Stone Mountain, Georgia, the same year, adopted some of the film's novel imagery, including burn-ing crosses, pointed hoods and robed horses. It was likely the first time an American vigilante group was directly inspired by and a reflection of pop culture, a phenomenon that would repeat many times over the next century. (Why, hello there, Christopher Nolan's Dark Knight Trilogy!)

The second Klan was better organized, employing full-time paid recruiters and a publicity department. Though still political, the organization broadened the focus of its violence to a wider array of opponents, including Jews, black people, Catholics and newly arriving immigrants from southern European countries such as Italy. At its height in the mid-twenties, the Klan claimed up to four million members.[13] Internal divisions, criminal activities by members and public opposition caused the group to fade over the next two decades before reviving once again in the fifties and sixties in lockstep with the civil rights movement. The third Klan was also notable for its close ties to southern police departments.

The unifying force behind each iteration of the Klan, including its resurgence in recent years, is members' common perception that authorities and institutions weren't (or aren't) upholding the will of their constituents—in their case, predominantly white Protestants. Members felt justified to take matters into their own hands in the absence of enforcement of the supposedly higher rules they believed to be self-evident. Members were also motivated by the belief that those who weren't white Protestants were imperiling their way of life. Whether or not that belief was supported by facts was irrelevant.

Despite the Klan's co-opting and distortion of the concept, American vigilantism hasn't remained a solely white-supremacist pursuit. At the other end of the spectrum, the Black Panthers emerged in Oakland in 1966 as a group that sought to protect African Americans from police brutality. The group was primarily defensive in nature, though they brazenly carried rifles and shotguns in the streets as a warning—and implicit threat—to police, with whom they engaged in several firefights. Across the bay in San Francisco, the Lavender Panthers formed in 1973 as a response to attacks on gay men and women in the Tenderloin, the city's infamous slum. The group patrolled the city armed with shotguns, looking for gangs or police officers who were hassling gay individuals. They never shot anyone, but they did engage in numerous street fights.[14]

The motivations of these groups, regardless of who they were representing or protecting, were similar on a basic level: when there is no one in power to do to the job, it's incumbent on citizens to do it for themselves. This self-help, do-it-yourself attitude has—for good or for ill—become fundamental to many aspects of the American experience; it is integral to the founding of the country and remained omnipresent through its growing pains, continuing to the present day. As Abrahams suggests, the strong early adoption of vigilantism by Americans "partly shows that their emergence reflects freedom from, rather than simply absence of recourse to, state control."[15] Citing Richard Maxwell Brown, Abrahams posits,

> The vigilante tradition is a firmly established feature of American society and culture. It arose... from the peculiar combination of a revolutionary tradition, the post-revolutionary inheritance and persistence of an outdated legal framework, the emphasis on "popular sovereignty" and the state's obligations to its citizens, and the special nature of the frontier and the accompanying ideas of "do-it-yourself" localism.... [Vigilantism is] an intrinsic, if informal, feature of the total social system, coexistent with the formal legal and judicial apparatus.[16]

Twentieth-century pop culture has played a large role in romanticizing vigilantism in the American consciousness. A steady stream of movies starring the likes of Clint Eastwood and Steve McQueen made heroes of Wild West regulators, while comic books and then films and television shows turned Batman, Wolverine and the Punisher into household names. Robert De Niro and Charles Bronson became stars in the seventies in vigilante films such as *Taxi Driver* and *Death Wish*, respectively, which reflected and capitalized on American society's growing angst about inner-city crime and moral decay. Audiences and readers ate up these fictional works about heroes, super and otherwise, ostensibly serving a higher good and making the world safer for the average Joe. Today's superhero movies tap into the same vein, inspiring a certain strain of individuals to step up and make a difference.

SUPER ANGELS

SLIWA, WITH HIS ANIMATED RHETORIC DELIVERED THROUGH A TOUGH-guy Bronx accent, has consistently been sharp in his criticism of the status quo. He told a documentary crew in 2017 that the time in which the Guardian Angels were founded was "an era of Uzi-toting, dope-sucking, psychopathic killing machines laying siege to the outer boroughs and Manhattan itself." The Guardian Angels were a movement against political indifference—and not one that would stay rooted as merely an intellectual exercise. "Bronson in *Death Wish*, De Niro in *Taxi Driver*—I wasn't going to live vicariously through these vigilante movies that were hits in the seventies," he said. "We would bring together young men and women, the least likely to get together, the ones that you were generally afraid of, paralyzed of, and we would proactively get them to preemptively stop crime and if necessary grab the individuals responsible and be positive role models. If that meant I was going to be labeled with the scarlet letter, the big V, a vigilante, so be it."[17]

Talking to Sliwa directly, I found him to be no less animated, even four decades on. Guardian Angel chapters have launched and folded in numerous cities over the years, but the group remains active today. Sliwa estimates overall membership at about five thousand, though it's difficult to verify that claim. He sees a direct link between his group and the Wild West regulators. "When you're a student of history, you understand how important vigilantes were. The birth of the nation was filled with this constant battle of good versus evil," he says. "If I existed in those times, would I have been a vigilante? Absolutely. Would I have joined together a posse comitatus to protect the little town that I lived in? Without a doubt." A good portion of Americans, it turns out, have always felt beleaguered—the challenger or under-dog mentality is ingrained in the psyche of having to establish a new country out of nothing. Or perhaps fear has simply become part of the national consciousness. "What were these people to do? They were being victimized time and time again," Sliwa says. "Rather than fight it, if people insist you're a vigilante, then yeah, okay. If you want to call me a vigilante, fine, I can deal with it, but it's nothing compared to what you think it is."[18]

Distrust of authorities has also been a distinguishing and unify-ing feature of entrepreneurial law enforcement throughout its history in the United States. Official crime rates in New York have declined dramatically since the days of Fear City, but Sliwa argues that the numbers don't necessarily reflect the reality. The Guardian Angels resumed patrols in Central Park in 2015, for example, because of that perceived discord. "I saw a noticeable difference, the number of crimes, particularly that involve assault and robbery at night, had skyrock-eted," he says. "The police certainly don't want us here because they take it as if it's a suggestion that they're not doing their jobs. Tough noogies. The cops don't want to get out of their cars, they don't want to get out on their mountain bikes, they don't want to go undercover, they don't want to go up these hills, they don't want to be in the dark... They know, with proper policing, the Guardian Angels would not be needed in Central Park. Don't blame the messengers because you don't like the sound of the message."[19]

Though crime was the catalyst for the group's formation, super-hero fiction was also a major motivator for many recruits. "Not so much for myself," Sliwa says. "But definitely for a lot of our members who would live vicariously through comic-book characters and had no way of exemplifying what they found to be the best characteristics of crime fighting in those characters... They felt this was a transition from fantasy into reality as a crimefighter."

The Guardian Angels also set the template that many real-life superheroes would adopt in the years to come in terms of approach, patrol tactics and community outreach efforts. Some prominent real-life superheroes, including Mr. Xtreme in San Diego, got their starts in entrepreneurial law enforcement as members of the Guardian Angels. Some, such as New York's Dark Guardian, continue to moonlight as both. "We're considered the grandfather of these types of efforts," Sliwa says. "People start saying, 'yeah, if we [try to stop crime] we'll get killed out there. People will set upon us and attack us.' But then other people will say, 'Well, the Guardian Angels have been doing it for some time and that's not the case.'"

Sliwa says he respects the basic motivation driving many real-life superheroes—to make their communities better and safer—but he questions what's really at the heart of their activities; he isn't convinced that altruism is the true spark. "They're more into a 'I and me' kind of thing. Our motto is 'us and we.' In our situation, a lot of people join because they want to use the vehicle of the Guardian Angels to make a change in their community," he says. "Being a particular character is so important to [RLSH]. In the Guardian Angels, you have to play the role you're designated. You may be the medic or the one who runs to [emergency] response when everyone else is running to a problem. It requires that you come in without a pre-fixed idea. If someone were to say to you, 'No, you can't be Batman, you have to be Robin,' I think they'd be crestfallen."

Phil Hui, Sliwa's onetime disciple, is more charitable when it comes to the real-life superhero phenomenon. He doesn't consider his past actions with the Guardian Angels—beating up and chasing off subway muggers—to be superheroic, but he's otherwise proud of the fact that he helped some people feel safer during their nighttime commutes, and that the group as a whole played at least some role in New York shedding its "Fear City" moniker. Sitting at his desk at Fordham Comics, a shop that somehow finds itself at an odd, almost mystical nexus between where Batman was created and where the Guardian Angels were born, he gives his blessing to today's real-life superheroes, the latest inheritors of the spirit of American entrepreneurial law enforcement. "They're great," he says, "as long as they learn to protect themselves and patrol in groups."

CHAPTER 4

YEAR ONE

IT'S A QUIET AND CHILLY APRIL MORNING IN AURORA, ILLINOIS. A LONE goose, freshly returned from its winter pilgrimage south, spreads its wings and glides in for a landing on the gently flowing Fox River. Landing with the graceful *splish* of an Olympic diver, the goose pierces the calm with a loud, strained "Honnnnnk!" Anyone watching could be forgiven for wondering if it's cursing out of shock, like a person might when gingerly stepping into freezing water.

The Fox River, which cuts through this city of two hundred thousand on its way to join the larger Illinois River, is cold but vital. The section between Aurora and Yorkville, thirteen miles south, is one of the best stretches of smallmouth bass fishing in the state. It's a key recreational asset for this sleepy suburban region an hour west of Chicago. But it wasn't always so. Just a few decades ago, the Fox River was a sewer—a literal dump for the region's then-burgeoning manufacturing industry. With scant regulations preventing them from doing so, soap factories, aluminum foundries and steel mills pumped noxious gases into the air and effluent directly into the water. Dead fish bobbed in the river, swimming pools in the area were covered with soot and residents stayed indoors to hide from the pervasive stench. It was an ecological disaster in the making.

In 1969, Jim Phillips was a junior high school science teacher. Like many people in the area, he was fed up with the pollution and wished someone would do something about it. Fatefully, a friend relayed to him a story about a dispute between two local men over their home sewage situation. One of the men didn't have a septic system and was instead running his waste through a pipe directly into the other man's garden. The aggrieved man retaliated by stuffing a bag of oats into the pipe, causing the toilets in his thoughtless neighbor's house to back up. A physical fight between the two men nearly ensued, but the offending party finally backed off and installed a proper drainage system.

Phillips thought a similar stratagem might work with Armour-Dial, the big soap company that owned a factory in Montgomery, just south of Aurora. The plant was one of many in the area that was brazenly spewing toxic sludge into the environment. So, one cold night in March, Phillips stole through a hole in the fence around the factory and found a pipe that was spewing sludge out into the river. Furtively, he filled it with bags of randomly strewn garbage and cement mix. Satisfied that the pipe was clogged, he penned a note to remind the company of its social responsibilities and left it nearby. He signed it "Fox," with a cartoon animal face representing the O, a symbol he had thought up after coming across a fox in the woods a few days prior. Just as Bruce Wayne was inspired by a chance encounter with a bat while considering his crime-fighting persona, Phillips took his meeting as an omen. As he would later write in his pseudonymous memoir, "My message was in place and the Fox River had a spokesman."[1]

The blockage worked temporarily, but Armour-Dial employees managed to clear it the next day. Phillips went back a few weeks later and re-plugged the pipe, leaving another note. Workers again cleared the obstruction.

Spring was arriving and new life was popping up. On one of his frequent walks along the river, Phillips noted a mother duck swimming in the river with her new brood of ducklings. Something in him snapped a few days later when he found them in a pool of soap bilge:

> Floating upside down with their orange legs relaxed in death was the mallard hen and all of her baby ducks. The shock of seeing such carnage gave way to sorrow and then rage. Wading into the glop, I saw one tiny duckling's foot feebly kick. Scooping it up and stripping soap waste off its partly fuzzy body, I tried to open its little beak and blow breath into its lungs. It was the only thing I could do, but it wasn't enough. The little body went limp in my hand as the final spark of life flickered out. Everything got blurry as tears of sorrow and anger rolled down my cheek.... For the first time in my life, I was beginning to feel myself slipping away from the legions of law-abiding citizens into the realm of those who felt a gut-driven need to follow another set of laws. Maybe those of a higher set than statutory law.... I was feeling that I wasn't part of the world that followed the rules and wondered whether the soap company felt the same way.[2]

Phillips had had it. He had monitored local efforts to force some sort of environmental action, but, frustrated with inaction from the authorities, he decided he would have to step up. Like the long string of American do-it-yourselfers before him, he felt he had no recourse but to enact his own brand of entrepreneurial law enforcement. The situation also echoed Batman's fictional origin story, where a young

Bruce Wayne is spurred into action by the senseless murder of his parents. The ducks certainly weren't as personally connected to Phillips, but their deaths were no less enraging.

Under the mantle of the Fox, Phillips spent the next two years escalating his discrete acts of vigilante sabotage into an all-out eco-war that ranged from humorous mischief to outright—albeit good-intentioned—criminality. He hung banners in shopping malls that read, "Stop me before I kill more environment, signed: Armour-Dial" and "Armour-Dial murders our air and water for pure profit." He smuggled a cap onto the local aluminum foundry's chimney, filling the building with smoke. He tossed dead skunks onto the roof of a factory owner's home. He dumped a bucket of sewage and roadkill onto the floor of steel producer American Reduction's headquarters in Gary, Indiana; hung a protest poster on the Picasso sculpture in Chicago's Daley Plaza; padlocked the doors to an asphalt factory; and held a mock funeral for the Fox River in reaction to a proposed dam project. All told, he hit twenty-six different corporations and businesses in fifteen cities across five states.[3]

Through it all, he maintained a code: property damage was acceptable, but not if it resulted in harm to people. Like Batman—post–Golden Age, anyway—the Fox opposed extreme justice: "If you have to kill or brutalize to make your point, then you and your point aren't worth much," he wrote.[4]

The media picked up on his activities, which garnered him allies. Mike Royko, a Pulitzer Prize–winning columnist at the *Chicago Daily News*, routinely wrote about the Fox's exploits in a favorable light, which in turn prompted articles in *Newsweek*, *Time* and *National Geographic*. *Life* magazine ran a feature on the eco-vigilante after he dumped sewage on the floor of US Steel offices in Chicago. In all cases, his real identity was either unknown by reporters or withheld on purpose.

The Pine Hill Improvement Association also partnered with the Fox to distribute stickers to its friends across the country. Recipients of the stickers, which read, "Armour-Dial kills our water," and "Armour-Dial kills our air," clandestinely affixed them to soap products in stores. Children's writer Clifford B. Hicks penned *Alvin Fernald, Superweasel*, a kids' book based on exploits of the Fox. Phillips himself produced *Tales of the Fox: Pollution Fighter*, a thirty-page comic book depicting a cartoon version of his alter ego and his escapades. He distributed the comic—printed on recycled paper, of course—to local children in an effort to teach them about pollution.

Aurora's police chief and the Cook County state's attorney both wanted to arrest the mysterious figure who was inducing so many corporate headaches, but they couldn't figure out who he was. Many residents of the area, including journalists and rank-and-file police, were indeed aware that Phillips was the man behind the persona, but they didn't rat him out. Much like his Wild West forebears, the Fox had tacit support from the public for his war against wrong-doers. He even inspired a copycat—someone calling themselves the Beaver, who plugged up a sewage treatment plant near O'Hare airport in Chicago.

Phillips's efforts proved highly effective in raising awareness of the region's pollution problem and in turning public sentiment against the culprits. The soap sticker campaign led to a national boycott of Armour-Dial products and a strengthening of the Illinois Environmental Protection Agency. In 1975, the state sued the soap company for violating pollution standards at its Montgomery plant. And rather than looking for the copycat Beaver who had sabotaged the O'Hare plant, authorities instead fined the owner for polluting and turned him over to the EPA. Cleanup followed slowly but surely and by the late eighties the Fox River had mostly recovered from years of ecological abuse. Children could once again swim in its waters and ducklings no longer keeled over. Bald eagles even returned to discover a replenished feast of fish.

Phillips eventually took his fight to a higher level by joining the government as an inspector in charge of pollution investigations. He never publicly admitted to his alter ego, though friends and family finally copped to it after his death at the age of seventy from diabetes complications in 2001. Phillips never married and left no heirs, but conservationists honored his legacy by spreading his ashes along the river. In 2006, the Oswegoland Park District enshrined his contributions with a series of memorial plaques at Violet Patch Park, just south of Montgomery. His efforts unquestionably helped clean up the region. Now, the only threat geese face from the river is frozen tail feathers.

While he never wore a mask or costume—though he did sometimes disguise his voice when talking to reporters on the phone— Phillips can be considered the first known real-life American superhero, or at least a prototype of the concept. His persona and strategies served as a template for those who followed—the use of symbolism to attract attention to problems; the obviation of existing authorities to deal with issues in a vigilante fashion; the courting of the media to spread the message; the selflessness required to do it all; and the playfully self-aware sense of humor that kept regular people from fearing him.

"I've talked to a lot of people who are part of this real-life superhero thing who consider him to be one of their major influences," says Nellie Bly Workman, a Milwaukee filmmaker working on a documentary about the Fox. Workman cites Michigan's Citizen and Arkansas's Wolf Paradox as a few examples. "Even though he didn't use a costume or disguise, he did use a larger-than-life identity to draw attention to what he was doing. I see a direct connection between Jim and his Fox persona and what a lot of these heroes are doing."[5]

Roger Matile, who considered the Fox a friend and reported on his activities as editor of the Oswego *Ledger-Sentinel*, thinks Phillips would be pleased to learn of his status among real-life superheroes. "If he thought he was inspiring people to do positive things, he'd really be proud of that. I think he'd be touched, really," Matile says. "I think he would have been proud that his legacy is being carried on."[6]

THAT'S INCREDIBLE

"I AM AMERICA'S ONLY PRACTICING CAPED CRUSADER," RICHARD PESTA told the San Diego *Evening Tribune* in 1984. "That is the role I desire to maintain for the rest of my life." Better known as Captain Sticky, Pesta picked up where the Fox had left off.

Born in Pittsburgh in 1946, Pesta made a fortune in the early seventies selling corrugated fiberglass, a key material used in buildings at the time. At the age of twenty-eight, he retired and settled in California to pursue his dream of being a full-time superhero. To that end, he bought and heavily modified a Lincoln Continental. The "Stickymobile" was painted gold and had plastic bubbles on its roof like the eyes of a bee, plus two guns hidden next to its front headlights. The guns didn't fire bullets, but rather streams of peanut butter and jelly, at a range of about five feet. Dressed in a blue jumpsuit with a big S on the chest, along with gold boots and a cape, Pesta would drive up to teenagers who were stealing hubcaps from parked cars or spray-painting graffiti onto walls and shoot them with his concoction, hence the nom de guerre Captain Sticky. It helped that the 350-pound wannabe superhero was also fond of peanut butter and jelly sandwiches.

Aside from patrolling the streets of San Diego looking for misbehaving teens, Captain Sticky was also a consumer advocate. He used his flamboyant persona to expose dishonest auto mechanics and car rental shops that were ripping off customers. In 1977, he was credited with spurring the launch of an investigation into substandard care at nursing homes, which resulted in stricter statewide regulations. "If I were to wear a pinstripe suit while trying to aid the oppressed, I would have no efficiency," he told the *New Musical Express* in 1975. "When I stage a surprise raid in my costume, you can be sure I'm not ignored."[7]

As with the Fox before him, Captain Sticky's effectiveness was hard to dispute. "He got results largely by just showing up at the crime scene," wrote comic book artist Mark Evanier on his blog. "He was one of those colorful characters that no reporter could resist. If he pulled up outside your business, so did the TV cameras. If you had a lick of sense, you'd just correct whatever he thought needed correction."[8]

Pesta retired Captain Sticky in the early nineties to pursue other interests. He sold eco-friendly gardening products. He also indulged his seedier side: he invested in a chain of brothels in Nevada and was investigated by police for allowing one of his homes to be used in porn productions. He also promoted the "Real Man's Midlife Crisis Tour of Thailand," offering "drinking, debauchery and fun stuff," an endeavor the Thai government promptly shut down.[9] Pesta died in Thailand in 2003 of complications from emergency bypass surgery at the age of fifty-seven. "His dream was to alter the course of history," his fiancée, Lynne Shiloh, told the press at the time. "He was a huge man with a huge heart filled with love for everyone."[10]

Meanwhile in Birmingham, Alabama... Willie Perry was working as a manager at a furniture assembly shop. He was shocked to hear a news report one day about a group of men who had raped a woman whose car had broken down. As a husband and father, he was determined to prevent such crimes from happening and to prove that there were still good people who could be trusted. To that end, he bought and modified a 1971 Thunderbird, cramming it with every amenity he could think of—a record player, toaster oven, television, even an Atari game console. He painted the car, which he dubbed the "Rescue Ship," with white-and-red racing stripes and affixed the message *Will help anyone in distress* to the front bumper and side doors. Perry himself donned a white-and-brown jumpsuit and a racing helmet emblazoned with a familiar bat logo. With his vehicle and uniform set, the Birmingham Batman was good to go—another entrepreneurial law enforcer and good Samaritan hitting the streets.

In addition to helping out motorists, Perry gave rides to individuals who'd had too much to drink, took elderly people to doctor appointments, drove kids to McDonald's, assisted with guiding traffic around road hazards, taxied mothers carrying groceries and even paid for stranded travelers' motel rooms. As a report on *al.com* put it, he "knew the birthdays of every kid in the neighborhood and would show up at their parties with bags of candy and cookies. If he drove past and saw kids jumping rope, he would stop and play music for them to jump to from the loudspeaker of his car."[11]

Perry's activities made him a local hero and celebrity. In 1982, Birmingham mayor Richard Arrington declared August 3 "Willie Perry Day." An episode of the ABC TV show *That's Incredible* the same year featured a segment on the Birmingham Batman. "There is no comic book about Willie Perry, but there should be," said host Fran Tarkenton. "He's the most incredible superhero of them all because he's real."

Perry died in the winter of 1985 at the age of forty-five from carbon monoxide poisoning. He was working on the Rescue Ship and either closed his garage door to keep out the cold, or didn't notice when it accidentally shut. Either way, the car in which he did so much good ended up killing him. The Birmingham Batman's legacy lives on through the Willie J. Perry Foundation, steered by his daughter Marquetta Hill-King. The organization holds community education and anti-bullying events and donates restored cars to single parents. "He just gave so much of himself," Hill-King told *Alabama Newscenter* in 2016. "Everything he'd make he would basically give it away in helping somebody else."[12] Sheila Tyson, a Birmingham city councilor, remembers Perry helping her mother home with groceries. "We thought he was actually Batman," she told a reporter. "He was an inspiration to me. It made me feel humble doing volunteer work. He inspired me and made me feel like it was alright to volunteer without being paid."[13]

Meanwhile in St. Petersburg, Florida... a darker hero was prowling the streets and back alleys looking for criminals to thwart and homeless people to help. Knight-Hood claims he began his activities in 1989 after his wife of twelve years died and, two weeks later, his house burned down. Living in a van with nothing left to lose, he says he decided to throw himself into helping others. The blockbuster *Batman* also happened to be raking it in at the box office. "I saw it twelve times that year," he told author Tea Krulos in Krulos's book *Heroes in the Night*.[14] Wearing a black face mask with a knight chess piece symbol on it, Knight-Hood called in crimes to police, kept watch over the city's homeless and counseled prostitutes and drug dealers in an effort to help them reform. Or so he said. Unlike Captain Sticky and the Birmingham Batman, Knight-Hood shied away from the media and never revealed his identity. As such, there is scant evidence of his activities. He did respond to one email message I sent and revealed that he's now retired, in his sixties, living in Louisville, Kentucky. "I still feed the homeless here of course whenever I come across them," he wrote. "Old habits are hard to break and I still report crime when I see it."

Knight-Hood's place in the history of real-life superheroes is important, however, specifically for his reference to the 1989 *Batman* movie as a source of inspiration. The superhero comic-book boom that followed, coupled with the earlier media sensations generated by the Fox, Captain Sticky and Birmingham Batman, meant that the real-life superhero phenomenon was starting to stir. Inspired by the fame and impact of the early do-gooders and emboldened by the growing nerd culture, a few costumed individuals—such as Master Legend in Orlando, Florida, and Captain Jackson in Jackson, Michigan—were popping up around the country. They were soon joined by Dark Guardian and Terrifica in New York City; Superhero in Clearwater, Florida; Civitron in Salem, Massachusetts; Shadow Hare in Cincinnati and others. For the most part, these individuals were isolated and unaware of each other. The internet changed all that.

WEB OF SPIDER-MAN

IT ALL STARTED WITH AN INNOCUOUS POST IN 2004 BY COMPUTER PRO-grammer Mark Schmidt on his personal blog, titled "Calling All Superheroes." Acting on the same curiosity that spawned this book, Schmidt idly posed the question: why weren't there more people try-ing to be real-life Batmen and Batwomen? The query brought some of those isolated individuals, who perhaps hadn't received the same media attention as their forebears, out of the woodwork. Schmidt's post garnered hundreds of comments, many from actual real-life superheroes and those considering taking up the mask. For some, it was their first realization they weren't alone. "That blog was the start of it," says Dark Guardian. "It helps when you realize you're not the only one."[15]

In response, Kevlex, a real-life superhero in Phoenix, launched the online World Superhero Registry in 2005, a site where costumed individuals could enroll themselves and make their presence known to the world. "There was almost nobody out there doing this," Kevlex said on a podcast in 2009. "There were people there saying, 'I'm tak-ing this seriously and I'm going to go out and do this, it's a good idea.' Since there seemed to be a little spark there... I decided to fan the spark until something happened, and indeed it did."[16] Myspace, which helped kick off the concept of social networking the same year, also enabled individuals to create their own pages, complete with profiles and photos. The Heroes Network, also started in 2005 by New Jersey real-life superhero Tothian, created a proper forum for interested indi-viduals to connect and converse. All of the online activity created a snowball effect, connecting existing real-life superheroes and spur-ring new ones into being. "It was this whole world I had discovered," says San Diego's Urban Avenger. "It was almost like watching *Star Wars* for the first time."[17]

The fledging movement got some inadvertent help from Stan Lee the following year in the form of *Who Wants to Be a Superhero?*, a real-ity show on the Sci Fi Channel hosted by the Marvel Comics legend. Contestants dressed up as superhero characters of their own devis-ing to compete in comic book–inspired challenges, such as quickly changing in and out of costumes, shutting off water valves and solving thefts. The show ran for just two seasons, but it spawned some unin-tended spinoffs. Several individuals who had unsuccessfully audi-tioned stayed in touch and formed the SkiffyTown League of Heroes, a group that creates superhero characters for the purpose of encourag-ing good ethics and morals in children. Some, including Citizen Prime in Salt Lake City, Utah, and Geist in Rochester, Minnesota, took it a step further by patrolling the streets of their respective cities, looking for crime and people in need, as real-life superheroes. "When you ask the question, 'Who wants to be a superhero?' Well, who doesn't?" says the cowboy-themed Geist. "When I didn't get cast, I had this suit and I thought, 'What am I going to do?' I ended up going over to the other side of the line and got real with it."[18]

In 2007, Chaim Lazaros and Ben Goldman were students at Columbia University in New York. Like Schmidt the blogger, they wondered why superheroes weren't real, only to be surprised when they learned the opposite. "We found these people on Myspace and were blown away," Lazaros says.[19] The duo wanted to film a documentary project on the emerging subculture, but as students they couldn't afford to travel around the country to meet these disparate people. Their solution was to have the characters come to them instead, to Superheroes Anonymous, likely the first convention of its kind—a meeting of the minds for do-gooder types where participants could network, partake in workshops devoted to costume design and self-defense techniques, and patrol together. Thirteen superheroes attended, and, when the planned host dropped out at the last minute, Lazaros decided to fill in himself. He cobbled together a costume and dubbed himself Life, the translation of his Hebrew first name, Chaim. "I woke up the next morning after not having slept for months and I was a real-life superhero," he says. "I'd done it, I'd dived in, I was wet." Superheroes Anonymous has since turned into a periodic event, with gatherings also held in Massachusetts and Louisiana.

Kick-Ass, a comic book by writer Mark Millar and artist John Romita Jr. first published in 2008, brought the real-life superhero concept full circle—back to fiction. Starring an ordinary teenager named Dave Lizewski, the first issue starts with the protagonist asking some by-now familiar questions:

> I always wondered why nobody did it before me. I mean, all those comic book movies and television shows, you'd think at least one eccentric loner would have stitched himself a costume. Is everyday life really so exciting? Are schools and offices really so thrilling that I'm the only one who ever

fantasized about this? C'mon. Be honest with yourself. We all planned to be a superhero at some point in our lives.

In the comic's early pages, Lizewksi spends his evenings thinking up superhero names before finally settling on "Kick-Ass." He assembles a costume centered on a wetsuit he orders on eBay, then gets thrills from secretly wearing it under his clothes at school. Eventually, he admits that "like a murderer, simply fantasizing would only cut it for so long. After a while, I had to engage." In his first encounter, Lizewski tries to stop a trio of teens from spray-painting graffiti on an alleyway wall, but instead ends up in the hospital after the hoodlums pummel and stab him. He recovers and later intervenes in a street fight, only to be beaten once again. This time, the skirmish ends up on the internet after an onlooker records it on his cellphone. The incident goes viral, turning Kick-Ass into an internet sensation and something of a local celebrity. From there, he hooks up with other like-minded costumed heroes and manages to actually foil some crimes.

The comic book and the movie that followed in 2010 at first offered a simple answer to the question of why there weren't more real-life Batmen—that it would be dangerous and potentially fatal for anyone foolish enough to try it—before ultimately glorifying the idea. If Kick-Ass didn't inspire real people to go after hardened criminals and gangsters, it at least tempted some to think it could be possible, and suggested how it might be done. "It did have a very interesting message buried beneath it, which is: What's actually stopping people from dressing up in costumes and doing their best to better society?" says Nameless Crusader, a real-life superhero based in Oshawa, Canada. "It doesn't have to be literally going out and fighting crime. It could be something as simple as what me and the Justice Crew of Oshawa did on occasion, which is go out and do night patrols on a weekly basis."[20]

By 2011, the growing real-life superhero movement had attracted the attention of filmmaker Michael Barnett. Barnett's simply titled documentary *Superheroes*, which aired on HBO, cast a sympathetic eye on the phenomenon and followed the exploits of a variety of characters, from Mr. Xtreme's mission to apprehend a sex offender in San Diego and the Black Monday Society's street patrols in Salt Lake City to the New York Initiative's training sessions and Master Legend's work with the homeless in Orlando. Barnett was struck by the costumed characters' entrepreneurialism. "Help just wasn't coming," he says. "This movement was born out of that, not waiting around for bureaucracy."[21] His film further galvanized momentum, with numerous real-life superheroes citing it as inspiration for their decision to join the movement. Canadian Justice, in Windsor, Ontario, for example, says he was particularly amused by Mr. Xtreme, who comes across as haplessly earnest despite repeated setbacks, like being forced to live in his van. But on repeated viewings, "it stopped being funny and started being inspirational," he says.[22] Crimson Canuck, also in Windsor, was prompted to action by the one-two punch of *Kick-Ass* and *Superheroes*, which he says he watched "five million times." "It really resonated," he says of the *Kick-Ass* movie. "What if everyone just adopted that ethos?"

THE DARK PHOENIX SAGA

ON OCTOBER 13, 2011, A SEATTLE JUDGE ORDERED TWENTY-THREE-YEAR-old Benjamin Fodor to remove his mask to address assault charges stemming from an incident in which he had allegedly pepper-sprayed people fighting outside a nightclub. Fodor complied and took off his black-and-yellow molded-rubber cowl, revealing in public for the first time the identity of the famous Phoenix Jones.

Fodor had decided to become a real-life superhero a year earlier, after discovering that his car had been broken into. His young son had cut himself on the broken glass and required stitches. Fodor was later told that several people had witnessed the break-in, but had done nothing about it. Then one of his friends was assaulted at a bar and was left with permanent facial damage. Again, no one intervened.

Fed up with bystander apathy, Fodor started breaking up fights at bars. As an amateur mixed martial artist, he was effective, which drew attention. He realized he was becoming known as "the guy who stops fights" and that he was putting himself in danger because of it. "They'd recognize me and pick me out. I couldn't do regular, everyday things anymore," he told Seattle's KOMO News. "So I started wearing the mask."[23] Fodor was thus "reborn" as Phoenix Jones, a butt-kicking street fighter in customized, black-and-yellow bullet-proof Dragon Skin armor—the brand favored by the CIA and the US military—and matching rubber cowl. On his belt: a stun baton, pepper spray, tear gas, handcuffs and a first-aid kit. By look, equipment and capability—physical, at least—he was the closest thing yet to a real-life Batman.

Jones joined forces with a group of like-minded individuals including Buster Doe, Thorn, Green Reaper, Gemini, No Name, Catastrophe and Thunder 88 to patrol the streets of Seattle as the Rain City Superhero Movement. Like a gang of costumed Guardian Angels, the team broke up fights outside bars, chased down thieves and petty criminals, and performed everyday good deeds like helping ordinary citizens to get taxis or to cross the street. As with the Fox, Captain Sticky and the Birmingham Batman before them, they became fast celebrities, locally and globally. "Vigilante justice has come to Seattle, and the caped crusaders drive a Kia," proclaimed the Seattle Post-Intelligencer.[24] "The case mirrors that of Kick-Ass, last year's Hollywood film directed by Matthew Vaughn, in which an ordinary teenager tries to become a real-life superhero," reported the *Telegraph* in the UK.[25] The team even earned a mention, albeit a mocking one, on *Saturday Night Live* after a fight gone wrong in early 2011. "A man in Seattle who calls himself Phoenix Jones and dresses up in a homemade superhero costume while fighting crime had his nose broken in a fight," said Seth Meyers in the "Weekend Update" sketch. "So it seems evil has found Phoenix Jones's only weakness: weakness."

The incident that landed Fodor in court happened on the night of October 9, 2011. As per his account, two groups of club-goers were brawling outside the venue, which necessitated his involvement and the discharging of pepper spray. The official police report stated that no fight had in fact happened and that the partiers were simply dancing and walking to their respective cars. Fodor was charged with four counts of assault and released on bail of $3,800 after spending the night in jail. In court a few days later, the prosecutor declined to press charges after video footage showed Fodor was in the right. Wasting no time, Fodor donned his cowl and ripped off his dress shirt, Superman-style, to reveal his black-and-gold armor underneath. "I will continue to patrol with my team, probably tonight," Fodor told reporters waiting outside the courthouse. "In addition to being Phoenix Jones, I am also Ben Fodor, father and brother. I am just like everybody else. The only difference is that I try to stop crime in my neighborhood and everywhere else."[26]

The court appearance fueled Jones's fame. The case drew worldwide media attention, making him a sought-after interviewee. "Being a superhero is the best way I can serve my community," he said on *Fox News*. "It's time for people to stand up and defend themselves and what they believe in," an unmasked Fodor, with his real-life superhero wife, Purple Reign, by his side, told BBC's *Newsnight* while visiting the UK. Television network AMC came calling and filmed a Phoenix Jones pilot, though it never aired.[27]

The notoriety reached a fever pitch in 2012 when a video of Jones in a street fight went viral. Police looked on as the costumed fighter beat on an unidentified man who had challenged him. Authorities allowed the bout to happen without intervening on account of Washington state's mutual combat law, which permits fights between consenting individuals. Mirroring Kick-Ass, except with the super-hero as the victor, various versions of the video quickly amassed more than fourteen million views on YouTube.

Public opinion of Jones's activities was generally supportive, but authorities felt differently. Seattle police maintained they didn't want anyone besides sworn officers putting themselves in danger. In at least one case, members of the Rain City Superhero Movement broke up a fight, but refused to press charges, not wanting to reveal their identities by appearing as witnesses in court. "There's nothing wrong with citizens getting involved with the criminal justice process as long as they follow it all the way through," a police spokesperson said.[28] Seattle prosecutor Pete Holmes was less charitable to Jones. "Mr. Fodor is no hero, just a deeply misguided individual," he said in a press release following the court appearance. "He has been warned that his actions put himself in danger and this latest episode demonstrates that innocent bystanders can also be harmed."[29]

Phoenix Jones isn't the only self-styled do-gooder to run afoul of the law. In 2005, a few years before Fodor's run-in, factory worker Thomas Frankini—better known as the purple-cape-wearing Captain Jackson—was arrested for drunk driving in Jackson, Michigan. The Captain was forced to hang up his tights after the local newspaper published his identity. Also in Michigan, the Petoskey Batman was busted just a few months before Fodor after police found him hanging off the wall of a building. Petoskey Batman (Mark Wayne Williams), was arrested for trespassing and possession of dangerous weapons, which included a baton, a can of pepper spray and a pair of lead-lined gloves. He was sentenced to six months' probation, during which he was forbidden from wearing his Batman costume. Williams was arrested again the following year after he was found nosing around an area that police had cordoned off after a car crash. "He wouldn't clear the scene and we had a canine out there and he kept screwing up the scent," a police sergeant told the *Petoskey News-Review*. Williams ultimately sold his Batman suit for $152 to help cover his legal fees.

Williams's Michigan Protectors teammate Bee Sting (Adam Besso) also managed to get himself into trouble. Bee Sting was in a trailer park in Burton, Michigan, and found himself annoyed by a man loudly revving his motorcycle. He asked the man to cut it out and, when he didn't, a struggle ensued. Bee Sting's shotgun went off—no one was hurt, but it was enough to earn him 102 days in jail and two years of probation, not to mention universal enmity among the media and his peers. What exactly was a self-styled real-life superhero doing with a shotgun anyway?

Then there was Matthew Argintar, a twenty-three-year-old man who got himself arrested outside a Home Depot in Mansfield Township, Ohio, in 2012. Argintar, a former military policeman, was offering shoppers a helping hand in his Beast guise, wearing a Batman-like mask, armor and cape. The problem was, he was doing this less than two weeks after a masked gunman had killed twelve people and wounded fifty-eight others during a midnight screening of *The Dark Knight Rises* in a Colorado movie theater. It's worth noting that Argintar cited Phoenix Jones as his inspiration.[30]

CIVIL WAR

IF REAL-LIFE SUPERHEROES ARE SOME FORM OF ENTREPRENEURIAL response to perceived societal needs, then real-life super villains are, similarly, a reaction to market demand. They aren't homicidal world-conquering comic-book madmen like Lex Luthor or Doctor Doom, nor are they actual bad guys like real-world dictators, drug lords and greedy corporatists. A real-life super villain is instead just an internet troll with a gimmick. Their raison d'être isn't to perform acts of evil, but to act as foils to real-life superheroes—to criticize and expose their failings and hypocrisies.

According to Tea Krulos, they started appearing around the end of the aughts. A man calling himself Dark Horizon, dressed in a trench coat and fedora with pantyhose stretched across his face, posted a YouTube video in 2008 in which he taunted several heroes. He referred to Florida's Amazonia as "a beast of a woman" and threatened to crush Minnesota's Geist "like an insect."[31] Meanwhile the debut of hero Shadow Hare in Cincinnati in 2009, which garnered local TV news coverage, kicked off a wave of criticism on Myspace and YouTube by self-styled villains calling themselves Dr. Sadistique, Sword Kane, Executrix, Tiny Terror, Street Shock and Gravestar. Much of the commentary took the form of poorly filmed rants in low-rent disguises. The criticisms, however, were sharp. "These people claim to be heroes, but honestly they do very little that is heroic," Gravestar said on an internet radio show produced by Portland, Oregon's hero/villain Apocalypse Meow.

Real-life super villains ultimately gave voice to the questions and concerns that ordinary people tend to have when it comes to real-life superheroes. "Everyday citizens go about their lives and help people," Lord Malignance told Krulos. "To say that one must put on a costume to inspire others is to seek to elevate themselves at the expense of ordinary people. If one wanted to fight crime, become police. If one wants to help the hungry, work in a soup kitchen. The reason they are superheroes is ego, and ego alone."[32] Purple Lotus, a Florida villain who started as a real-life superhero before switching sides, is less charitable. "The superhero community is full of self-righteous schizophrenics," he says. "Come on, look at you: you look like a multi-colored ninja."[33]

If the villains found Shadow Hare and his ilk irksome, they really *hated* Phoenix Jones. Rex Velvet, in actuality Seattle filmmaker Ryan Cory, took Fodor to task in a series of videos he posted on the internet. Unlike most villain missives, Cory's videos had professional-quality production, makeup and costuming. "Now, our city is not protected by our once-respected police force, but by a tormented, delusional freak in a mask. How did this happen?" the mustachioed and eyepatch-wearing Velvet asked in one slickly produced short. "When I see that our boys in blue are being replaced by a hobo snitch in a mask galli-vanting around with a slew of nerds in tights, I have to wonder: What direction is our fair city heading in? For far too long we've watched as our nation buys in to its childish charade and it has run its course."

Lord Mole, a villain based in the United Kingdom, was especially angered by Fodor's attempt in 2012 to crowdfund ten thousand dol-lars for a new, high-tech suit of armor. He pointed out the irony in a sarcastic response video: "All you have to do is get out there and spray some people in the face! If you don't spray them in the face, tase them! Kick them in the nuts! And then you will be worthy of a super suit too," he said. "Come on American superheroes, get your act together! Be a Phoenix Jones role model, break some children's fingers today!" Mole is more soft-spoken in person these days, but no less critical. He points to the viral video of Jones in mutual combat as everything that was wrong with what he and others like him were doing. "There's noth-ing superheroic about it," he says. "There's nothing about it that looks like a superhero making things better. It just looks like a guy who's really good at fighting beating up someone else who's drunk."[34]

The villains were ultimately effective in that they sparked inter-nal dialogue within the real-life superhero community. They may in fact have been too effective, with the heroes themselves becoming their own harshest critics, thus putting the villains out of their jobs. Phoenix Jones in particular has become a lightning rod for criticism from fellow heroes. "The kid was an affront to whatever I stand for—being yourself and not lying to the world," says Zero, cofounder of the New York Initiative.[35] Even his own teammates turned on him. "He would try to instigate the situation instead of defusing whatever we came upon," says Skyman. "He was born aggressive, already looking for the next fight."[36] "I don't trust the guy anymore, I'm very skeptical of his intentions," says El Caballero. "He'd roll into a place and all of a sudden there'd be some sort of craziness. It was almost as if his energy was bringing that in a way."[37]

The feelings were mutual. Jones seemed to delight in denigrating his more charitable-minded compatriots. "When you wake up one day and decide to put on spandex and give out sandwiches, something's a little off," he told writer Jon Ronson. "I call them real-life sandwich handlers."[38] Jones disbanded the Rain City Superhero Movement over social media in 2014, saying that some members were disloyal and/or were carrying illegal weaponry, but then quickly reformed the group with new qualifying criteria. Members would have to be able to perform five pull-ups and twenty-five sit-ups in a two-minute stretch, he said.

His purged teammates tell a different story. The actual dissolution of the Rain City Superhero Movement occurred after May Day, an annual protest event for worker and immigrant rights, in Seattle in 2014. According to Evocatus (James Marx), the team had scouted downtown locations ahead of time and had planned to use a hotel room as their base of operations. Their plan was to watch the proceedings on television and spring into action at the first sign of trouble. Jones was "in one of his moods" when the day actually arrived, according to Marx, refusing to talk to his teammates and seemingly uninterested in the whole affair. He led them into a large throng of people, where a shouting match over the team's presence ensued. A group of about sixty protestors, angry that a group of masked individuals was drawing attention away from their cause, surrounded the team and the situation escalated into shoving and punches. The costumed group was lucky to escape without serious injuries. "We were clearly making things worse by being there," says Marx, who had served ten years in the army including a tour in Iraq, where he developed post-traumatic stress disorder. "We had crossed that Rubicon of no longer being a benefit to the city. We were actually turning them violent. I was getting really triggered."[39]

The team had a group chat on Facebook shortly after and it was evident that everyone in the group was mad at everyone else—especially Jones. In response, Jones announced that new rules, including fitness requirements, would be forthcoming. "I was just seething—it was the worst disappointment," Marx says, "the worst and most poorly executed May Day we'd ever had. Any time he did something wrong he'd throw a completely unrelated curveball." Marx knew he was done, as did other members. El Caballero quit and formed a new team, the Emerald City Heroes Organization, similarly angry at Jones. "He's a grown-ass man," El Caballero says. "He's got to do what he's got to do, but I just couldn't work with him anymore."

Jones's life was already unraveling by this point. A year earlier his wife, Purple Reign, had announced they were splitting. His teammates were now questioning him about the money they had given to him to secure liability insurance and armor. He had failed to deliver on either count. "If anyone ever brought it up, he would just shut down," Marx says. "The final total was like eight people who he had taken money from and never gave them their armor," El Caballero says. "That was so disrespectful." His teammates suspected he had personal problems, judging from his frequent social media posts emanating from casinos and parties. Marx remembers seeing Jones tweeting that he was out on a solo patrol, when in reality he was sitting next to him at home playing video games. "He's always got a different story based on who he's talking to," he says. Jones's patrols became less frequent, until he disappeared from the streets altogether. In early 2019, he posted what looked to be a cry for help on his Instagram account, commenting on how he was at a weird point in his life and needed to be alone. "I don't think I've met enough people I would get shot to save, I don't think people would get shot to save me," he wrote. "I was wrong, maybe everything I've ever believed in was wrong."

Shortly after that, he tearfully told the NW NERD Podcast that he had lost in faith in people and in himself, leading to his hanging up his rubber armor. "I didn't make a difference. The people who saw it were not supposed to act this way anymore and they have not gotten that lesson... I'm not going to win. Who plays a game not to win?" Despite that, later in 2019, he was showing signs of reconsidering by making noise on social media about coming out of retirement.

His situation deteriorated further in January 2020, when news broke of his arrest for selling MDMA—a street drug known as Ecstasy or Molly—to a police officer in Seattle. Police said an undercover agent contacted Fodor via text message, posing as a buyer, after receiving tips that the former real-life superhero was selling drugs. Fodor requested three hundred dollars be paid up front to his online Venmo account, then met "Mike," the undercover agent, in a Starbucks. He collected the remaining two hundred dollars he was owed, placed a paper bag on the table in front of Mike and left. Police tested the contents and confirmed them as just over seven grams of MDMA. Mike tried to contact Fodor again to buy cocaine, but he got no response. Police tried again using a new identity, "Laura," and successfully made contact. Fodor and his girlfriend, Andrea Berendsen, were then taken into custody when they showed up at a hotel to make the exchange.[40]

Fodor had yet to appear in court to answer the charges as of this writing, but the news set off a wave of discussion amongst the real-life superhero community online. Many expressed disappointment and feelings of betrayal, but others pointed out that the arrest wasn't entirely unexpected. "I believe he may have had some good intentions as a real-life superhero, but he cared more for his ego and chasing fame than actually doing good," said New York's Dark Guardian on Twitter. "Him being arrested for dealing drugs is no surprise to people that knew him."[41]

Fodor initially did not respond to my multiple attempts over the course of two years to get in touch, though he did reply once to suggest contacting Peter Tangen, the Los Angeles photographer who had previously acted as his de facto publicist. Tangen didn't get a response from him on my behalf either.

How the saga of Phoenix Jones ends is, as of this writing, unknown. But his legacy is a key chapter in the history of real-life superheroes. Despite his shortcomings and his apparent downfall, his former teammates nevertheless recall his charisma and intelligence. He was a force on the streets and an erudite spokesman in front of the cameras who brought an unprecedented spotlight to what the hundreds of real-life superheroes were trying to do, even if not all of that attention was positive. "He wasn't the first, but he was the first to be marketable," Marx says. "Without that over-the-top personality, none of that would have happened." With his overt and aggressive style, Fodor also unintentionally did much to galvanize the community into policing itself, which in turn led to the kinder and gentler wave of real-life superheroes that would follow. "The superheroes themselves are as good, if not better, than the villains were at pruning the branches of the heroes who were too far out or dangerous," says Lord Mole. "Before, it was sort of a vigilante core that was leading them. Now, it's a community-focused core."

CHAPTER 5

THE HERO GOTHAM NEEDS

IT'S JUST AFTER TWO IN THE MORNING ON SATURDAY OF MEMORIAL DAY weekend and the Xtreme Justice League, or XJL for short, is in action. The real-life superheroes are moving in patrol formation down Fourth Avenue in downtown San Diego. Nyght and Grim are in the lead; Mr. Xtreme is in the middle; Nyghtingale and Freedom Fighter are bringing up the rear.

Suddenly, Nyght spots an altercation up ahead by the Balboa Theatre. Two young men are bumping chests, yelling at each other and threatening to brawl. "Code Xtreme, everyone," he says with urgency, "Code Xtreme!" The men are in their early twenties; one is wearing a yellow T-shirt and green cargo shorts, the other is in a grey shirt and blue jeans. Both have buzzcuts and reddened cheeks and are staggering from side to side, signaling the likelihood of inebriation. They're also mad as hell.

"She died and you didn't even call me, you motherfucker!" the yellow-shirted aggressor shouts, pushing the other provocatively. The man on the receiving end shoves back. "Fuck you, man, I'll kill you!"

Nyght, a barrel-chested tank of a man in thick ballistic armor and a half-face mask, barks orders to his team. "Grim, you're on de-escalation; Nyghtingale, stand by; Freedom Fighter, watch our backs!" Without missing a beat, Mr. Xtreme maneuvers between the two men. He puts his arms up and tries to create space between them. "It's only words, man, it's only words," he says. Grim moves in and tries to strike up a conversation with the man in the grey shirt. "Hey dude, what's going on?" he asks calmly. "Can you tell me about it?" Nyghtingale, looking on from the side, settles in for a show. "Grim is amazing at this, he's really good at talking people down," she tells me as we watch from the sidelines. "He once broke up a fight by getting a guy to talk about his shoes."

Grim manages to maneuver the grey-shirted man, who looks startled by the sudden appearance of a stranger in a blue skull mask, away from the scene. Now isolated, Mr. Xtreme and Nyght convince the apparent instigator to explain why he's angry. He's emotional, it turns out, from the recent passing of his aunt. He feels like his friends haven't been supportive and he has chosen this moment, when inhibitions have been lowered, to let them know. But he's also puzzled by these interlopers, one of whom is wearing a purple cape and military helmet while the other looks a bit like Darth Vader.

"Why don't you guys talk about this tomorrow," Mr. Xtreme says, "when you're sober." The yellow-shirted man takes a step backward and lowers his fists a few inches. "It's not worth it," Mr. Xtreme says. "This'll make more sense in the morning." Grim, meanwhile, has walked the other man to the end of the block. We can't hear what he's saying from where we're standing, but he later tells us he distracted the man with idle chitchat. Peace slowly returns as tempers ebb. Both parties go their separate ways; a crisis is averted.

The xjl members walk a few yards as a group to the entrance of the Balboa Theatre for a debriefing. Nyght asks the team members for their assessments. "We did an adequate job of de-escalating the situation," Mr. Xtreme says. Grim, however, says Freedom Fighter was lax in his backup role. Tasked with crowd control, he was supposed to ensure that Mr. Xtreme's back was covered. He instead focused on the conversations happening in front of him, which meant the team could have been attacked from behind had the situation gone awry.

Chastened, Freedom Fighter—who wears an American flag motif on his half-mask and chest—apologizes and says he'll do better next time. Nyght wraps up the conversation with a round of kudos. "In any case, good job everyone," he says.

Incidents like these—and far worse when they aren't successfully defused—happen nightly in the Gaslamp Quarter, a powder keg of a district thanks to San Diego's unique demographic mix and tightly concentrated nightlife. The city is home to seven Marine, Navy and Coast Guard bases and has one of the biggest military populations in the country.[1] It is also a vacation hotspot, ranking as one of the most popular American tourist cities.[2] Colleges and universities contribute more than a hundred thousand students to the mix.[3] Petco Park stadium, at the southern tip of downtown, also adds thousands of baseball fans on game nights. Topping it off are the city's estimated four thousand gang members.[4] On weekends all of these disparate groups converge in the Gaslamp to form one big bomb that can go off at any time.

The Gaslamp has served as San Diego's entertainment-cum-red-light-district since the mid-nineteenth century, when it was established as New Town, a destination sought out by sailors for alcohol, drugs, massage parlors and prostitution. Redevelopment in recent years has driven much of the overt criminality under the surface, but the area remains ground zero for the city's vices. With more than a hundred bars, restaurants and nightclubs packed into just sixteen blocks, alcohol and drug-fueled violence flares up frequently. The chances of witnessing a bar fight on any given night are estimated to be as high as 90 per cent.[5] Fatalities, like the young man we learned about earlier who died in a punching game at Jolt'n Joe's, are common.

The police, meanwhile, are chronically understaffed—about 243 officers short as of 2018, the worst it's ever been according to longtime
members of the force.[6] They're overwhelmed by the sheer volume of
people in the Gaslamp, which can heave with up to thirty thousand
revelers on a busy night. As in the Wild West, conditions are ripe for
entrepreneurial law enforcement.

The xjl is the self-appointed response, a triage unit of sorts. The
team patrols the Gaslamp most weekends looking to defuse fights,
prevent vandalism, administer first aid and, as we saw in the prologue,
carry drunken tourists back to their hotels. "It's a perfect... I almost
want to say cesspool, although I don't want to refer to my town as
that," says Nyghtingale. She estimates the xjl encounters five potential altercations per night, which usually involve between five and ten
people each. Situations can easily escalate to twenty or thirty individuals. "The fights here tend to get very big. If one buddy is going to
fight, they're all going to fight. If a marine sees another guy who looks
like a marine getting beat up, he's going to join in even if he doesn't
know the guy," she says. "It starts with two guys yelling at each other
and next thing you know it's an entire mob being pushed out into a
busy street."[7]

Nyghtingale believes the police can use the help with de-
escalation and medical assistance or simply with warm bodies and
eyeballs. xjl members wear body cameras to record "Code Xtreme"
incidents, in case evidence is needed later. Grim turned his on the
moment the team approached the brewing altercation by the Balboa
Theatre. Nyght says he has turned over evidence to police in the form
of video recorded on memory cards at least two dozen times. xjl members routinely appear in court—unmasked—to provide testimony and
press charges.

Their efforts have won fans in the community. Will Sam, proprietor of the Doner Mediterranean Grill fast-food joint on Fifth Avenue,

greets the team warmly when they patrol by his shop. Guy Harrington, manager of the parking lot at the corner of Sixth and Broadway, says street gangs used to use his space as a meeting point until the XJL helped chase them off. "They are the saviors of downtown!" he says. A homeless man thanks Nyghtingale for checking on him during the Memorial Day weekend patrol. "You guys are awesome, I really appreciate it," he says. "You guys be safe, man!" An African-American couple stop the team and ask Grim to pose for photos. "This is better than Comic-Con," the man says, "because Comic-Con don't have black folks!" Even some rank-and-file police are appreciative. "We see these guys every weekend," says patrolman Daryl Cox. "It's fantastic."[8] His comments aren't necessarily reflective of the entire local police department's attitude, but the XJL has at least achieved a level of tacit tolerance by authorities, if their continuing, regular patrols are any indication.

The XJL purposely tries to differentiate itself from Phoenix Jones and the Rain City Superhero Movement, whose less than positive notoriety has spread across the country. The group has carefully cultivated its image with authorities and the public and distances itself from the early vigilante stylings of the real-life superhero phenomenon. The team more closely resembles the Guardian Angels, both in protocols and societal role. Like the Angels, the XJL has similarly insinuated itself as a community institution of sorts, tolerated at worst and cheered on at best. The parallels aren't accidental.

ANGELS AND DEMONS

THE XTREME JUSTICE LEAGUE HAS BEEN A THING, MORE OR LESS, SINCE 2006, which is when founder Mr. Xtreme (Erick Wong) began his side career as a real-life superhero. The police would routinely pull Wong over in his early days, force him to unmask and produce identification. Each time, he would explain he was trying to help them by providing another watchful eye on the streets. Bemused, officers tolerated him, but mostly they tried to discourage him. They regularly told him to leave crime fighting to the professionals.

Wong's anti-crime activities actually go back further, to the late nineties, when he joined the San Diego chapter of the Guardian Angels at the age of twenty-two. His parents say that he was a happy child until his younger brother was born, which divided their attention.[9] His demeanor further soured when, as a youth, he was jumped and beaten by gang members. It was a catalytic moment in which he developed an anti-victim mentality. He took up martial arts and has since earned a purple belt in jujitsu. He also found escape and inspiration in comic books. He fell in love with superheroes such as Captain America and Iron Man. He idolized Bruce Lee, the Power Rangers and professional wrestlers. "I wanted to go out there and do something positive and be part of something bigger," he says. "Even when I was a kid, I wanted to be a Green Beret or some type of a hero."[10]

When dwindling membership forced the San Diego Guardian Angels to shut down, Wong commuted to Los Angeles to patrol with the chapter there. On a visit to New York, he met with Curtis Sliwa and convinced the organization's founder to let him reopen and lead a new division in San Diego. Wong's stock within the Angels rose and he was soon made regional director for California, overseeing chapters up and down the state. He then helped the organization expand to South Africa and England, at first as an unpaid volunteer then later as the recipient of a stipend to help cover expenses on the road.

All of this activity was taking its toll. Guardian Angels members must follow strict rules and protocols; they have to be expert in local laws, train in self-defense and patrol frequently. Wong was burning out, tiring of the Angels' demands and starting to wonder if there was another way he could fight crime independently. Fatefully, he came across the World Superhero Registry, the online forum that catalogued and connected real-life superheroes around the globe. He struck up conversations with Dark Guardian in New York and Mr. Silent in Indianapolis, both of whom encouraged him to create a costume and hit the streets solo. "I was wanting to try something different, something new where I could use the same reason why I joined the Guardian Angels, but maybe something a little more raw," Wong says.

He decided to start his own team of real-life superheroes, the Xtreme Justice League—creating the name as a hybrid of DC's Justice League of America and wrestling impresario Vince McMahon's Xtreme Football League. The XJL would have the same goals as the Guardian Angels, but the team would be freer, more fluid and unshackled from the rules of a larger organization. Wong decided to call himself Mr. Xtreme, an homage to Marvel's Fantastic Four and their leader, Mr. Fantastic.

His solo patrols drew local media attention, which in turn attracted like-minded individuals. Before long, the fledgling Xtreme Justice League had its first members: Urban Avenger and Vigilante Spider. Their patrols netted some results. In 2011, Wong and his partners passed out flyers as part of an awareness campaign in the manhunt for a local sexual predator, who the media had dubbed the Chula Vista Groper. Police caught the man, which earned Mr. Xtreme praise in some official circles. "It's all stuff that contributes in a positive way," San Diego deputy mayor Rudy Ramirez said at the time. "Public awareness is something he can be very valuable in."[11]

Wong hadn't told Sliwa and the Angels about his alter ego, but they figured it out, leading to a rift. Before long, the organization's leaders stopped communicating. Wong feels the schism was influenced by the 2012 wrongful shooting of African-American teenager

Trayvon Martin in a gated Florida community by neighborhood-watch coordinator George Zimmerman. "They were thinking that if people were discovering that a Guardian Angel leader was going around dressing up like a superhero, it might bring controversy because of what was going on with that situation. They're a little political," Wong says. "They just stopped responding to my emails and my calls so I just said, 'Fuck it, I've already put in all this time, I already got this going so let me go ahead and just keep rolling.'"

Sliwa has a different take on the falling-out. He says Wong claimed he was patrolling as a Guardian Angel when he was actually on the streets as Mr. Xtreme. "He wasn't being honest with us," he says. "He was using the Guardian Angels as a cover. It really struck us the wrong way."[12]

Wong registered the XJL as a charity in 2014, which made his identity public by virtue of his name being on the documentation. On the plus side, the status helped develop legitimacy with authorities and the public. Media coverage and membership grew.

Grim, who was working as a civilian security specialist after six years in the Navy, recalls hearing about Mr. Xtreme in 2011. He was joking with coworkers about how he might someday become a superhero, so one of them showed him a story in a local magazine. "I read the article and said, 'This dude sounds legit!'" He found Mr. Xtreme's email address, sent him a message and got a phone call shortly after. Wong asked about his work history, skills and background. It felt like a job interview. "I now understand it, but back then I thought it was weird as hell. I was like, 'What kind of skills would I need to do this? I don't even know what you guys do!'"[13] He signed up and got to work on creating a costume. He dusted off an old Masters of the Universe Skeletor mask he had once worn to Comic-Con and painted it blue, then paired it with some motocross pads. The "Grim" persona came from a nickname he'd gained after an incident where his girlfriend's angry ex-boyfriend slashed his car tires. Determined to retaliate, he found the ex's house and began carving *Grrrr...* into the front door with a knife, only to have second thoughts. "I decided that was dumb, so I ended up scribbling, *Grrrr-m*. The ex ended up asking my girlfriend who 'Grim' was, so that stuck."

Nyghtingale's recruitment in 2014 also began randomly, when she ran into the xjl in the Gaslamp while part of a friend's bachelorette party. She initially thought the costumed characters were cosplayers—an honest mistake given that Comic-Con's presence is felt year-round in San Diego. The superheroes happily obliged when the drunken party of women asked to pose for photos. The next day, she couldn't recognize any of the people in the photos as existing comic-book characters. Her son, however, correctly identified them as real-life superheroes. "It was like brakes squealing in my head," she says. "I was like, 'Hold on, San Diego has what?' I was immediately down the rabbit hole." She posted one of the photos online along with the message, "Sign me up!" Mr. Xtreme got in touch the next day. "He wanted to make sure I wasn't one of those crazy people who wants to come out and beat up strangers." She quickly put together a costume. "I pulled some stuff out of my closet and said, 'Okay, this works.'" As a caregiver in real life, she chose her nom de guerre as an homage to Florence Nightingale, the founder of modern nursing.

Nyghtingale's costume has since evolved to include a mesh surgical-style mask and a gold-and-green corset. Her oldest son, a graduate of the Naval Station Great Lakes Navy boot camp near Chicago, also sometimes patrols with the team as Yce (pronounced "Ice"). Her youngest son, Osprey, wears a costume while participating in xjl charity food drives and supply handouts. "He's very self-aware for eleven years old," she says. "He knows it's way too late for him to patrol and he's just not prepared yet. Eventually one day he will, but now he's just not ready." Like many xjl members, Nyghtingale has a military background. Prior to becoming a nurse, she spent ten years as an aircraft mechanic working for the Department of Defense. Her stepfather is also a Navy man. She's in a relationship with Nyght, though they insist the similar spellings of their names is coincidental.

Nyght, for his part, is a former Marine and now a special education teacher in an elementary school. He says he did considerable research on the xjl before joining. He had been feeling despondent while on a year-long deployment in Afghanistan and was wondering if there was something positive he could do when his service time was up. When he returned home and learned of the xjl through the hbo *Superheroes* documentary, he decided to follow the self-styled superheroes covertly around the Gaslamp. "I'm not the type of person to jump right into something, I want to know what I'm getting into first," he says. "I saw the genuine sincerity in everything they did and I saw it consistently."[14] He asked former Marine colleagues who had become police officers for their thoughts. "They said, 'They're not awesome, but they don't hurt anything. They're just citizens who are helping citizens.'"

Satisfied, he contacted Mr. Xtreme in 2014 and joined. He put together a black-and-silver costume with a reflective Superman symbol on the back and a conspicuous *F*ck isis* patch on the front. He also wears a modified half-mask paintball helmet that gives him a distinct resemblance to Batman's nemesis, Bane, something Gaslamp revelers routinely point out.

Fallen Boy is unique in that, as of this writing, he's still on active duty with the Navy. An injury in Iraq forced him into a desk job, which in turn led to restlessness. He checked out his local neighborhood watch, but they weren't active enough for his liking. He discovered Mr. Xtreme through the media and, like most of his teammates, got recruited after reaching out. He joined in 2014 and chose his persona as a sort of redemption effort. "My [military] call sign used to be

'Golden Boy' because I did everything by the book, but in Iraq I kind of fell off the rocker, so people called me Fallen Boy. We did some things I wasn't proud of," he says. "It's a terrible name that's shadowed with darkness and bad stuff. But what happens if I bring it back and instead of thinking of all the stuff I did, I think of all the stuff I'm doing now in the community? Now when I hear it and think about it I don't associate it with what I did in Iraq. I associate it with what I'm doing now."[15] His superiors in the Navy are aware of his nocturnal activities and are supportive as long as he stays within the Uniform Code of Military Justice. That means leaving the Navy out of anything he might be doing.

All told, xjl membership has fluctuated between a dozen and twenty people in recent years—large, by real-life superhero standards. If New York City is the center of the fictional superhero universe, San Diego holds that distinction in the real world largely because of the xjl's public profile, active recruitment efforts and courting of media coverage—all tactics Wong learned as a Guardian Angels leader. The result is that more real-life superheroes call San Diego home than any other city in the world.

ARMOR WARS

XJL PATROLS GENERALLY CONSIST OF FOUR TO EIGHT MEMBERS, EACH OF whom has a specific role. The leader determines the route and gives orders while the medic attends to injuries or health issues that may arise with teammates or civilians. Another team member handles communications, calling police and emergency services if needed, while at least one other performs crowd control. The team works out together several times a week and each member is encouraged to take advantage of free self-defense lessons offered by the San Diego Krav Maga

Academy. Grim's father, a reserve deputy sheriff, periodically hosts training sessions on how to de-escalate situations. He is generally supportive of his son's activities. "I wouldn't say he was skeptical, he was more practical," Grim says of his father. "He asked, 'Do you have a bulletproof vest? Do you need some training?'"

Several members, including Grim, do indeed wear body armor. Nyght, who is almost as wide as he is tall, wears a level-four ballistic vest—capable of stopping armor-piercing rounds—on top of a level-three vest, totaling more than a hundred pounds of protection. When patrolling, the team stops at intersections and waits for a fresh green light before crossing the street. "I've got ballistic armor on," Nyght explains. "That's legal in California, but if I'm caught doing anything illegal—even jaywalking—it becomes a felony because of that." When the team stops, members form into a circle to protect each other's backs. The patrol leader uses hand signs to order stops and single-file formation when moving through crowds.[16]

The protocols are drawn from the members' respective backgrounds. Some derive from Guardian Angels procedures while others originate with the Army and Marines. "You get this amazing amalgam of street-level law enforcement from the Guardian Angels and the militaristic structure and organization," Nyght says. "It becomes this amazing beast."

Mr. Xtreme has difficulty quantifying the number of incidents the xjl has been involved in over the years. The team has broken up too many fights to count, he says. He does recall several difficult situations, such as a particularly tense patrol with Grim on the beach in the summer of 2014. The duo was investigating a commotion in a nearby parking lot where three men were threatening another on a bicycle. The real-life superheroes chased the antagonists off, only to have them return with backup. "The next thing you know, they've surrounded us," Mr. Xtreme says. "One guy tried to hit Grim with a chain and I just started pepper-spraying my way out of the situation. I told Grim, 'Let's go!' It was pretty tense."

He also recalls breaking up a fight between two large men in the Gaslamp, but not before one of them punched him in the side of the head. Spartan prevented the attack from escalating further by pepper-spraying the assailants, but Wong felt the blow clear through his helmet. "I had a headache for maybe two or three days," he says. "In this business, it's like feast or famine, right? Sometimes you'll have a slow night and then a lot of times we'll get a lot of small little situations, verbal de-escalation, a little punch-up and then full-on street brawls. Big situations seem to happen at least every few weeks."

Nyght, Grim and Mr. Xtreme have each appeared in court to provide evidence and testify against individuals involved in bigger situations. "We like to come across as professional so we wear our suit and tie," Nyght says. "I've never showed up to court wearing my uniform or anything like that." In one case, Nyght appeared to press charges against a man who had instigated a large fight in the Gaslamp, which resulted in injuries to several individuals. He supplied the court with video of the incident and a written summary. "They asked me more about my military service and credentials," he says. "They didn't ask too much about the superhero angle." In another case, he testified by phone against a homeless man who had pulled a gun on him. The man was sentenced to several months in jail and then remanded to a drug and alcohol treatment center.

The court appearances bring up a wrinkle in the secret-identity logic that many real-life superheroes, including most members of the XJL, subscribe to. Just as Peter Parker doesn't reveal that he's Spider-Man for fear that Doctor Octopus will take reprisals against his Aunt May, so too do many real-life superheroes hide their identities from the media in an effort to prevent repercussions; many say they don't want blowback in their civilian identities because of something they

did while in costume. Real-life superheroes are thus faced with a
choice: they can either choose to maintain their secret identities and
not press charges after intervening in incidents, in which case the
involved miscreants may escape punishment, or they follow through
and expose themselves to those they accuse. Nyght, for one, doesn't
seem worried by the latter, even though he insists on anonymity in
the media. "In those instances, [defendants] have a lot bigger things to
worry about than some dude dressed like Darth Vader," he says. "He
might remember my name, but whatever."

In either case, the xjl has pulled off an impressive feat. By co-
operating with police and the courts and practicing internal discipline
rooted in the military and quasi-militant Guardian Angels, the group
has gained a measure of institutional acceptance not previously seen
among real-life superheroes. They have won admiration from their colleagues elsewhere as a result, a major accomplishment given how frac-
tious and prone to infighting their kind is. "When the Xtreme Justice
League started, they were the joke of the rlsh community," says Rock
N Roll, leader of San Francisco's California Initiative. "To their credit,
they've pulled it up."[17]

By distancing and differentiating themselves from the Phoenix
Jones example, the xjl has also pulled the real-life superhero community's evolution into mirroring its fictional counterparts. Batman, after
all, started out as a loose-cannon vigilante who often enacted his own
sentences on criminals, so to speak, before ultimately settling in as a
friend and trusted ally of Police Commissioner Gordon. Once again,
life has imitated art.

DEFENDING THE STATUS QUO

ARE THE XJL VIGILANTES? THEY INSIST THEY AREN'T—"I CONSIDER myself to be a protector," Mr. Xtreme says. "I don't act as judge, jury and executioner"—because they cooperate with official enforcement authorities and make a concerted effort to avoid breaking the law. The group has good reason to avoid the term and its baggage. While vigilantes were generally admired in the Wild West frontier era, the Ku Klux Klan applied an irrevocable stain of racism to the concept. Periodic racially charged incidents in more recent years, such as the Trayvon Martin shooting, have only added to the public's soured perceptions about vigilantism. Outside of racism and within the specific context of real-life superheroes, Phoenix Jones and his polarizing methods also tarnished the brand.

But *not* being a vigilante isn't as simple as *not* considering oneself to be one, given that the definition changes as policing evolves. Criminology experts mirror Sliwa's comments in Chapter 3 when they point out that word doesn't mean what most people think it does today. In his book *Vigilant Citizens*, Ray Abrahams notes that the judge, jury and executioner aspect of classic vigilantism has changed to match modern times. Today's vigilantism, he writes, is more about self-reliance and unofficially enforcing the law than it is about punishment or taking revenge. Gavin Weston, an anthropology professor at Goldsmiths, University of London, who studies vigilantism, agrees with that assessment. "Expectations of policing today are higher, generally speaking, so the fantasy of the Wild West vigilante is perhaps anachronistic," he says. In the specific context of real-life superheroes,

> there's a really narrow gap in the law where it's not vigilantism if you don't want to call it vigilantism, but it certainly is taking justice into their own hands. There's also the

threat of violence in what they do. It's implicit rather than explicit. What you're doing actually falls within the law that covers everyone. You're acting in a way that is appropriate when other people are using force or violence or antagonistic behavior toward you. That's why they're not vigilantes if they don't want to be thought of as vigilantes.[18]

The nature of vigilantism is evolving, but its underlying causes aren't. It is still a reaction to the wilderness phenomenon, existing where the law doesn't—it's just that the frontier itself is different now. Rather than the definable geographical location it was in the Wild West, the frontier is now a more amorphous concept found within cities that is being exacerbated by rising inequality, poverty, racial discord and declining faith in institutions, including law enforcement. Many American cities now have clear divides within them—no-go zones for certain groups of people. "It fits with a very particular way in which the policing of violence is done in the United States that perhaps doesn't extend elsewhere," Weston says. "Frontiers aren't just in the heart of the country anymore, they're just as likely to pop up in a city where the police don't really want to go on a Saturday night. Vigilantism emerges in these frontier spaces—and that's quite American."

Regardless of whether real-life superheroes consider themselves to be vigilantes or not, it may not even be something they really need to be ashamed of. After all, despite the racial baggage, Americans have historically sympathized with vigilantes. Bernhard Goetz, the man who shot and wounded four youths who he claimed were trying to rob him on a New York subway in 1984, and Ellie Nesler, the California woman who in 1993 murdered a man accused of molesting her young son, both enjoyed widespread public support, as just two examples. As one study on the public acceptance of vigilantes notes, the police hotline in the Goetz case was "swamped with supporters rather than callers looking to provide information that could help in his arrest. Furthermore, out of the eighteen charges, the jury only found him guilty of illegal gun possession, despite his confession to the shooting."[19] Meanwhile, 60 per cent of respondents to a 1985 study on the effectiveness of the Guardian Angels—a group that is as debatably vigilante or not as the xjl—said they felt safer knowing they were in their community.

Basketball great Kareem Abdul-Jabbar, of all people, points at the recent superhero movie craze and other pop culture TV hits—such as *Dexter*, about a serial killer who only murders bad guys, or the BBC's modern *Sherlock*, which reimagines the detective as a trigger-happy executioner—as proof that Americans' love of vigilantism is only deepening. Abdul-Jabbar, a comic book fan who penned a page of the *Marvel Comics #1000* anniversary issue in 2019, believes the phenomenon has been developing since the seventies, in lockstep with declining trust in public institutions. "How did America go from admiring lovable police detective Columbo to admiring lovable serial killer Dexter?" he wrote in *Time* magazine. "To ignore the seismic shift in who we're elevating as heroes is like ignoring the backpack of meth you found in your teen's closet."[20]

This fevered obsession with pop-culture vigilantes indeed looks to be a reflection of what's happening in the real world. According to Gallup's 2017 Law and Order Index, which measures how safe citizens of 142 countries feel, Americans have good reason to be looking for law enforcement in whatever form it may take, however they can get it. "In most economically developed countries with strong rule of law, high majorities of residents say they feel safe walking alone in their areas at night," the report says. "This response is nearly universal in Singapore at 94% and tops eighty percent in many Western European countries. The U.S. is considerably farther down the list, at 72%."[21]

America's steady slide to the political right may very well be the cause of all these interrelated phenomena, or perhaps it's a reflection of them. As lawyers James Daily and Ryan Davidson point out in their book *The Law of Superheroes*, fictional heroes in comic books have been acting as government agents since their inception, whether their writers have been cognizant of it or not. The argument is also applicable to their real-life counterparts:

> Policing and investigation are traditional governmental functions, so by engaging in the same kind of work that the [Gotham City Police Department] does with their cooperation and approval, Batman may be fairly described as a state actor. Overall, the more closely Batman and other superheroes work with the police, the more likely they are to be described as state actors, which makes a certain amount of intuitive sense. There wouldn't be much value to the Constitution if the government could do an end run around it by having private parties break the law on its behalf.[22]

Others suggest that real-world vigilantes, wherever they are on the spectrum of the term, are effectively state actors who contribute more to the proper enforcement and preservation of the status quo than they do to changing or abolishing it. As Abrahams writes in *Vigilant Citizens*, "rather than reject the state, vigilantism commonly thrives on the idea that the state's legitimacy at any point in time depends on its ability to provide citizens with the levels of law and order they demand."[23]

Some pundits have gone so far as to suggest that Batman, Superman and other fictional superheroes have, for most of their history, been symbols of fascism. Writing for NPR, pop culture commentator Glen Weldon says that, "although conceived in a progressive spirit,

the superhero genre's central narrative has always been one of defend-
ing the status quo through overpowering might."[24] Damien Walter,
writing for the *Guardian*, suggests the same of Frank Miller's 1986
landmark *The Dark Knight Returns* comic-book series: "Everyone in the
city is guilty, and Bruce Wayne is the only man worthy to sit in judgment over them, dishing out violent retribution as he sees fit."[25] Plenty
of critics have suggested fascist themes in Christopher Nolan's Dark
Knight Trilogy. "Bane's henchmen literally attack Wall Street, savagely
beat the rich and promise the good people of Gotham that 'tomorrow,
you claim what is rightfully yours,'" writes Mark Fisher, also for the
Guardian.[26] That is, until Batman restores the status quo by beating
everyone involved within an inch of their lives.

Real-life superheroes don't possess that overpowering might in
the sense of superpowers, nor do they necessarily dish out violent
retribution, but the XJL—with its armored, trained and pepper spray—
toting members—are certainly more mighty than the average Gaslamp
drunkard, and they don't shy away from taking such offenders down
when they deem it necessary.

Vigilantism, entrepreneurial law enforcement or whatever we
want to call it, is a conservative impulse—an acceptance of control
and a desire for its proper application, rather than a rejection of it. As
historian and American violence scholar Richard Maxwell Brown sees
it, vigilantism is driven by a desire to restore order and stability: "The
sources of instability vary throughout history—crime, demographic
shifts, government corruption—but the impulse remains the same: to
restore stability to a world turned upside down, and reinforce those
values at risk in a rapidly changing world."[27]

Abdul-Jabbar, who in 2012 was chosen by then–secretary of
state Hillary Clinton to be a US global cultural ambassador, writes
that the popular obsession with vigilantism and entrepreneurial
law enforcement is indeed pulling the United States in a worrisome

direction—toward the fascism that some fear is represented by super-heroes. Not only does the fantasy perpetuate the belief that it's okay to skirt the law to fight corruption—fighting fire with fire, as it were—it also stunts reasoned debate and encourages violence. Most worryingly, Abdul-Jabbar writes in his *Time* piece, it chips away at the fundamental base of democracy:

> Many fictional vigilante heroes rationalize their actions because the villains "got out on a technicality" or "beat it through a legal loophole." Nothing infuriates us more and we angrily blame our judicial system for these "technicalities" and "loopholes." And yet, often the technicality or loophole that we so hate is actually something important, like searching without a warrant, racially profiling, or not reading Miranda rights. These aren't minor "technicalities," they are the foundation of the American ideal of protecting our people against the abuses of power. They are defending our Constitution as legitimately as soldiers on a front line. Yes, there will be miscarriages of justice because of these technicalities, but that doesn't mean we dismantle the judicial system any more than abandoning soldiers in a just cause just because we lose some to the miscarriage of friendly fire.

A possible descent into fascism is the furthest thing from the minds of the Xtreme Justice League members. They are likely to take offense at such a suggestion; their supporters would view it as a great disservice to their efforts. It's a conversation that might seem prudent in the detached realms of the media and academia, but on the streets—where help is needed—it makes no sense at all.

Political discussions and debates on XJL patrols are indeed discouraged. With a diverse membership coming from different races, creeds and religions, views differ dramatically. The mission is all that matters. "You look at the bigger picture, what are you here for, what binds you together?" Fallen Boy says. "When you really focus on that, it overshadows everything else. Don't get me wrong, sometimes certain things will pop up, but the senior guys or the people with the bigger image smash it. They'll say, 'Hey we're not going to go down that road.'"

Nyghtingale disputes the notion that real-life superheroes are agents of the status quo—they are, in fact, the exact opposite. The biggest reason for why they wear costumes is to draw attention to their actions and how they fly in the face of widespread social apathy. If anything, being a real-life superhero is about motivating change, rather than promoting the continuation of the norm. "I want to be the change that the world needs," she says. "The world needs more kindness, it needs more people to stand up and say, 'This is wrong!' This is how we need to be, this is how the world heals."

CHAPTER 6

TRUTH, JUSTICE AND THE AMERICAN WAY

RELATIVELY FEW PEOPLE VENTURE INTO LOWER WACKER. IF THEY COME at all it's fleetingly in their cars, zipping through to bypass the traffic above in Chicago's downtown Loop. There isn't much here to warrant a visit otherwise, just a subterranean warren of roads, alleys, sewers and pillars, all bathed in a dull, orange light. There are no stores, restaurants, trees or grass—just concrete and the dull *shoom-shoom-shoom* of cars and trucks going by. It's austere and bleak.

The Windy City is cold and inhospitable for many months of the year, which is when Lower Wacker becomes appealing to a certain segment of the population. This frigid weekend in early April is a case in point. With temperatures hovering in the low thirties, several hundred beleaguered individuals have fled here to seek protection from the elements above. The tunnels and pillars block the worst of the wind, rain and sleet, making a bone-chilling night slightly more survivable for Chicago's homeless population.

Lower Wacker also serves another purpose when it comes to these marginalized people—it hides them from sight. Like the shunned, subterranean Morlocks in X-Men comics (themselves an homage to H.G. Wells's *The Time Machine*), people are effectively invisible here, freeing more fortunate Chicagoans and tourists alike from having to confront the societal issue. For the people who run the city, it's a unique asset that other municipalities, struggling with the negative optics of their own respective homeless problems, are quietly envious of. But to anyone with a social conscience, it's a postmodern dystopia where the have-nots are literally living beneath the haves.

It's an unfortunate side effect of a civil engineering marvel that was initially built out of necessity. For much of the nineteenth century, the city's roads were prone to flooding from the Chicago River and Lake Michigan. Officials decided to fix the problem by raising the street and building levels in the downtown Loop by several feet, which created enough space to install a proper sewer and drainage system. The Illinois Center development in the eastern section of downtown expanded the plan in the early twentieth century. Michigan Avenue, running through the heart of the city, was then constructed with three levels. The surface section was intended to accommodate pedestrians and local traffic while the two levels underneath were reserved for commercial vehicles. A number of other streets in the area adopted the same strategy. Wacker Drive, running east-west along the river, became the longest and last to be completed, in 1926. The megaproject, which now spans many miles beneath Chicago and is colloquially known as Lower Wacker, has helped to control congestion downtown ever since by quietly serving as a pressure release valve for vehicular traffic.

The development has resulted in some unexpected by-products. Lower Lower Wacker, the name by which the remote and largely forgotten third sublevel is known, has in recent years become a hot spot for illegal drag racing. Police have been playing an ongoing game of whack-a-mole with teenaged gearheads, who attract weekend crowds with their *Fast & Furious*—style drag races.[1] The phenomenon led the producers of *The Dark Knight* to select the tunnels as the setting for one of the 2008 movie's key chase scenes. Director Christopher Nolan found the sublevels' bleakness irresistible: "It was such a perfectly natural place to capture the darkness we wanted for those mind-blowing, fast-action sequences," he told the *Chicago Sun-Times*.[2]

Film shoots aside, Lower Wacker's main by-product is homeless camps. During the Great Depression, thousands of unemployed men moved into the recently completed sublevels, which they dubbed the "Hoover Hotel" after President Herbert Hoover, who they blamed for their poverty.[3] Over the intervening decades, city officials have alternately tolerated or cracked down on the camps, at times erecting fences to prevent homeless people from entering the tunnels or sending police to evict them after the fact. The dilemma persists today, as inhabitants don't have anywhere else to go. If they are blocked or evicted, they inevitably end up on the streets above. And the situation is getting worse.

Official government statistics peg the number of homeless people in the city at about six thousand, but the Chicago Coalition for the Homeless believes it to be much higher. When individuals living with friends and family are counted, the number easily exceeds a hundred thousand.[4] About nineteen thousand of those are students who have registered in schools to receive social services. Nearly half the people on the street or in the tunnels are between the ages of fourteen and twenty-four. Families make up nearly half of the total homeless population and represent the fastest-growing segment.

Mental health issues, addiction and abuse at home are all contributors, but the overriding factor is the skyrocketing cost of living. Rents are shooting up in many urban centers. In Chicago, they ballooned more than 60 per cent between 2000 and 2015. More than half the renters in the city are devoting 30 per cent or more of their income to housing, a portion the federal government considers unaffordable.[5] Wages, meanwhile, are not growing at anywhere near the same pace.

Paul Hamann, president and chief executive of the Night Ministry, a local homeless outreach group, says it's a humanitarian crisis in the making. "We have so many individuals who are living on the edge," he says. "They are literally one paycheck away from being homeless."[6] It's a seemingly hopeless situation crying out for a solution—for help from any quarter.

HOPE IN DARKNESS

ON THIS COLD APRIL MORNING, A GROUP OF FOURTEEN REAL-LIFE SUPER-heroes are determined to deliver at least a little bit of that much-needed help. Assembled from around the Midwest and farther afield, the colorful assemblage is meeting at Millennium Park for an event known as Chicago Hope, an annual spring tradition in which real-life superheroes hand out sleeping bags, blankets and other essentials to homeless people. It's a big, costume-clad charity mission.

Night Vision is unmistakable in his neon-green spandex suit, a large eyeball logo emblazoned on his chest. He's philosophical in explaining his chosen persona: "I want to shine a light on what goes on." West Devil, with his bright-red hair, black-and-red tunic and domino mask, is no less conspicuous. Civil Defender is dressed in black-and-white motorcycle leathers, with goggles and an engineer's hard hat. Frost is also sporting a motorcycle jacket, black and blue, and a fearsome mask reminiscent of Spawn, the demonic comic-book superhero. He raps his knuckles on his chest to indicate the ballistic armor underneath. All four of these real-life superheroes are from the Chicago area.[7]

Samael is from Iowa City, a four-hour drive away. He wears a black leather jacket with red-and-blue accents and a chain bandolier across his chest. A blue-and-red skull adorns his mask, making him look like a cross between Ghost Rider, another demonic comic-book hero, and a member of Slipknot, the theatrical heavy metal band that also hails from Iowa. He says he's a fan.

Patchwork, from Wisconsin, is draped in a costume that looks like rags sewn together. "I get 'Scarecrow' a lot," he says, referring to the Batman villain. Reverb, who actually resembles Batman in his black outfit and cape, is from Lansing, Michigan. Nyghtingale, from the Xtreme Justice League, has made the trip from San Diego to take part in the mission and to attend her son's graduation from the nearby Navy boot camp.

Citizen Tiger, a former paratrooper, has driven in from Huntington, Indiana, three hours away. He wears two tiger masks—one a tight-fitting Mexican luchador mask that covers the top of his face, the second a full-faced Black Panther mask that he's painted orange, white and black. "Someone was still able to recognize me with just the one, so I'm not taking any chances," he says. Canadian Justice, who wears a camouflage balaclava and wields a heavy wooden walking stick, has taken the bus in from Windsor, Canada.

Geist and RazorHawk are veritable royalty among the assemblage by virtue of their seniority. With more than two decades of real-life superhero activity between them, they are respected veterans of the community. RazorHawk is used to the cold. The frigid winters in his hometown of Minneapolis have informed his costume design—he's wearing several layers, with his trademark orange-and-yellow vest on top. Geist, also from Minnesota, sports a green leather trench coat, cowboy hat and armored gauntlets. Sunglasses and a bandana disguise his identity.

Crusader Prime and Wraith, the brothers who organized this event, are the last to arrive. They've driven in from northwestern Indiana, about an hour away, and have just parked a rented U-Haul truck containing the cargo that the group will give away. Crusader

Prime is tall; red-and-white medieval crosses adorn his smock and mask. Wraith wears a long beige trench coat, the kind stereotypically associated with news reporters, along with ninja boots and a full green mask that covers his face.

Their truck contains a sizeable stash of goods: 250 blue tote bags and a hundred red sleeping bags in plastic wrappers. The tote bags each contain an assortment of toiletries, socks, granola bars and bottles of water. Most of the goods are donations from Crusader Prime's work colleagues—the forty-nine-year-old is a manager at an undisclosed health care provider in Indiana. Many of his colleagues know about his alter ego, which he protectively hides from journalists like me. The socks, he explains, are from Bombas, a manufacturer in New York that supports the real-life superheroes' charity missions. "Socks are the number one item requested by homeless people," Crusader Prime says. "They constantly need them because they're getting wet or worn out." The sleeping bags are from Warm Wishes, a charity organization in Bartlett, an hour west of Chicago. The truck itself has been paid for by Impact and Nyght, two real-life superheroes who weren't able to attend in person. Crusader Prime is kicking himself because he learned, belatedly, that U-Haul offers free rentals for charity events.

Many of the real-life superheroes know each other, either from online conversations or previous group missions. They exchange hugs and pleasantries by the Cloud Gate, otherwise known as Chicago's big bean sculpture, and get down to business. They head north toward East Randolph Street, then descend a flight of stairs into Lower Wacker, where the truck is parked. West Devil climbs into the back and tosses sleeping bags to the others. Citizen Tiger ties a seemingly impossible number of them to his rucksack. Patchwork stuffs half a dozen into a shopping cart. Everyone else tucks one under each arm, then grabs as many blue bags as they can carry in each hand. The brothers lock the truck and the team heads into the bowels of the city.

They don't make it very far before encountering an encampment. Situated away from the sublevel's main arteries and stretching a half-mile into the darkness, the alleyway is filled with people. Sleeping bags, blankets, tents and garbage bags containing possessions line the road, each delineating someone's personal, claimed space. Several dozen people have made this area their base. It's quiet, just before noon. Some of the temporary residents are sleeping. The superheroes file down the line quietly, solemnly handing blue bags to the few individuals who are awake, carefully placing goods on spots that otherwise look occupied. The smell of urine and rotting trash hangs in the air like an unmoving cloud. One man, roused from sleep, cheerfully greets Frost. "Thanks man, that's a sweet sleeping bag!" he says.

The group moves on, arriving at a busy intersection. Patchwork glimpses a blanket and garbage bag hidden mostly out of sight behind a pillar on the opposite corner, a sign that someone is probably calling that spot home. Some homeless people congregate together for social and safety reasons, he explains, but others prefer to be by themselves. He grabs a sleeping bag from his cart and dashes across the intersection. A few seconds later, his drop-off completed, he rejoins the group.

A similar situation presents itself a couple minutes later. A lone sleeping bag rests on top of a grate, against a pillar on a traffic island in the middle of a busy thoroughfare. Cars rush by, the dull *shoom*ing noise providing a constant drone of white noise. Someone is bundled up, sleeping, though their face is hidden from view. A road sign reading *End Detour* stands a foot away. Patchwork drops off another tote bag.

The team continues on. Wraith points out a bright-yellow notice affixed to one of the concrete pillars, informing of "off-street cleaning" scheduled to take place in a week. "It's like an eviction notice," he says. Citizen Tiger notices a hypodermic needle on the ground and warns his teammates to watch where they're stepping.

Nyghtingale is becoming despondent. She explains that the homeless people she encounters in San Diego are generally more upbeat. "We have this guy who always plays his trumpet for us. They'll come up and give us hugs, they're always super excited to see us," she says. Here, the mood is bleak. "They're curled up in little balls and just trying to fight to stay warm. That sleeping bag could absolutely mean the difference between life and death."

Several respites break up the gravity of the day, like the cigarette break that a few of the heroes now stop for. Samael shocks Citizen Tiger by removing his mask to reveal that he's Asian underneath. "He thought I was going to be some Irish dude!" Samael laughs. It's a needed moment of levity before the mission resumes.

The group continues and comes across a man and woman bundled up together. They're leaning against a wall, sheltering under the adjacent highway on-ramp. They're both white—a rarity among Lower Wacker's predominantly African-American population. "What the hell is going on here?" the man snarls. Wraith offers him a tote bag, but he waves it off. "I got pretty much everything I need," he barks defensively.

Geist, the veteran, steps forward and explains that he and his teammates are dressed in costumes because they want to attract public attention to homelessness. He also tells him that they don't take themselves too seriously and that they're hoping to bring some mirth to the people they're trying to help. The man warms to the explanation; his hostility shifts to bemusement. He introduces himself as Tony and his partner as Deanna. He chats with Geist for a few minutes, then shakes his hand. "I appreciate you, cowboy!" he says.

A few minutes later, the real-life superheroes come across another line of tents and sleeping bags, denoting several dozen more inhabitants. Citizen Tiger hands a tote bag to a man just rising from sleep. The man nervously smiles as he reaches for it, a sublime moment that captures the bizarreness of the day. An observer passing by might have difficulty making sense of the scene, where a middle-class white man dressed in a tiger costume is handing socks and toothbrushes to an impoverished African-American man living in the bowels of a frozen city. The recipient's sheepish laugh is a suitable reaction. As Tony put it a few minutes earlier: What the hell is going on here?

THE DOUBLE-EDGED SWORD

CHICAGO'S HOMELESS SITUATION IS NOT UNIQUE IN THE UNITED STATES, nor is it even particularly bad when compared to other American cities. The Night Ministry pegs Chicago in the sixtieth percentile when it comes to homelessness, which jibes with official statistics; the city and state of Illinois don't even make the federal government's top ten. In absolute numbers of people on the street, New York City leads the way with more than seventy-six thousand, followed by Los Angeles with fifty-five thousand. When measured by homeless rate per ten thousand residents, Washington, DC, is first, followed by Boston and New York.[8]

Several cities have resorted to unusual measures to cope. San Diego, for one, erected giant tents downtown in 2017 to act as temporary housing for its nine thousand plus homeless denizens. That was in response to an outbreak of Hepatitis A on the streets, which led to twenty reported deaths and nearly four hundred hospitalizations. City workers sprayed the streets with bleach in an effort to contain the epidemic.[9] Hawaii, which ranks first as a state in homelessness per ten thousand residents, built similar temporary shelters after declaring a state of emergency in 2015. The state saw a 23 per cent increase in its unsheltered homeless population between 2014 and 2015, and a 46 per cent rise in the number of unsheltered families. As is the case elsewhere, the skyrocketing cost of living is the main culprit.[10]

The US compares favorably to other developed countries in terms of per-capita homeless rates—only about 0.18 per cent of the total population, compared to 0.94 per cent in New Zealand, the leader. But those figures are distorted by overall population sizes. In absolute numbers, the US dwarfs its peers with more than half a million people living on the streets. The next closest country, Germany, has 330 thousand. New Zealand has forty-one thousand.[11]

Going hand in hand with out-of-control cost of living is inequality, another measure in which the US fares poorly. The US is paradoxically the richest country in the world, but also the most unequal, according to financial services provider Allianz. The country scores eighty in the Gini coefficient—which uses zero to indicate perfect equality and one hundred as full inequality—thanks to a gap between rich and poor that has been growing unabated since the seventies. The Organisation for Economic Co-operation and Development ranks the US as the fourth most unequal country among advanced economies, after Turkey, Mexico and Chile.[12]

Like vigilantism, homelessness obviously isn't an exclusively American phenomenon. But there is something unique to American homelessness, which is rooted in similar origins. "We have the bootstraps approach in this country; it comes out of our pilgrim heritage," says the Night Ministry's Hamann. "Our ancestors came to this country, landed here in a boat and made something out of nothing. They pulled themselves up by their bootstraps and they made it. That is the pervasive American attitude. People feel that by the time you're an adult, you should not be in that homeless situation, or you've chosen to be there. You haven't been resilient enough to pull yourself up." The prevailing view, he says, is that homelessness in America is seen either as a choice or as a personal failure.

The problem is sparking grassroots efforts such as Chicago Hope and similar charity missions by people who reject that bootstraps view.

Growing homelessness is thus providing an opportunity for progressively minded individuals to partake in the real-life superhero community without having to engage in the crime prevention that has historically defined the movement. Many modern-day real-life superheroes either aren't interested in the crime fighting side of things or simply prefer to steer clear of its potential dangers. Some also reject the status-quo protection associated with vigilantism, as well as the legacy of Phoenix Jones—who has derogatorily referred to charity-minded heroes as "real-life sandwich handlers."[13] If entrepreneurial crime prevention is to be considered conservative in nature, this newer form of real-life superheroism has emerged as the progressive wing of the party, so to speak.

The progressive aspect began to rise in earnest in 2007, with the first Superheroes Anonymous meetup in New York City. Attended by thirteen real-life superheroes, the event saw the arrival of organizer Chaim Lazaros (whom we briefly heard from in Chapter 4) onto the scene. Filling in as master of ceremonies after a last-minute cancellation, he came up with the nom de guerre Life, complete with a fedora-and-domino-mask disguise inspired by film noir—era heroes such as the Shadow and the Spirit. The group engaged in crime patrols together and shared techniques, but Lazaros quickly discovered it wasn't for him. He found it difficult to catch crimes in progress, which made his patrols feel pointless. Along with fellow New York hero Dark Guardian, he would occasionally stumble upon drug dealers and chase them off, only to see them return shortly thereafter. "For all of the risk, the reward wasn't all that great," he says. "It's not like I cleaned up the city—*that's it, no more crack in New York!* I'm just not going to be as effective as a trained and armed police force in doing that."[14]

Lazaros found greater fulfillment in spending time with the destitute. "I was walking around with this new set of eyes, looking at, who could I help? I started seeing homeless people, but more importantly, I started talking to them," he says. He learned about their needs. "Food is usually not such a huge problem for the homeless. They can often get food. People would ask me a lot for socks, so I'd ask them, 'What are the things you need?'" The answers he received informed his creation of "Life Packs," which contain many of the same toiletries and essentials as the blue tote bags passed out at Chicago Hope. He also gained an understanding of the uniqueness of American homelessness by learning about how the people he encountered arrived at their respective situations. "In Denmark, you don't become homeless because you had some medical thing," he says. "In New York, I hear, 'I got sick, I lost my job, I lost my health insurance, I couldn't pay the rent, I got evicted, my only relative is a sister in Toledo and I haven't spoken to her in twenty years, so I landed on the street.' Some version of that is very common." Anger swells in his voice as he continues: "It really bothered me to see so many people lacking the basic necessities in such a rich country. There are literally billionaires on the sidewalk passing homeless people with nothing. It's severely unjust."

Lazaros says he has been fortunate in life. He has a wife and child and has worked as a radio producer since 2006. He considers his family to be middle-class, but he's cognizant of how his life could easily have turned out differently. He recalls a young man telling him about how he had been attending college, only to suffer an accident that required him to be taken to the hospital by helicopter. The experience ruined him financially and landed him on the streets. All that separated Lazaros from this unfortunate man was a random twist of fate. "If you don't have insurance, you can get hit with a bill of fifteen thousand dollars for that ride—and they'll collect it like credit-card debt or a gambling debt," he says. "That's the Jekyll-and-Hyde thing about America. You can become Bill Gates, but you can also become homeless from getting ill.'"

Lazaros has tried engaging in charitable acts in regular street clothes, but he has found his costume confers several benefits. "A police officer, when he gets out of his bathrobe in the morning and puts on his uniform and straightens his tie in the mirror, he probably feels like he becomes something bigger and greater and stands for something," he says. "Me becoming Life is probably more powerful than the priest or police officer. I'm becoming my higher self. That's an extremely powerful feeling. 'Life' is certain parts of Chaim. It's much more of my charitable side, my righteous side. It's much less of my selfish side, my lazy side. I become a different version of myself."

Wearing the costume also has practical effects, he says. Homeless people can easily recognize him and immediately know he isn't part of a religious group or government agency. "They don't question my motivation and they accept my help," he says. "The idea of superheroes is so known and so powerful that it transcends language and culture. A superhero just helps people. They know, 'He's not going to ask me for money, he's not going to bring me into a church. Okay, it's a little weird, but I understand the deal.' The deal is: I'm a superhero and this is for you."

Lazaros has been one of the more forceful voices online and through the Superheroes Anonymous platform in advocating the charity side of the real-life superhero movement. His messaging has run counter to Phoenix Jones's sandwich-handler put-down—that it's okay for real-life superheroes to focus on homeless outreach and charity rather than crime patrols. "It's quantitative," he says. "On a given day I know I've helped fifty people. They have clean, dry feet now and they're happy. I'm not trying to project or live out some unrealistic fantasy about vigilantism or anything like that."

The origin of the Hope missions began with a visit by RazorHawk to the 2010 San Diego Comic-Con. Up until that point, RazorHawk—a former professional wrestler who got his start in the community by making costumes and gear for other real-life superheroes—had been focused on crime and safety patrols. Mr. Xtreme invited him to join the Xtreme Justice League in a charity handout following Comic-Con, and he was immediately struck by the scale of homelessness in the city. "We didn't have that big of a homeless population on the street here at home [Minneapolis]," he says. "I had only seen pics. There's something different when it's in your face and you see people huddled in the doorways of abandoned businesses."

The proverbial lightbulb turned on and he decided to organize Project Hope, a group outreach mission that would coincide with Comic-Con the following year. He spent the intervening months entreating real-life superheroes across the country and in Canada to come out, and to bring goods to pass out. The event was ultimately a big success by his estimation, with forty-six real-life superheroes congregating to distribute hundreds of food items, bottles of water and other basics. The Hope missions have become an annual institution in San Diego and have since expanded to a number of cities around the country, including Chicago, Portland and Seattle, as well as to London and Liverpool in England.

Besides the planned events, charity has also since become part of the standard operating procedure for many real-life superheroes, regardless of political leanings. "There are a lot of folks still doing crime/safety patrols and I think a lot of them carry supplies to help out the homeless so they have something to do while they patrol," RazorHawk says.

THE NEXT MEN

THE EVOLUTION IS EVIDENT HERE AT THE SUPERHERO BAKERY, A POP-UP shop set up at the entrance of the Pottery Barn factory outlet on

Alameda Island. The cavernous store, situated in an unused Navy hangar just south of Oakland and across the bay from San Francisco, contains what seem like acres of chairs, tables and other assorted furniture. Just a few minutes' walk away is the Sea, Air and Space Museum, housed in the World War II–era USS *Hornet* aircraft carrier, the main attraction of a former military base that is rapidly gentrifying into an offbeat shopping destination.

Manning the bakery's counter are Rock N Roll and Night Bug, two of San Francisco's best-known real-life superheroes. Neither is masked right now, but a picture of the couple in full costumed regalia sits next to the muffins, cupcakes and scones that they spent hours baking earlier this morning. *Tired of watching the world and wishing someone would do something?* asks a sign on the counter. *The California Initiative is doing something.*

The California Initiative is far removed from Phoenix Jones and the Rain City Superhero Movement in both temperament and activities, the pink-haired Rock N Roll explains. The team holds free self-defense seminars, performs used-needle pickups and conducts night-time crime patrols, though they only rarely get involved despite the fact that both she and Night Bug have been martial arts instructors since the nineties. Indeed, they often engage in "grey-man" patrols, the term real-life superheroes use for out-of-costume activities. "We're not the ones who run in and try to kick someone's ass," Rock N Roll says. "We've been on patrol with people who have and they scare us. Mostly, we're eyes and ears for the police. We hope to not do anything in a night. We don't want to run into a crime in progress. If you want to go out and save the day, you're hoping for someone to have their worst day ever just so you can be that hero. We don't subscribe to that. We hope that every night is a quiet night."

A portion of all the bakery's sales goes to buying supplies for homeless people, which the duo and their teammates distribute.

Rock N Roll and Night Bug are very serious about homelessness, as they know several people personally who have struggled to make ends meet. One of them is their close friend Krystal Marx, who has flown in for a weekend visit from her home in Burien, near Seattle. Marx heads up the Washington Initiative, an affiliate of the San Francisco group, under the alias Temper. Her husband, James, used to be known as Evocatus, or Phoenix Jones's right-hand man in the Rain City Superhero Movement.

Marx's mother had Munchausen Syndrome by Proxy, which meant that she made up illnesses for her daughter in order to get attention. The two were homeless while Marx was young for months-long stretches, couch surfing with different families they knew in Aberdeen. Eventually, child services removed her from the situation and sent her to live with her father in Bellevue, Washington. Marx hasn't seen her mother since she was ten years old. "That instilled in me really early on that who you present yourself to be in public may not be who you really are," she says. "Being homeless doesn't mean that you're dumb or lazy."

Her family continues to struggle financially despite the fact that she was elected to Burien's city council in 2017. The job pays $550 a month after taxes, she says. Her husband, meanwhile, is mainly a homemaker who takes care of their four kids. He's still recovering from his tour of Iraq, where a mortar attack left him with a traumatic brain injury and post-traumatic stress disorder. Both are familiar with how easy it is to become homeless in the US, and how close to the edge many families are. Superheroes, especially real-life ones, are an increasingly needed beacon of hope. "Reality sucks right now, at least for a lot of people in America," she says. "This is an escape to a better time when we were kids, or into a world where maybe, just maybe, there's a possibility that something will come along and save us from it."

The Bay Coast Guardians, meanwhile, are a newer team of real-life superheroes in St. Petersburg, Florida. Formed in 2017, the group began with core members Impact, who works in environmental remediation; Jaguar, a physical trainer; Good Samaritan, who's in film production; and Ikon, a systems engineer. All four are white, middle-class and progressive in their views. The team routinely patrols the outskirts of St. Pete's bar district on weekends. Downtown is the polar opposite of San Diego's Gaslamp District—it's immaculately clean, spans just a few blocks and is heavily policed. Revelers are generally well behaved as a result, which means the town's resident real-life superheroes choose to occupy themselves in other ways.

Bay Coast Guardian patrols instead consist mainly of handing out granola bars and water bottles to the homeless people scattered around the core. On the pleasantly warm summer evening I spend with them, the team members help a pair of men figure out what's wrong with their car engine, give directions to a woman looking for a bar and pose for pictures with drunken merrymakers. St. Pete's actually has a higher-than-normal crime rate as far as Florida is concerned, particularly in the gang-heavy south part of the city, but that isn't the team's scene. Since their mission is mainly charitable, no one feels the need to wear a ballistic vest. "Going into a bad area dressed like we are is asking to get shot," Impact explains. Tending to St. Pete's destitute, he adds, is a far better use of the team's time. "You could consider homelessness a disease. It's something that can happen to you whether or not you do everything right, and it's hard to get out of. It's the least charismatic public issue out there," he says. "In the grand scheme of things, we've had next to no impact. Very little. But, I'm doing something. I don't do a lot, but for those who I do it for, it is a lot."

Ikon agrees. "People are so self-absorbed, they don't understand what it's like to give something that is so small to someone that has so much nothing," he says. "To see that smile is just an amazing thing. And when you dress up in a costume, that brings them even more joy."

IN BRIGHTEST DAY

MEANWHILE, BACK IN CHICAGO, SUPPLIES ARE DWINDLING. AFTER FIVE hours of trudging through Lower Wacker, Crusader Prime estimates his team has provided at least a hundred homeless people with useful goods, plus some immeasurable amount of amusement from seeing grown men and women in garish costumes. It's late afternoon and he says it's time to go topside, back into the sunlight and Chicago's hustle and bustle; there might be homeless people around the downtown Loop who can use the last of the handout supplies. It's also an opportunity for the group to accomplish the other part of their mission—spreading awareness of what they're doing.

The superheroes file up a stairwell and emerge into the daylight near North State Street and West Wacker Drive. The second part of their plan nets results immediately. A pair of women in their twenties ask the real-life superheroes for photos as they wait for the traffic light to change. Someone leans out of the side of a passing car and yells, "Why are you dressed like that?" Similar reactions multiply as the team moves south through downtown. On each occasion, the heroes stop to chat with people about what they're doing.

As Crusader Prime later explains, "A guy in jeans and a T-shirt walking down the street who hands a homeless guy a sandwich or a dollar, by the time he gets to the next corner, who's going to remember that? If you have a squad of ten people dressed in superhero costumes doing the same thing, that may have an impact on somebody. They may remember and maybe they'll do a good deed next."

Many real-life superheroes believe that striving to inspire is as important as passing out supplies, if not more so—it gets to the core of what they're truly fighting: apathy. It's obvious in cities such as Chicago, where people have become inured to the sight of homelessness. Residents and visitors alike walk past needy individuals holding signs asking for help without giving them a second thought or without even acknowledging their existence. "A lot of people turn a blind eye to stuff like this," Crusader Prime says. "When the weather is nice, there are people out on every corner and hundreds and thousands of people walk by them and... nothing. That's kind of a sad feeling even if it's not you who's on the street, that you can treat other humans so poorly. So let's make ourselves stand out so other people notice the problem."

Despite the issue being self-evident, American apathy doesn't necessarily show up in empirical measures. The US ranks highly in charitableness, according to the UK-based Charities Aid Foundation. The country ranked fifth on the organization's 2017 World Giving Index—which measures dollars donated, strangers helped and hours volunteered—and second over a five-year span. Americans are also tops in the world when it comes to helping strangers.[15] The two realities seem to be incongruent, but both can and do exist at the same time. Americans are charitable when it comes to helping those who need it; but the scope of that need may just be too large to handle.

None of the real-life superheroes taking part in Chicago Hope are under the illusion that their actions will change the larger systemic problems, but they want to help regardless. "We're trying to put a patch on the world," Geist says. "We can't be bystanders. I can't. I just can't be that person and live with myself."[16] Crusader Prime echoes that sentiment. "We don't take care of our own," he says. "A lot of us are one catastrophic event away from being the people that we're helping."

CHAPTER 7

A SUIT OF ARMOR AROUND THE WORLD

AS FAR AS FLAT MAN KNOWS, HE IS NEW ZEALAND'S ONLY REAL-LIFE superhero. In a country with fewer than five million people and one of the lowest population densities in the world, that's not surprising. Given the Pacific nation's socially harmonious image, even one might seem like too many.

Flat Man got his start following the 2011 earthquake in Christchurch, a disaster that killed nearly two hundred people and caused an estimated eleven billion dollars in damage. Feeling the need to help in some way, he assembled some food packages and delivered them to friends living in residence at a nearby university. The deed left him feeling good, so he decided to keep at it. As a lifelong superhero fan— he broke his collarbone when he was three years old by jumping off the roof of his family's two-storey house dressed as Superman—he figured it might be fun to deliver food in costume. He put together a uniform consisting of a red-and-black spandex bodysuit, a cape and a Mexican wrestling mask, then dubbed himself Flat Man after the flats where his school pals resided.

Flat Man has since engaged in some unique heroics. His main activity involves knocking on random doors in residential neighborhoods and handing food packages to whoever answers. "I'd probably get shot if I tried that in the US," he jokes.[1] He also plays a version of the kids' prank Ding Dong Ditch, where he rings doorbells and runs off before anyone can respond.[2] Instead of a flaming sack of poop on the doorstep, though, he leaves behind a bag of groceries. He also darts in and out of gridlock to deliver snacks to frustrated drivers. All told, Flat Man estimates his giveaways have cost him up to four hundred dollars a month. Schools and hospitals have taken notice of his activities and regularly invite him to give inspirational talks to kids. A local car dealership has loaned him a tricked-out car, the "Flatmobile," to use in his charity missions. He says even his "Flatmum" approves of his actions, which are intended to spread positivity. "My superhero powers are all about kindness and generosity," he says. "My motto is 'be a bruv, share the love.' The simple act of a card or flowers or chocolate can change someone's day or week. If someone is out there doing positive things it affects the amount of positivity in the world."

All things considered, New Zealand's need for figurative superheroes is relatively low. Despite the aberration of the horrific Christchurch mosque shootings in 2019, which left fifty-one dead, the country ranks as peaceful and law-abiding in just about every global crime and safety index, and routinely places at the top of happiness surveys. Per-capita homelessness is higher than the US rate, but the situation isn't nearly as grim. An estimated 10 per cent of the country's forty thousand plus homeless people suffer from mental health and addiction issues, but infrastructure mismanagement appears to be the main cause.[3] Escalating real estate prices are driving people into the street, as they are elsewhere, but local experts say it's mainly because the government hasn't facilitated the construction of enough new housing to keep pace with population growth.[4] The crisis certainly doesn't stem from people being unable to pay their medical bills, as it does in the US. Health care is free or heavily subsidized for all

New Zealand residents—even tourists get emergency treatment without having to pay for it.

Still, there isn't a country in the world that can't use more positivity; hence Flat Man's heroics. His demeanor starkly contrasts with Phoenix Jones's aggressiveness or even the Xtreme Justice League's stern efforts to maintain order in San Diego's bar district. Those sorts of physical approaches may not have a place in New Zealand. "We've got crime, but it tends not to be in your face like it is in other countries," Flat Man says. "Even when you go out at night in the bar areas you don't see that kind of anger. It wouldn't go down here. There just isn't the need for it. I don't know what you'd be trying to achieve."

COMMONWEALTH CONFORMITY

NEW ZEALAND IS A SMALL, ISOLATED EXAMPLE, BUT IT HELPS TO EXPLAIN why real-life superheroes are fewer and farther between outside of the United States. Costumed do-gooders have indeed popped up around the globe, from Heroi Ordem in Brazil and Capitán Menganno in Argentina, to Storm Dragon in Australia and Street Spirit in Costa Rica, to Entomo in Italy and Chibatman in Japan, just to name a few, but for the most part the phenomenon is fundamentally American. A proxy estimate for geographic dispersion can be taken from a 2016 survey of real-life superheroes by researchers at the University of Sydney in Australia, which found that about three-quarters of respondents were American, while the remainder were scattered around the world. Fewer people, smaller population densities and larger geographies are factors, as are less pressing social needs resulting from stronger laws and enforcement and safety nets such as unemployment insurance and health care. There is less push and pull—less supply and demand—in most countries for real-life superheroes.

Differing cultural values are also a significant factor. In many countries, authorities and the public alike are more likely to reject the physicality that has underpinned the real-life superhero movement in the US since its beginnings, even as it has evolved toward a more charitable bent. The idea of a superhero who operates on his own cognizance and not necessarily within existing social structures, while just as popular in fiction around the world, isn't as accepted in most other countries. The overwhelming sentiment is that the activities real-life superheroes engage in—whether oriented toward charity or fighting crime—are best left to professionals or institutional organizations. That can be oppressive to anyone thinking about dressing up in a costume to fight crime or to hand out supplies to homeless people.

The United Kingdom is a prime example—just ask Roger Hayhurst. The fledgling real-life superhero learned about social resistance the hard way in 2013 after appearing on television as his alter ego, Knight Warrior, where he talked about patrolling the streets of Manchester looking for bad guys to thwart. A group of local youths saw the interview, figured out who the self-styled superhero was under his mask, then found him and gave him a beating till he was as black and blue as his costume. Humiliated, his face swollen, the slight, twenty-year-old Hayhurst called it quits. He briefly returned to the scene five years later by organizing a Hope-branded homeless handout mission in Liverpool, this time with a new resolve—to focus on charitable work instead of crime patrols. "I really didn't know what I was doing," he says. "I look back at it now and think, 'What was I thinking?'"[5] Shortly after the mission, he appeared to once again hang up his tights, taking up stage magic and paranormal investigation instead.

The UK has had its share of real-life superheroes, if the definition can be stretched somewhat, starting with Angle Grinder Man around the turn of the millennium. An odd-job laborer by day, he patrolled the streets of Kent and London by night dressed in a blue-and-gold

The Xtreme Justice League guards the streets of San Diego's Gaslamp District. Left to right: Grim, Edgerunner, Light Fist, Fallen Boy, Mr. Xtreme, Midnight Highwayman, Brick and Violet Valkyrie. *Peter Nowak photo*

The Guardian Angels, a volunteer crime-fighting group and precursor to the real-life superhero phenomenon, patrol the streets of New York in the early 1980s. *Curtis Sliwa photo*

A memorial to environmental activist Jim Phillips, a.k.a. the Fox, was created in Violet Patch Park on the shore of the Fox River in Oswego, Illinois. *Peter Nowak photo*

Phoenix Jones (left) has gained notoriety for his hands-on approach to tackling crime. Here he joins forces with Evocatus in Seattle. *James Marx photo*

The Xtreme Justice League's Nyght pauses for a photo with a shop owner in San Diego's Gaslamp District. The group has attracted fans in the community by breaking up fights and patrolling the streets. *Peter Nowak photo*

Nyghtingale (left) and Freedom Fighter work with the rest of the Xtreme Justice League to keep the streets of San Diego safe. *Peter Nowak photo*

Real-life superheroes prepare for a homeless handout mission in Chicago's Lower Wacker. Left to right: Reverb, Geist, RazorHawk, Frost and Patchwork. *Peter Nowak photo*

Samael takes a break from a Chicago mission to catch up on his comics. *Peter Nowak photo*

Superhero duties for the Bay Coast Guardians include hamming it up with tourists. Left to right: Good Samaritan, Ikon, an innocent bystander, Jaguar and Impact. *Peter Nowak photo*

The Bay Coast Guardians' Impact makes a friend on the streets of St. Petersburg, Florida. *Peter Nowak photo*

Knight Warrior displays the United Kingdom Initiative banner in London. *Lord Mole photo*

The members of Canada's Trillium Guard show off their weatherized gear during a mission in Toronto. Left to right: T.O. Ronin, Canadian Justice, Nameless Crusader and Urban Knight. *Peter Nowak photo*

Peatonito, an activist who spray-paints DIY crosswalks on dangerous intersections, helps pedestrians in Mexico City. *Felix Canez photo*

Luchador, activist and public speaker Tacubo leaves his mask on while riding the subway in Mexico City. *Edgar Olguín photo*

The polarizing real-life superhero Master Legend poses on the streets of Orlando, Florida. *Peter Nowak photo*

The members of the California Initiative fight homelessness but avoid physical altercations on the streets of San Francisco. Left to right: Vector, Shadarko, Temper, Night Bug, Rock N Roll and Draco. *Peter Nowak photo*

costume looking for wheel clamps that police had affixed to parked cars, which he would then saw off with his grinder tool. He even maintained a hotline number that motorists could call to request his services. He considered himself a vigilante freedom fighter. "I may not be able to single-handedly and totally cast off the repressive shackles of a corrupt government, but I can cut off your wheel-clamps for you," he told the BBC in 2003. "My obsession with wheel-clamping is actually a rebellion against a much deeper malaise. Namely, the arrogant contempt that politicians hold for the people who put them into power, and whom they claim to represent."[6]

Angle Grinder Man soon disappeared from the public eye, but not before inspiring a colorful cavalcade of similarly short-lived British real-life superheroes, including Statesman, Vague, Swift, Black Arrow, Lionheart, Terrorvision, Onyx Avenger, Shipwreck and others. In 2015, a black-clad individual wearing a bandana over his face began intervening in attempted muggings in South London. Dubbed the Bromley Batman by the media, but reportedly preferring the name "Shadow," the mystery man was active for about two years until he disappeared without a trace, much like Angle Grinder Man.

Local crime experts say it's difficult to engage in American-style vigilantism because of the UK's ubiquitous surveillance and the illegality of carrying weapons or armor, as many real-life superheroes do in the United States. Citizens aren't allowed to possess flak jackets, pepper spray and the like, which makes such individuals more vulnerable in physical situations. "The British police make them go away a lot quicker, the gaps in the law are a lot smaller," says Gavin Weston, the vigilantism expert. "The risk factors are higher, the threat from the police is a lot higher."[7] The British public is also generally more hostile toward self-styled heroes, as evidenced by the attack on Knight Warrior. "People like to say 'I told you so' when people who have been successful fall, they like to see people brought down," says Lord Mole, who has straddled the line between charity-oriented real-life super-hero and online real-life super-villain. "People end up challenging that behavior: 'You're a superhero? Let's see what your super powers are!'"[8]

Black Mercer, a real-life superhero in Liverpool, thinks this resistance might be rooted in the requirement for children to wear uniforms in school, which conditions them to stay within the status quo. "It's a lot more formal," he says. "Watch the way you dress, watch the way you speak."[9] This uniformity speaks to a larger phenomenon found in many English-speaking countries that aren't the United States—the so-called tall poppy syndrome, where people of high status are often resented, criticized and cut down by those below them. The concept is rooted in old British classism, where individuals are socially punished—not necessarily for succeeding, but for flaunting their success. Commonwealth countries have generally retained this sensibility, along with both the good and ill associated with it. On the plus side, it's a form of culturally sanctioned humility that acts as a curb on arrogance. On the down side, as several studies in New Zealand and Canada have found, it can be a drag on business performance and productivity, especially for women, who disproportionately find themselves being cut down in the workplace. Tall poppy syndrome is also common in other cultures, where it is known by different names or idioms. The Law of Jante, for example, is the unspoken code of conduct in Nordic countries that deems nonconformity and overt ambition unworthy and inappropriate. In Asia, the traditional proverb that "the nail that sticks up gets hammered down" is pervasive.

Such social leveling mechanisms are anathema in the United States, where the opposite is often true—the taller the poppy, the better. The difference has its roots again in the very founding of the country, in the rebellion by pilgrims against British rigidity. American settlers, unbound by generations of tradition and classism, adopted a different attitude—that success is something to be celebrated.

Benjamin Franklin Fairless offered perhaps the best articulation of this divergent worldview, as well as the inherent problem with tall poppy syndrome, when he said that "You cannot add to the stature of a dwarf by cutting off the legs of a giant."[10] Americans thus have no problem standing out from the crowd. The impulse to rise above is in their country's DNA.

Historian Richard Maxwell Brown suggests the relative lack of entrepreneurial law enforcement efforts in Britain is an outgrowth of national evolution—the country simply doesn't have a tradition of vigilantism the way the United States does. It's a relatively small country with a long history of dense and stable settlements with a healthy respect for the rule of law.[11] If anyone is familiar with this, it's Curtis Sliwa. The Guardian Angels founder has tried repeatedly to establish his group in the country, with little luck. It isn't just Britain, he says—the same has held true across the Commonwealth, including Canada, Australia and New Zealand. "Any countries that flew the Union Jack or were still basically somewhat under the British system were always the most opposed to the start of a Guardian Angels chapter because it was this 'American' thing," he says. "They would say, 'We don't have American-style problems,' and for the most part they didn't. But there's more violent crime now in London than in New York City. Who would have ever thought that?"[12] He isn't exaggerating—violent crime rates in the United Kingdom have been rising. Fifteen people were murdered in London in February 2018 alone, versus fourteen in New York, the first month in modern history where the British capital surpassed the American city in that measure.[13]

Sliwa also finds Canada's resistance to the Guardian Angels exasperating. The group has been trying to establish a chapter in Toronto, the country's biggest city, since the early eighties, but has been stymied on multiple occasions. Reacting to one such attempt in 2006, Toronto mayor Mel Lastman likened the organization to criminals: "The Mafia got started by originally wanting to do good and then they became the gangster organization," he said. "I'm very concerned about people who are coming into areas, who are not asked to come into those areas."[14] Lastman refused to meet with Sliwa, but he did pose for photos and shake hands with members of the Hells Angels in 2002. He later claimed he didn't know the motorcycle gang was involved in murders and the illegal drug trade. "How do you like that?" Sliwa says.

Canada is similar to New Zealand and Britain in its cultural and institutional resistance to vigilantism and entrepreneurial law enforcement, which means the few real-life superheroes who have popped up have typically focused on charity and goodwill. Thanatos, clad in black with a green skull mask, patrolled Vancouver's streets for years, helping homeless people and handing out supplies. Polar Man, meanwhile, was perhaps the most Canadian of real-life superheroes—he'd show up at people's houses in Iqaluit, the remote capital of Nunavut, dressed in a black-and-white costume and mask, and shovel snow from their driveways. "We're more about community service," he says. "Down in the states they're kind of like bounty hunters."[15]

Ark Guard, an inactive real-life superhero in Toronto whose day job is in security, says the crime-fighting aspect of the phenomenon is a nonstarter. "Starting off with that sales pitch is not good," he says. "It's not as accepted in Canada."[16] He recalls one of the first group missions he took part in shortly after he began patrolling in 2012. About a dozen real-life superheroes had met up in a downtown Toronto alley and were changing into their costumes, only to be interrupted by police who had been summoned by nervous security guards from the university campus nearby. The heroes were made to unmask and produce identification, then warned to alert authorities whenever they assembled. "The police were then joking around with us and taking photos. I don't know if that was a good thing or a bad thing," he says.

"Everyone is so sensitive, they always expect the worst. If I show up wearing all black, right away everyone thinks: Terrorist."

Crimson Canuck's experiences in Windsor, just across the border from Detroit, have been similar. He's mostly retired now, but in the four years in which he was active, police routinely stopped him and made him unmask and produce identification. It became enough of a hassle that he stopped wearing his mask and eventually his red-and-black costume altogether, opting instead to go "grey man." On top of that, he discovered the other realities of trying to fight crime independently in Canada. "Patrolling in Windsor sucks. No one goes outside in winter except for you because you're crazy," he says. "Literally every patrol was boring, the vast majority of them were wet and cold. Ninety-five per cent of the minutes spent patrolling were miserable and me questioning myself, asking 'Why the frick am I doing this?'"

These experiences aren't endemic to Canadian real-life superheroes—their American counterparts must also deal with police resistance and boredom on patrol. The best way to get past police issues, according to American veterans like Mr. Xtreme, is to prove one's good intentions by sticking with it and staying within the law. Boredom can be alleviated by finding comrades to patrol with.

Neither of those options is necessarily practical in many countries. Smaller populations and greater distances between cities, both of which are especially true in Canada, make it harder to congregate and organize regular patrols. That in turn makes it difficult to develop a rapport with local authorities. Fewer real-life superheroes overall also means it's harder to find patrol partners, which relegates the few who do suit up to the inevitable boredom that goes with the gig. In a country like Canada, the forces discouraging people from becoming real-life superheroes are great indeed.

WINTER SOLDIERS

STILL, SOME DO IT. THOSE WHO DO TEND TO BE A KINDER AND GENTLER representation of the American archetype, which fits well with Canada's reputation as a nation of polite and friendly hosers. The Trillium Guard of Ontario, for example, focuses almost exclusively on homeless outreach. It takes only one patrol with the team to see the difference in tone and demeanor from their American counterparts. The team members don't have military backgrounds and don't usually wear functional armour. They don't sport *F*ck ISIS* badges, nor are they even likely to curse in public (remember Crimson Canuck saying "frick" just a few sentences ago?). They don't go near bars or clubs. They're more likely to give the people they encounter a hug than a face full of pepper spray. Heck, the team is even named after a flower.

It's a cold Saturday afternoon in February in downtown Toronto; the Trillium Guard's four members have picked the most Canadian of times to engage in a charity mission. Snow is falling onto the slush already covering the sidewalks, adding to the wet mess blanketing the city. Traffic snarls slowly across Yonge Street, the downtown core's central artery, as drivers struggle to navigate the barely visible roads. Hordes of shoppers step gingerly, afraid of slipping and falling.

The team manages to make it just a few steps from the Silver Snail comic shop, their meetup spot, before encountering an elderly woman bundled in a parka and giant wool scarf, holding a sign asking for food. Canadian Justice, who sports a military utility vest and camouflage balaclava, asks if she wants socks, water or toiletries. The woman happily accepts them all. T.O. Ronin, who resembles a ninja in her black costume, gives the woman a granola bar and a heart-shaped lollipop. An attached note reminds her, *You're not forgotten!*—a timely message of love, given that it's almost Valentine's Day.

A few steps farther on, the team comes across a man sitting on the ground, puffing a cigarette. Nameless Crusader, who wears a paintball mask and red-and-white camouflage gear, offers him a T-shirt from his pushcart of supplies. The man asks if he has any hooded sweatshirts, but no luck. "You guys know me, right? I used to be a protestor and activist," the man says. "My father is George Chuvalo," referring to the Canadian heavyweight boxer. "He kind of forgot about me. I don't deserve nothing." No one is quite sure what he's talking about, but T.O. Ronin steps forward regardless. "Yes, you do," she says. "Everyone deserves something. Don't give up the fight."

Nearby, a panhandler elicits chuckles from passersby with a sign that reads, *I'm too ugly to strip and I'm too nice to steal.* He explains to Urban Knight, clad in a steel medieval breastplate and chainmail hood, that he isn't actually homeless. Skyrocketing property rates mean all of his income goes to rent, so he's forced to beg for money to pay for food and laundry. Urban Knight gives him a bottle of water and a pair of socks and gets a compliment on his armor in return. "I used to dress up as a Klingon," the man laughs.

The Trillium Guard members range in age from late twenties to early forties, each starting as real-life superheroes in 2012 or 2013. Canadian Justice and Urban Knight are brothers, a university student and a car parts technician, respectively. Both were inspired by the HBO *Superheroes* documentary and *Kick-Ass* movie, although Urban Knight says his brother initially pressured him into suiting up. Both loved comic books and role-playing games growing up, so the move into the participatory aspect of that part of pop culture was natural for them. "It's a break in the normal routine of life," Urban Knight says. "It enables me to be charitable, but also dress up oddly with partners. There's also the notion of directly delivering help to those who need it. It's a great deal of self-satisfaction, it makes me feel like I'm doing a good thing. And I might as well do it while dressed up funny."[17]

Nameless Crusader works in the digital entertainment industry. The Trillium Guard is his second real-life superhero team; the Justice Crew of Oshawa, a city about an hour east of Toronto, was his first. His old team, which dissolved as members drifted away, received a certificate of appreciation from the city for cleaning up trash at a local park. T.O. Ronin, meanwhile, is originally from Ottawa, the nation's capital, about four hours northeast of Toronto. She says she was motivated to don her ninja-like attire after her martial arts teacher died. An odd-job laborer by day, her charitable activities also bring personal satisfaction. "It was a pretty dark time in my life," she says. "I'm just grateful that the universe reached out to me... and helped me out and kept me alive all this time."[18]

The group continues down Yonge Street, then bears east toward the public park in front of Metropolitan United Church. The benches and tables here are a popular spot for the less fortunate to congregate in warmer months. On the team's previous visit in the summer, the area was busy with people playing chess or surreptitiously drinking beer out of cans hidden in paper bags. On this snowy Saturday, it's deserted. The team members don't mind because they're now close to their secondary destination, the McDonald's across the street. They pool their money and send Urban Knight inside to order as many hamburgers as he can afford.

While we wait, Canadian Justice recounts a tragedy he and his teammates encountered on their previous patrol at this same McDonald's. He had headed inside to use the bathroom, but found it occupied. The restaurant manager realized that someone had been tying it up for a long time, so he knocked on the door. When the manager got no response, he unlocked it and discovered a man unconscious on the floor. His lips were blue and he wasn't breathing, the telltale signs of a fentanyl overdose, a common occurrence in the area. Canadian Justice offered up a naloxone injection kit that he had with him, but the manager refused it, not wanting to risk liability. Paramedics and police arrived soon after, but the man ended up dying. "We could have saved him, but the manager wouldn't let me," Canadian Justice says angrily. The incident led him to swap out the needle kit for a nasal spray, which he shows me. "This should be much easier to use and probably less intimidating than a needle," he says. "Hopefully I'll be allowed to help next time."

With a bag of burgers secured, the team heads east to Queen and Sherbourne, one of the most notorious intersections in Toronto. The northeast corner is home to Moss Park, a baseball diamond and adjoining green space where drug use is rampant. A FOR LEASE sign has gone up in the window of the former Libertarian Public House on the southeast corner. Just a few months earlier, a masked gunman casually strolled into the bar's patio and opened fire, leaving one person dead and four wounded. An abandoned building sits on the southwest corner while the northeast corner hosts an array of downtrodden businesses: a discount convenience store, a tattoo parlor and a dive bar. With a shelter just around the corner and a drug haven across the street, the front stoop of the bar is a magnet for homeless people and junkies, even now in the driving snow. The Trillium Guard head straight for this congregation; their offers of free McDonald's hamburgers are received warmly.

The real-life superheroes spend the next twenty minutes unloading much of the gear they've brought with them: clothes, granola bars, bottles of water, care packages containing toothbrushes and other toiletries. More people filter out of the bar and ask for specific items— hooded sweatshirts are again a popular request. Canadian Justice makes a mental note to stock up for next time. The bustle continues as the heroes round the corner to the Salvation Army shelter, where another group greets them cheerily. Urban Knight draws more attention with his shiny armor. "I played a lot of Dungeons & Dragons back in the day," a man named Robert tells him. T.O. Ronin offers hugs to anyone who wants them and gets several takers.

With much of their gear handed out, the group heads north toward All Saints Anglican Church, one of four warming centers in Toronto where homeless individuals can shelter from the cold overnight. The church sits on the southeast corner of Sherbourne and Dundas, an even more notorious junction than the one a few blocks south. Based on sheer volume and crime per square kilometer, it was ranked the most violent intersection in the city in 2009. "That's what happens when you put all the city's poorest people together on the same block," a janitor living in the area told the Toronto *Star* newspaper.[19]

A few people are milling about outside the church, some chatting, others puffing on cigarettes. None seem interested in the Trillium Guard's goods. Suddenly, a conversation between two men gets heated; one starts shouting unintelligibly at the other. It's now early evening, a time when tensions tend to rise here. The church has 150 spots and several dozen people get turned away every night. Arguments and fights over those spaces are common. No one wants to be stuck outside, especially when the weather is as poor as it is today.

T.O. Ronin moves to intercede in the brewing fight, but Canadian Justice cuts her off. "Let's move," he says, raising his voice. "It's time for us to go!" The other three heroes cross the street; reluctantly, she follows. A few blocks later, Canadian Justice explains that developing a sense for danger is part of the real-life superhero gig. Avoiding conflict is often their best course of action, since it doesn't antagonize an existing situation into something worse. It also keeps the real-life superheroes off authorities' radar, which allows them to continue their charitable activities.

This approach stands in stark contrast with how teams patrol in places such as San Diego and Seattle. It's a fact of life for real-life superheroes in Canada, who are only just barely tolerated by both authorities and the public. It highlights the culturally sanctioned humility—the tall poppy syndrome—prevalent in countries other than the US. "When you go outside the bounds of the law and piss off the police, not only do you create a bad name for the community as a whole, you also risk legislation being put in place to prevent this sort of thing from happening," Nameless Crusader says. "If they can argue that you're putting yourself or other people in danger by doing this, then the next thing you know, this legislation comes out about outlawing dressing up in costumes at night or things of that nature."[20]

FROM CIRCUS TO UNESCO

IF THERE'S ANY COUNTRY IN THE WORLD WHERE SUPERHEROES ARE AS beloved as they are in the United States and where their real-world counterparts may be just as tolerated, or even encouraged, it's Mexico. That's because Mexican superheroes are very different entities from how they are generally known in the rest of the world. Mexican archetypes aren't necessarily superpowered aliens or Norse gods or even teenagers who have been bitten by radioactive spiders. Rather, they're professional wrestlers. Real-life superheroes in Mexico are also very different from how we've come to know them so far in this story.

Coming from humble beginnings in the 1930s, *lucha libre* professional wrestling—literally "free fighting"—has evolved into a cultural institution in the country. Its practitioners, or *luchadores*, are venerated as nothing short of real-life superheroes, albeit in the truer, less ironic sense of the term. They aren't seen just as hulking men who bash each other with chairs on television each week; they're symbolic characters who represent the never-ending battle between good and evil. Like their American superhero counterparts, they have permeated Mexican pop culture to the point where regular people are adopting their own *luchador* personas to promote social causes and combat injustices. In modern Mexican society, *luchadores* have as much power to inspire people to do good as Batman, Superman and other comic book superheroes do in the United States.

Like superhero comic books, pro wrestling is an American invention. It originated in P.T. Barnum's nineteenth-century touring circus. In between lion-taming acts and acrobatics displays, Barnum's skilled Greco-Roman wrestlers would solicit challenges from random audience members. These were untrained marks at first, but Barnum eventually figured out that the matches were more interesting when the wrestlers engaged with capable plants instead. The wrestling match thus changed from being a proper contest to a representation of a contest. Audiences bought in to this new form of entertainment, which became known as "professional wrestling," and the phenomenon grew into a system of intercity circuits in the United States and Europe. By the 1920s, wrestlers were traveling internationally and adopting characters to make themselves more memorable. In the US, it became fashionable for practitioners to use their heritages as their nom de guerre gimmicks, hence the likes of Italian Joe Savoldi, Jimmy "The Greek" Thepos and Turkish Ali Baba.[21]

In 1933, Salvador Lutteroth, a Mexican government property inspector, was immediately smitten while taking in one of these events in the tiny Texas border town of Eagle Pass. Along with a financial partner, he imported wrestling to Mexico City under the banner of their newly formed company, *Empresa Mexicana de la Lucha Libre* (EMLL). The organization staged regular cards that proved to be as successful south of the border as they were north of it. Performers were initially drawn from the United States, but local talent eventually emerged to Mexicanize the quasi-sport.

American wrestling was typified at the time as a battle between social classes, or of homegrown good guys versus foreign bad guys. As historian Heather Levi puts it in her book *The World of Lucha Libre*, confrontations in American wrestling typically took place between "the working stiff and the egghead or the Italian and the hillbilly." With Mexico having a different social organization and different demographics, wrestling characters necessarily evolved in a different direction. Performers donned masks to embody not just social types, but also animals, supernatural entities and forces of nature, becoming something more comic book-ish in the process. As Levi writes,

> Like magical realist fiction, lucha libre portrays a world in which human agency is limited and supplemented by the intervention of (natural and supernatural) force beyond human control. Masking, in this context, is a convention that allows wrestlers to represent the abstract, mythological levels of reality. Lucha libre thus portrays a world view that recognizes human agency is ultimately constrained the forces of history, nature, and the world beyond.[22]

Just as disguised superheroes in comic books allowed readers to project themselves onto their adventures, masked *luchadores* provided audiences someone heroic to identify with. Mexican wrestling thus became even more participatory than its American counterpart, with spectators living vicariously through the performers. As writer and *lucha libre* fan Salvador Novo puts it,

> Each rheumatic and bald owner of a two-peso ticket at ringside loses the kilos and years necessary to transform himself, during a quarter of an hour, into [heroic wrestler] Jimmy el Apolo, and with equal ease, find in El Hombre Montana or

in Alberto Corral his enemies scattered around the world—
the landlord, the section chief, his own father-in-law—and
contributes from his seat to exterminate them, to kick them,
to throw them out of the ring.[23]

Lucha libre found its way onto Mexican television in 1948, where
it grew in popularity until 1954. But then, coinciding with the publication of Fredric Wertham's *Seduction of the Innocent*, which kicked off
the Great Comic Book Scare north of the border, Mexican authorities
enforced a crackdown of their own on wrestling. Fearing that children
would injure themselves by imitating the moves being performed by
professionals, the government restricted minors from attending live
matches and banned *lucha libre* from television. The various *empresas*
that had sprung up didn't object much, because they feared that the
new medium would cannibalize attendance at their live events anyway.
The ban, they felt, would be good for business.

Movies stepped into the void and further mythologized *luchadores*.
Films put wrestlers such as El Santo, Blue Demon and Mil Máscaras
into all manner of melodramas, comedies, science-fiction and horror
stories. The masked protagonists fought gangsters, drug smugglers,
evil scientists, zombies, vampires, Martians and every other B-movie
villain imaginable. Production companies cranked these super-low-
budget films out to satisfy the explosive demand, with an estimated
three hundred films running in theaters through to the mid-eighties.
El Santo—literally, the Saint—appeared in no fewer than fifty of them,
making him the king of the genre and cementing his status as a pop
culture icon akin to Superman or Mickey Mouse. As Levi writes, the
movies elevated flesh-and-blood wrestlers to mythic status, presenting
the *luchador* as "a vision of stability, an incorruptible hero immune to
the ravages of time."[24] It was like Mexico had superseded the current
superhero movie craze by several decades.

The lack of televised matches also led to Mexican wrestling diverging stylistically from its American origins. Rather than developing the ability to escalate feuds verbally, as American wrestlers did, *luchadores* instead improved their physical acumen to become more agile and acrobatic than their northern counterparts. This also helped them in movies where they effectively became the special effects that producers couldn't otherwise afford, which further contributed to their perceived superheroism. On screen and in person, they were characters that viewers or spectators could fantasize about inhabiting, capable of superhuman feats. "They were the only types of figures that could compete with the likes of Superman and Batman," says Luis Coronado Guel, a history professor at the University of Arizona, who specializes in Mexican pop culture. "It's how those movies became masterpieces."[25]

Wrestling returned to television in Mexico in the early nineties and continued its ascent into mainstream pop culture. By this point, *lucha libre* was increasingly viewed within Mexico as something uniquely Mexican. In the eyes of many fans, it was also seen as superior to its American counterpart by virtue of its athleticism. It also carried the social connotation of being a phenomenon associated with the common masses, which made it more real to its audience despite its fantastical characters. Since there had never been much money in *lucha libre*, *luchadores* were still considered members of the general population, rather than members of a class of wealthy celebrities, which meant that the costumed individual back-flipping off the top rope on television could very well be your next-door neighbor or coworker. *Lucha libre* became accepted as a form of entertainment uniquely developed in Mexico and representative of the country's particular idiosyncrasies. Whereas pro wrestling in the United States continued to be shamefully associated with the poor and uneducated masses, in Mexico that connection was considered a badge of honor for fans.

The veneration of El Santo (Rodolfo Guzmán Huerta) is proof. The wrestler and movie star was honored with a statue in his hometown of Tulancingo after his death in 1984. Huerta was again honored in 2017, the centennial of his birth, with a ceremony at which Roberto Shimizu, art director for the Antique Toy Museum in Mexico City, spelled out what he meant to the country: "For us Mexicans, El Santo is a figure of rectitude, of integrity, of dedication. He represents every virtue." Felipe Carrillo Montiel, an El Santo expert, also highlighted his impact: "While Americans had Superman, Batman or Spider-Man, we had Rodolfo Guzmán, El Santo, fighting everybody from the mummies to the Nazis.... But unlike those American superheroes, he was a real man—you could read his comics during the week and then go see him wrestle on the weekend at your local arena."[26]

Lucha libre is now a legitimate cultural export, with luchadores a fixture of wrestling shows in the United States, Europe and Japan. In 2018, Mexico City mayor José Ramón Amieva gave the quasi-sport Intangible Cultural Heritage status, a decree that grants it special UNESCO protections on the same level as Chinese calligraphy, Indian Yoga and Japanese Kabuki theater. Given their cultural importance and prevalence in the United States, American superheroes might someday find themselves on that list, but for the time being—just like in the movies—Mexican luchadores have beaten them to the punch.

LOS VENGADORES MONTAR

IT WAS PERHAPS INEVITABLE, THEN, THAT SOMEONE, SOMEWHERE WOULD think to use the image of the luchador to do good in the real world. The first to do so was likely Fray Tormenta in 1973, who in actuality was Sergio Gutiérrez Benítez, a reformed drug addict and alcoholic turned priest. After teaching philosophy and history at Catholic universities in Mexico, Benítez founded an orphanage that served as a home to hundreds of children. Chronically short of funds to run the operation, he was inspired by a pair of sixties *luchador* films in which the protagonists were priests who wrestled for money. Donning red-and-yellow tights and a matching mask, Benítez became Fray Tormenta, "Friar Storm" in English—a humble *padre* by day, an evil-fighting, fan-favorite *luchador* by night. If the story sounds familiar, it might be because it was retold in the US in the 2006 film *Nacho Libre*, in which Jack Black plays a comically inept monastery cook who secretly wrestles as the titular character to buy food for children.[27] Benítez officially retired in 2011, but one of the kids from his orphanage continues his legacy as Fray Tormenta Jr.

Next up was Superbarrio, who in the late eighties became Mexico's first "social wrestler"—a *luchador*-themed real-life superhero who didn't necessarily get his start in the ring. Superbarrio was instead the creation of journalist and social activist Marco Rascón as a reaction to the 1985 Mexico City earthquake, which killed more than ten thousand people and left over a quarter million homeless. Frustrated by government inaction in finding homes for the displaced, Rascón had Superbarrio—dressed in a red-and-yellow costume, mask and cape—show up at protests to demand action. The *luchador* also intervened in tenant evictions by rallying people to counter thugs hired by landlords. When the goons went into homes and moved occupants' belongings onto the street, Superbarrio and his followers shoved the items back inside through the windows. The character became a media sensation as a result, succeeding in his mission to draw attention to tenant rights. Rascón escalated the character's activities over time, ultimately declaring him as an unofficial presidential candidate in both Mexican and U.S. elections. He went so far as to hold mock rallies in which he denounced social inequity in the Americas and U.S. influence in Mexico, criticizing President Bill Clinton and his

Republican challenger, Bob Dole, in 1996 for their "madness" and supposedly racist policies.[28]

Rascón, who runs a seafood restaurant in Mexico City, is cagey about whether he ever actually wore the Superbarrio costume. He says more than fifty people have assumed the identity in the thirty plus years since he created it. "Superbarrio is a symbol, an image, a hero," he tells me through a translator. "It's not important who is under the mask. What's important is that people believe and use the symbol of Superbarrio to defend their rights."[29]

The character was effective in drawing attention to the plight of ordinary tenants, he says, because of *lucha libre*'s low cultural status in the late eighties. It wasn't yet part of the mainstream and was instead, like its US counterpart, still associated with the lower classes, which made it poignant to the people Rascón was seeking to represent. "It was a synonym to saying it's where the poor live," he says. "It became a symbol for the lower-class neighborhoods in Mexico City." Almost as importantly, the campiness of *luchadores* established through decades of low-budget B movies meant there was an element of humor attached to them. Rascón says this satirical aspect was—and is—necessary when rabble-rousing in a country as politically dangerous as Mexico. He recalls one protest in which Superbarrio challenged the chief of police to a wrestling match; he obviously wasn't serious, but the stunt helped defuse growing tension at the event. "Masked superheroes are an expression to the crisis of political parties; it's a way for citizens to fight for their rights, and not through the traditional political process," he says. "It puts it into another dimension. You have to take care of Superbarrio because if he disappears, the violence will come."

Superbarrio's effectiveness in spurring change is evidenced by the wave of social wrestlers that followed throughout the eighties and nineties. Ecologista Universal, in his green-and-yellow costume, used similar tactics to draw attention to environmental issues. Super Animal, in a black-and-gold getup, worked to have bullfights banned in Mexico. Super Gay, wearing pink tights and a rainbow-colored cape, encouraged gay and lesbian individuals to come out of the closet. In recent years, they have been joined by the likes of Peatonito, who was created by pedestrian activist Jorge Cáñez in 2012. Dressed in a black, white and green costume, Peatonito spray-paints his own crosswalks onto busy intersections that otherwise lack them. City officials sometimes erase his work, but other times they accept the unprompted suggestion and make the impromptu crosswalk permanent. "Sometimes road safety is very difficult to communicate, so this became a funny, great way to communicate the message that we have destroyed our cities just to make more room for cars," Cáñez says.[30] Like Rascón, he says the Peatonito idea is catching on—especially now that *lucha libre* is trendy—with a number of people assuming the identity since he first debuted it. Mexico City officials also invited Cáñez to create a road safety program for children, which he dubbed Peatonitos. The program seeks to fully or partially close some roads to create safe places for kids to play.

Tacubo is another social wrestler, though he is also an actual *luchador*. When he isn't performing flips in the ring, he's delivering anti-bullying talks in primary schools. He tells children about how wrestling helped him overcome being picked on. As a short and skinny kid, he lacked self-confidence. Learning how to wrestle taught him to tap into reserves of inner strength. He says his message resonates with children because of their veneration of wrestlers as superheroes. "My ideas are disruptive, not just to the students, but to the teachers and the schools, because I go out of the stereotype boxes," he says through a translator. "They come with PowerPoint presentations or scholarly speeches and they can't connect with students. One of my superpowers is connecting directly with students."[31]

Tacubo is aware of the authority granted by his status. He sounds like Spider-Man, with his mantra of great power conferring great responsibility, when talking about it. "*Luchadores* have filled that need for superheroes for Mexican audiences," he says. "When I realized the power of being a communicator and all the features of being a super-hero, I saw the positive side of it. I saw that label would be useful to make more people aware and get more visibility in helping people's lives, and even saving lives."

The results these social wrestlers get are varied and can be diffi-cult to measure, but their effectiveness is tangible nevertheless. "They are cultural flash points," Levi says. "They're not claiming victory, because it's a mode of communication. They're drawing attention to the issue that they're involved with. The fact that we've even heard of them shows they've succeeded." Guel says Mexican real-life superheroes are more effective than their northern counterparts because they aim higher. "There's no political boundaries for these superheroes because they come out of a community's need," he says. "They use whatever fame they have to advocate for their social causes. They started to understand the power they had by being famous among the community and using that to solve problems. That makes them uncomfortable for certain political figures."

One thing real-life superheroes in Mexico don't do, however, is patrol for crime. It's just too dangerous. The Guardian Angels came to Mexico City in the early aughts, with the chapter founded—of course—by a wrestler. Unlike their experiences in Commonwealth countries, the Angels were encouraged and welcomed by the local government as part of an exported initiative launched by former New York mayor Rudolph Giuliani to make Mexico City safer. The group had no trouble attracting recruits locally, but they soon found signifi-cant limitations to what they could do. "There are parts of Mexico City where you can't fuck around," says Canadian-born Ian Hodgkinson, the chapter founder who is better known as the *luchador* star Vampiro. "You can't look sideways because if you do the wrong thing, you're not going to make it out."[32] Hodgkinson says he was kidnapped, beaten and tortured by corrupt police on two separate occasions after expanding the Angels to Guadalajara. He said he was also threatened with death unless he left the country. He complied, though he eventually returned after a time in both instances.[33] The Guardian Angels have since shifted their focus in Mexico toward charity work and neighborhood cleanup. "There's no crime fighting. You can't. This is cartel heaven," Hodgkinson says. "You say the wrong thing, you've got a convoy of fifteen suvs pulling up on your house and your whole family, with machine guns." Needless to say, if the Guardian Angels aren't trying to fight crime on Mexican streets, neither are spandex-clad superheroes.

The Mexican experience highlights some truths about the overall real-life superhero phenomenon and its innate Americanness. While costumed do-gooders universally subscribe to a belief in the power of symbolism to promote social causes, those outside the United States tend to share a greater cognizance of the limitations of symbols. Whether imposed externally by social opposition and official authorities or internalized by fear or simple good sense, non-Americans generally do their best to avoid even the hint of danger—or they learn to do so soon after starting out. That avoidance is driven not just by a fear of physical injury, but also by cultural norms and the potential of ending up on the wrong side of authorities. In other words, the respect—or fear—of the status quo is much stronger in most other countries. Unlike in the United States, this keeps more people from putting on costumes and hitting the streets. American real-life superheroes are thus uniquely brave—or is it foolish?—in this regard.

But they could soon have some company...

CHAPTER 8

WAKANDA FOREVER

EDWARD OKEKE WAS A NOTORIOUS CHARACTER IN SOUTHEAST NIGERIA in the late 1990s. Better known as Prophet Eddy or "Jesus from Nawgu," Okeke ran a healing center at his compound near the market town of Onitsha. Statues of Jesus, Moses, the prophet Elias and Eddy himself—depicted rising over a fallen devil—greeted visitors. Okeke billed himself as a prophet of god, gifted with healing powers that could alleviate injuries and illnesses—for a fee, of course. Locals believed in his abilities and made him wealthy as a result, which elevated him to associating with powerful businessmen and politicians. He lived on a large property with his wife and eight children and had several cars, including a limo.

According to local folklore, Prophet Eddy came by his fortune through nefariously supernatural means. His supposed powers, which ranged from healing and hypnotism to invisibility and teleportation, were fueled by body parts harvested from dead bodies. One newspaper report accused him of ninety-three murders and the theft of sixteen babies, who he also used in his dark rituals.[1] Okeke was no ordinary mortal, media reports suggested, but rather a strange hybrid of man and spirit. Posters put up in town depicted him with two faces: one

human and one savagely animal. Police weren't interested in arrest-
ing him for his allegedly horrendous crimes because they had been
bewitched. It was clear that ordinary law enforcement could not stop
this villain—that something or someone special was needed.

Enter the Bakassi Boys, a group of local vigilante heroes who had
concurrently achieved similar mythical status. The young men wore
amulets that made them bulletproof and wielded machetes that could
determine if someone was a criminal. They would hold the weapon to
a person's chest and, if the blade turned red, they said it was proof that
he or she was guilty. They also had special tortoise shells that, when
hung around a suspect's neck, made it impossible for them to lie. Most
importantly, the Bakassi Boys were immune to greed and corruption,
which were great powers given the environment they operated in. If
anyone could apprehend the evil sorcerer who was preying on local
villagers, it would be them.

Okeke eluded capture by the Bakassi Boys on two separate
attempts, possibly by using his reputed teleportation ability. The vigilantes did indeed nab him on their third try and imprisoned him
in their headquarters, which they had dubbed the "White House."
Numerous government officials and business associates, obviously
ensorcelled, stopped by to offer riches and luxury goods in exchange
for their master's release, but his steadfast captors resisted their lures.
After several days of interrogation, Okeke admitted that he was in
fact a spirit who had enriched himself and his colleagues through evil
magic. At long last, Prophet Eddy was ready to be brought to justice.

It's a fantastical story that would be right at home in a superhero comic book were it not for its brutal and very real ending. With
Okeke's confession recorded on tape, the Bakassi Boys paraded him
into the center of Onitsha on November 9, 2000, and hacked him
to pieces with their machetes. About twenty thousand onlookers,
including many children, sang enthusiastic songs of support as the

executioners burnt his remains and played soccer with his severed head, to prove they weren't afraid of his ghost. In this poor, crime-ridden and superstitious part of Nigeria, this was the shape of justice.

The Bakassi Boys' story began on a slightly more benevolent note two years earlier in Aba, also a market town, about a hundred miles south of Onitsha. With Nigeria only just returning to democratic rule after fifteen years of military control, Aba was in disarray. The town had been carved up by criminal gangs and was beset by protection rackets, armed robbery, rape and murder. Residents heard gunshots nightly and slept with weapons at their side. Local police were either ineffective or as corrupt as the criminals. The whole place was reminiscent of "Fear City" New York of the 1970s. An estimated two hundred people were killed by armed robbers in the town between 1997 and 1999.[2] By all accounts, the situation was appalling.

The crime was starting to affect business in the Ariaria International Market, one of the largest commercial zones in West Africa, renowned for its leatherworks. Traders from neighboring Benin and Cameroon were staying away, while the leather workers themselves feared for their safety. The final straw came with the murder of a pregnant woman and two shoemakers in November 1998, which provoked a group of angry workers in the production zone known as Bakassi to declare war on Aba's criminality. The newly dubbed Bakassi Boys literally took no prisoners in their clashes with gangs. Fed up with living in fear and driven by righteous anger, they dismembered their tormentors with machetes and burned their bodies in public to serve as warnings to other criminals. Within just four months, they managed to largely stamp out crime and successfully reverse the tide of fear. Now, it was the would-be robbers and rapists who were afraid.

Cognizant that an ongoing security force was sorely needed in Aba, the Bakassi Boys formally organized. They named a chairman, secretary and treasurer and solicited friendly donations from townsfolk to fund their operations. They performed regular patrols and investigations and, when deemed necessary, executions. They also enforced a strict internal code of conduct, which helped them develop a reputation for fairness and honesty. Rather than appropriating and dividing the material spoils of the criminals they dealt with, they destroyed them. In one well-publicized case, a notorious robber named Jango offered the Bakassi Boys the equivalent of twenty thousand dollars to go free, but they rejected the bribe and burned his property instead.

The general public greeted the Bakassi Boys with overwhelming support. Many residents were relieved and said they were once again able to "sleep with both eyes closed," a local expression used to denote a sense of security.[3] With a lack of viable law enforcement alternatives, the vigilantes were welcomed despite their brutal, extrajudicial methods. As one Aba resident remarked, "Killing human beings is not good. The Bakassi Boys will go to Hell, but we thank God they're here."[4]

The group's success attracted attention from state governors, a number of whom had been clashing with the federal government over the right to set up their own police forces. Orji Uzor Kalu, a shady businessman who was governor of Abia state—where Aba is—tried to recruit the Bakassi Boys as a quasi-official law enforcement group. They rejected him, however, on the grounds that he, too, was corrupt. Nevertheless, the Abia government asked the group to journey to the nearby town of Umuahia to deal with a pair of violent robbers. They did so, but several members, including Chairman Ezeji Oguikpe, were subsequently arrested for murder by official authorities and thrown in jail. Some members later said the affair was a setup designed to eliminate the Bakassi Boys' more incorruptible elements. They may have been right.

New leadership reversed the group's stance on taking and keeping criminal spoils. The group also went to work for Kalu as the official Abia State Vigilance Service. Members were paid and supplied with cars, buses and weapons. Similarly, the governor of neighboring Anambra state, Chinwoke Mbadinuju, invited the Bakassi Boys to restore security there. They again made quick work of criminals, prompting the governor to sign an official law establishing them as the Anambra Vigilante Service, complete with government-supplied weapons, vehicles and salaries. They also expanded to adjacent states, Imo and Ebonyi. Wherever they went, whatever they were officially called, they continued to be known as the Bakassi Boys.

In Anambra, Mbadinuju quickly squeezed out the original members recruited from Aba in favor of disaffected locals and criminal elements, whom he then used for intimidation, extortion and political killings. In short, the Bakassi Boys were rapidly transformed into the governor's private army. One prime example involved a local police chief who happened to be Mbadinuju's political opponent. The original Boys investigated the chief on two separate occasions at the governor's request, but let him go both times after finding no evidence of corruption. He wasn't as lucky when he was interrogated a third time by the newly reconstituted vigilante group, who promptly executed him.

Similar changes happened in the other three states in which the group was active, eventually coming full circle in Aba in 2001, when government-sponsored Bakassi Boys attacked shoemakers for not paying protection money. By 2002, Amnesty International was criticizing Nigeria's federal government for allowing the vigilante groups' overt human rights abuses to continue, estimating their extrajudicial killings at more than two thousand people. Officials in Lagos agreed to put a halt to the group, but reversed course in the face of public backlash. It wasn't until 2006 that Nigeria took definitive action by outlawing the Bakassi Boys as a terrorist organization. Most members escaped punishment, although a trio was arrested and found guilty of murder the same year. Their cases wound through the system for years until finally, in 2018, the Supreme Court upheld their death sentences. In delivering the judgment, Justice Amina Augie said the Bakassi Boys "are nothing but outlaws... lawless persons operating outside the law who desecrate the laws of the land in their unlawful and misguided quest to dispense justice by killing alleged criminals."[5]

Despite that view and the country's official ban, the Bakassi Boys remained active throughout Nigeria. A 2018 investigation, for example, accused Kogi state governor Yahaya Bello of grooming a group of fifty Bakassi Boys as his personal militia. As one source told investigators, "It has become necessary to call on the Nigerian Government to rescue Ebira people from the evil of the group the state government is breeding, before it turns to another Boko Haram situation."[6]

THE NEW FRONTIER

THE BAKASSI BOYS AFFAIR IN NIGERIA SEEMS LIGHT-YEARS AWAY FROM the primarily American real-life superhero phenomenon, but it is surprisingly relevant. The similarity takes root in the fact that vigilantism occurs in many parts of Africa, an unavoidable growing pain for fledgling nations as they work to establish public institutions while emerging from decades of exploitative colonialism. Many of the continent's governments haven't yet figured out how to run effective law enforcement that can maintain legitimacy and public trust. The result in such a vacuum is that entrepreneurial efforts inevitably arise to become the only viable alternatives. Examples are numerous.

The Sungusungu was a justice organization that mobilized at village level in Tanzania in the 1980s to combat violent cattle theft, which subsequently expanded to neighboring Kenya before being banned by the government there in 2007. The Kamajors in Sierra Leone were a group of traditional hunters who transformed into vigilante soldiers during the country's civil war between 1991 and 2002. The Arrow Boys of Teso confronted the Lord's Resistance Army (LRA) in eastern Uganda between 2003 and 2007. The Zande Arrow Boys battled the LRA and South Sudan's Dinka-led regime in an ongoing conflagration that started in 2005. The Koglweogo "bush guardian" groups emerged in Burkina Faso in 2015 when it became clear that state authorities could do little to curb crime. Even Nigeria has continued to rely on vigilante groups, such as the Civilian Joint Task Force that has been working closely with government forces to counter Boko Haram ter-rorists in the northeast of the country since 2013, despite its previous troubles with the Bakassi Boys.

For weak governments and states, vigilantes can be an indispens-able tool that can quickly develop into an addiction—and a difficult one to shake at that. They're also a solution that can go bad quickly, as the Bakassi Boys illustrate. Finally, in the context of developed nations, their examples do much to explain why some officials in more established jurisdictions tend to resist the formation and incursion of entrepreneurial law enforcement. Or, as Toronto mayor Mel Lastman did with the Guardian Angels, why even borderline vigilantes inevita-bly get connected to criminality. Whether or not such fears hold any merit, there is a concern that the slope from community patrol to sum-mary justice is a slippery one.

Despite that, the vigilante experience in many African nations bears some resemblance to that of America during its own formative period. Practitioners in the Wild West may not have engaged in the same level of brutality as some of the groups mentioned above, but as we saw in Chapter 3, they similarly filled a void and performed extraju-dicial killings, enjoying general public support in the process. Readers in wealthier, less superstitious countries might also scoff at some of the occult overtones of African vigilantes, but it's worth remembering that their American counterparts weren't always completely grounded in the empirical world either. Cowboys in the Wild West had their own supernatural foibles, such as refusing to put their Stetson hats on beds for fear that bad luck would follow, or nailing horseshoes onto doors to ward off evil spirits.

Minor similarities aside, the overarching parallel is clear—many African nations have a vigilante tradition similar to the one America developed during its own early growing pains. This is a trait that many countries on the continent *do not* share with Europe or other English-speaking parts of the world, where rule-of-law traditions have either been long established or inherited and well enshrined.

In that context, it's fair to ask whether many African countries will follow America along a similar evolutionary path as they rise. Will the do-it-yourself mentality that develops around the provision of basic security take root and bloom into a larger entrepreneurial mind-set, as it did in the United States? And following that thought exercise further, is it possible that real-life superheroes could someday become a thing in Africa? We'll return to that second point in a minute, but in the meantime there is evidence that the potential outcome suggested by the first question isn't just possible, but already happening.

By several measures, entrepreneurialism in Africa is booming. Much of the continent is indeed in the midst of an entrepreneurial transition, according to a 2012 report by the Global Entrepreneurship Monitor (GEM). Most individuals in sub-Saharan Africa—about seven in ten—believed that opportunities for starting a business were good, which explains why so many had indeed done so. Intentional or opportunistic entrepreneurs—according to economists, the good kind of entrepreneurs, who are willingly self-employed rather than because they have no other choice—made up more than half of the overall total, a healthy and high proportion. Entrepreneurship is also seen as a good career choice in much of Africa, more so than in any other region except Latin America. Total early-stage entrepreneurial activity (TEA)—the prevalence of working-age individuals who are actively involved in business start-ups—was 28 per cent, or significantly higher than all other geographic regions. Countries such as Zambia at 41 per cent, Ghana at 37 per cent, Nigeria at 35 per cent and Angola at 32 per cent boasted some of the highest TEA rates in the world.[7] Many of these start-up businesses are likely to fail, but that doesn't appear to discourage their founders. Fewer than a quarter of individuals polled by GEM said that a fear of failure kept them from starting a business, which was lower than the 36 per cent of Brits and 31 per cent of Americans who said the same.[8]

This flourishing entrepreneurialism, as well as the overwhelming positive perception surrounding it, is contributing to strong overall growth. African nations including Libya, Nigeria, Ethiopia, Rwanda, Ghana and Ivory Coast are routinely placing in the top ten fastest-growing world economies.[9] The international community has more than taken notice, pushing investment in start-ups on the continent to nearly three-quarters of a billion dollars in 2018, a new record and a huge jump from just 125 million dollars in 2016.[10]

The entrepreneurial phenomenon is also fueling the sense that solutions to large and still-looming problems—including law enforcement—might come more from the grassroots level and develop organically by do-it-yourselfers. The phrase "African solutions for African problems" has gained cachet since it was coined by Ghanaian political economist George Ayittey in 1994. Or, as his country's vice president, Mahamudu Bawumia, told a 2017 business conference: "What we're realizing, and what many countries are understanding, is that if you're going to leapfrog, you really have to lead that charge yourself. Nobody else is going to come and say, 'Hey, you have to leapfrog,' because you're competing with everybody else. You're in a globally competitive environment. You have to do it yourself."

There's no way to definitively prove that early-stage, born-of-necessity, do-it-yourself law enforcement directly causes or leads to later economic entrepreneurialism, either in America or Africa, but there's no denying the strong correlation in both cases. So how do we get from here to real-life superheroes? A vigilante tradition and an entrepreneurial spirit are two strong causal elements that helped spawn the American phenomenon, but there were also other factors that needed to be in place before it could happen. As it happens, those are developing in many African nations too.

BROKEN WINDOWS

AS A CONSTABLE IN CAPE TOWN, CHARL VILJOEN HAD SEEN HIS SHARE OF crime. The South African city is routinely in the running for the title of murder capital of the world, a terrifying and frustrating reality not just for the people who live there, but also for those who police it. By 2006, Viljoen had decided he'd had enough of the lack of progress—despite proper law enforcement's best efforts, the murders, robberies and other violent crimes continued unabated. However, rather than rallying a group of like-minded individuals together to find and hack up criminals with machetes, he decided to import a less brutal strategy he'd seen on television. He sent Curtis Sliwa an email, asking how he might start a Guardian Angels chapter in South Africa. Sliwa's wife at the time, Mary, responded and asked for his phone number. Viljoen had never received an overseas call before, so he had to figure out how to do it. Once he did, it took just one conversation with Sliwa before the Guardian Angels had their first African chapter.

The point of the Guardian Angels in Cape Town, Viljoen explains, wasn't to fight crime as it happened or after the fact, but rather to try and prevent it in the first place. As a police officer, he agreed with

the notion that it was formal law enforcement's job to catch criminals, especially in a jurisdiction as dangerous as Cape Town. But he
was also aware that there wasn't much being done to eliminate the
root causes of crime. That had to change. "We could try to enforce
the laws as much as possible, but if there wasn't some civilian organization involved in changing the community, the police are going to
be involved in fighting a rearward battle," he says.[11] What impressed
Viljoen about the Guardian Angels' approach was their pioneering application of the broken windows theory, an idea suggested by
American social scientists James Wilson and George Kelling in a 1982
magazine article. They argued that major crime was ultimately rooted
in minor issues, such as vandalism, littering and graffiti:

> Consider a building with a few broken windows. If the win-
> dows are not repaired, the tendency is for vandals to break
> a few more windows. Eventually, they may even break into
> the building, and if it's unoccupied, perhaps become squat-
> ters or light fires inside. Or consider a pavement. Some lit-
> ter accumulates. Soon, more litter accumulates. Eventually,
> people even start leaving bags of refuse from take-out
> restaurants there or even break into cars.[12]

The Guardian Angels were obvious proponents of the theory.
Neighborhood cleanup had been among the group's central tenets
and activities since its beginnings as the Rock Brigade in the Bronx.
The theory also found support in the nineties with New York City
police commissioner William Bratton and mayor Rudy Giuliani, who
directed police to prevent and punish small infractions such as graffiti,
subway turnstile jumping and even aggressive squeegeeing at intersections. How much credit Bratton and Giulani deserve for cleaning
up New York is disputed, but there's no question they left the city

considerably safer than they found it, which has helped the broken windows theory gain traction in cities around the world.

Viljoen's Guardian Angels operation, which quickly grew to separate chapters in two different Cape Town neighborhoods, set the strategy in motion via street patrols. Following in the footsteps of their American forebears, members cleaned trash from the streets, removed graffiti from walls and performed general repairs where it was practical to do so. The results, Viljoen says, were immediate: "It changes the landscape, the physical environment. When we started doing it, I saw massive changes in the communities where we did it." Sliwa, in a 2007 interview, also said the impact was tremendous, that it gave neighborhood residents in Cape Town "a ray of hope" in fighting back against a seemingly intractable problem.[13]

As in New York City, Cape Town police officials became enamored with the strategy and entreated Viljoen to help with a broader implementation. The city instated Neighborhood Safety Officers, each of whom was charged with cleaning up a ward of five thousand residents. How much these NSOs helped is difficult to quantify, but the correlation was similar to what happened in New York. Stronger policing and better economic prospects helped Cape Town experience a big drop in its murder rate between 2006 and 2010, to forty-three people per hundred thousand residents from sixty-two.[14] That's still sizeable—Tokyo, the safest city in the world, has a murder rate of just 0.3—but it was a big improvement nevertheless.

Unfortunately, after its initial retreat, violent crime made a comeback in South Africa and Cape Town, especially over the course of the new millennium's second decade, with the city's murder rate soaring back up to sixty-nine in 2018. Officials placed the blame on a stagnating economy and a drop in police funding. "I can say the South African Police Service dropped the ball," Police Minister Bheki Cele told lawmakers in 2018. "A major problem is that the SAPS now only has

191,000 members, compared to the 200,000 we had in 2010. It could take us 10 years to get back to those numbers."[15] Whether the city and country can get back on the right track remains to be seen, but Viljoen maintains that community activism will continue to play a major role in any rehabilitation effort. Cape Town residents in particular need to see symbols of hope, he says, even if they are imported from the United States. South Africa may not be ready for real-life superheroes, but the symbolic foundation of the concept has been laid. "In a way, a guy who's on a Guardian Angels patrol is already a superhero," he says. "These are just normal people trying to do extraordinary things."

YIBAMBE! YIBAMBE!

POTENTIALLY LOST AMID ALL THIS DIRE TALK OF CRIME, MURDER AND poverty is the fact that nerd culture is exploding in Africa. Superhero movies are just as popular in major centers across the continent as they are in New York, London or Sydney. Theaters in cities such as Lagos, Nairobi and Johannesburg were running at all hours to accommodate the throngs of people lined up to see the latest Spider-Man, Batman and Avengers films even before Marvel Studios released *Black Panther* in 2018. Featuring a nearly all-black cast and set in the fictional African country of Wakanda, the film was the biggest global blockbuster of the year and set a new benchmark for the genre with a best picture nomination at the Oscars. In Africa, it was even more important than that. For South African journalist Sumeya Gasa, the story of Wakandan king T'Challa—the Black Panther superhero—was an emotional experience. "We were humanized, and that matters," she told the *Telegraph*. "It feels so good, too good." Nigerian tech developer Sani Yusuf tweeted that watching the film "felt like flying." Another viewer wrote on Facebook that the film was an "affirmation of what I had felt since I left my country for Cambridge and came back. I cried for my people and felt immense pride in being Ethiopian and most importantly African. We are truly resilient and beautiful."[16]

Attendance at African comic conventions was also booming prior to *Black Panther*, with new events multiplying. Lagos Comic Con in Nigeria was the first, drawing three hundred attendees in its augural year in 2012 before growing to more than four thousand by its fifth iteration. Comic Connect Africa, also in Lagos, launched in 2016 and drew five thousand in 2018. Nairobi Comic Con, in Kenya, had grown to more than four thousand attendees by 2018, four years after its founding. Zimbabwe also got its own convention, Comexposed, in 2015. Johannesburg then put every other city to shame in 2018. Headlined by a slew of actors from TV shows such as *American Gods*, *Vikings* and *Big Bang Theory* and fueled by *Black Panther*-mania, Comic Con Africa drew forty-five thousand people, an "unprecedented" result for an inaugural event, organizers said. Attendance nearly doubled the following year, prompting the scheduling of a second, separate convention in nearby Cape Town starting in 2020.

Just like everywhere else in the world, attendees come to these events in droves to share their love of superheroes and pop culture. The shift from passive consumption of superhero fiction to participation is well underway in Africa, a sign that not all is doom and gloom in countries across the continent. The economic growth happening in many of these countries is having some positive effects, the simple enjoyment of silly escapism among them.

There's just one problem with this superhero fare—much of it is imported, the vast majority from the United States. With the phrase "African solutions to African problems" continuing to have cachet, it's a situation that isn't likely to hold for long.

It certainly won't if Jide Martin has anything to say about it. Growing up in Nigeria as a comic book–obsessed kid, Martin always wondered why—Black Panther notwithstanding—there weren't more African superheroes. He didn't understand at the time that the comic books produced by Marvel and DC, while available in Africa if you were willing to hunt for them, were aimed primarily at white kids in North America. The heroes contained therein were thus designed to look like them, for those readers to identify with. It wasn't till much later, when the big publishers realized their audiences were universal and global, that they started to diversify characters and stories.

Still, despite strides in recent years, there's no getting around the fact that many of the most popular superheroes—Batman, Spider-Man and Captain America (*especially* Captain America)—are foreign characters who don't necessarily represent the African experience.

That's why Martin, after graduating from law school, decided to start a comic book company rather than become a lawyer. Comic Republic, which he founded in 2013, is an attempt to solve that African problem with an African solution. "What I see on TV, especially in western media, is completely far away from my reality," he says. "So why don't we push the African narrative the way we see it? It's not some dark corner or primitive place."[17] The publisher has grown quickly, employing dozens of artists and writers who have created a slew of African superheroes, including Guardian Prime, a sort of Nigerian Superman; the genius Nutech, who has telepathy and magnetism abilities; the warrior woman Ireti; and the lightning-fast Max Speed. The characters are locals and their adventures are set in real places, rather than in Metropolis, Gotham or even Wakanda. Just as with their American forebears in the mid-twentieth century, Comic Republic's plan is to create a mythology that is relevant to its audience—characters and stories that readers can identify with and relate to. Using a similar modus operandi, Martin is aiming to be the African Stan Lee.

Distribution continues to be a problem for African comic book creators, however. Not only is there no established system like there is in North America and Europe, it's also inordinately expensive to print comic books. The solution might be to leapfrog print and go straight to digital, which means that brick-and-mortar stores like Fordham Comics in the Bronx may never exist there. Only about a third of Africans had internet access as of 2019 compared to about 94 per cent of North Americans, but usage is skyrocketing—uptake grew by more than 10,000 per cent from 2010, most of it thanks to the spread of wireless networks.[18] Literacy is also growing quickly, with two-thirds of people in sub-Saharan Africa knowing how to read as of 2017, up from just half thirty years ago.[19] Comic books, well established as great tools for teaching literacy, are the perfect intersection of those two phenomena. It's reasonable to expect that generations of African kids will grow up much like their American counterparts—learning to read via superhero stories. And those kids will inevitably show up at comic conventions, perhaps dressed up as Spider-Man or Batman or, even better, Guardian Prime or Nutech. Maybe some of them will even become real-life superheroes.

The idea isn't so outlandish. As African cities go, Lagos isn't as dangerous as might be assumed by North Americans. Although, like any big city, it has its shady parts, it is indeed safer than some North American counterparts and considerably more so than other parts of Nigeria. In 2016, the city recorded 246 murders, for a rate of 2.7 per hundred thousand residents.[20] That's not bad for a city of twenty-one million people, and it's considerably lower than the national average of twenty. It's also much better than several US cities, such as St. Louis (population 308,000), which had 205 murders in 2017; Baltimore (population 611,000) with 343; and Detroit (population 673,000) with 267. A 2016 report prepared by the University of Ibadan, the Nigeria Stability and Reconciliation Programme and the French Institute for Research in Africa went so far as to suggest that "anyone walking in the streets of Lagos would thus be quite surprised to learn that the city is almost as safe as Stockholm in Sweden or Geneva [in Switzerland]."[21] Martin agrees with the assessment. "You don't just walk around and get robbed," he says. "It's pretty rare. I'm wondering why we have that kind of reputation."

Despite being steeped in comic books, Martin admits that his knowledge of the real-life superhero phenomenon is limited. He does remember hearing about one costumed individual in Seattle. "Some black guy," he laughs, unknowingly referring to Phoenix Jones. "I hope he's still alive." Nigeria certainly has the entrepreneurial spirit necessary to drive such individuals, the cumulative cultural result of years of government ineffectiveness. "Most of our officials are corrupt and self-serving, so most people have the mentality that you have to do it yourself," he says. "You provide your own electricity, your own water. It's become so normal. If you have to build a house, you know you have to have your own generator. Even the smallest home has those services that they've provided for themselves." Real-life superheroes are an inevitability, he believes. "I think it would be pretty safe to be a superhero here; you're just going to get laughed at a lot, but I'm sure someone is going to do it. Very soon someone is going to get the idea."

Someone already has, except not in Nigeria. It's happening on the other side of the continent, in Kenya. And it's not happening as anyone might expect.

CHILD HEROES

A SET OF TRAIN TRACKS RUNS THROUGH THE CENTER OF KIBERA, A neighborhood just southwest of central Nairobi. The phrase "wrong side of the tracks" has no meaning here because abject squalor is all around. Estimates of Kibera's population typically range from five hundred thousand to a million people, but either way, it's the largest

slum in Africa. The majority of residents live in extreme poverty, earn-
ing less than a dollar a day. A majority lack access to basic services
such as electricity, running water and medical care. Many have HIV
and AIDS. Dilapidated, tin-roofed shanties stretch as far as the eye
can see and open sewers flow through the streets past stinking piles
of trash. Unemployment is as high as 50 per cent; assaults, rapes and
murders are rampant. Kibera is, unfortunately, the stereotypical image
that many North Americans picture when they think of urban Africa.

It's an unusual place to find real-life superheroes. Even more
surprising is that they're kids. "My superpower is to help out when
there is fire in the slum, I bring water and help people get to safety,"
says Precious Subira, who calls herself Squid 1. "Kibera has lots of
liars and criminals," says Ashley Joy, who goes by the name Wonder
Woman. "If I can get people to be honest, we can live peacefully."[22]

The kids are part of a project called Superheroes of Kibera, a
community-improvement effort started by a local arts club in 2017.
The idea is to get the slum's children thinking positively about their
environment and believing that they can change things for the better.
"You can be everything you want to be," says Steve Kyenze, one of the
project's organizers. "Even if you're coming from a poor background,
you can still do something good for the community. That's how you
can be a superhero."[23]

The elementary school–age kids spend their weekends creating characters and brightly colored costumes to go with them, using
cardboard, plastic water bottles, discarded computer keyboards and
any other junk they find lying around. They come up with names and
"superpowers," which typically include helping women with their groceries, putting out minor fires and community cleanup. By 2019, about
eighty kids had been through the program, which runs when school
is out and when organizers can find funding. The children have never
heard of Phoenix Jones or the Guardian Angels, but they are well

acquainted with Spider-Man, the Avengers and all the other American superheroes, from watching them on DVDs. Aside from developing community service, the program also seeks to spur local pride. "It's about getting them to stop focusing on Batman and Superman and things like that and start internalizing that they can be superheroes," Kyenze says.

Kyenze hopes the program can change external attitudes toward Kibera. "Most people are ashamed to say 'I'm from there,'" he continues. "Nobody cares about them. It's in everyone's minds that we're nobodies. This gets into the kids' minds. If you tell someone you're from here, they say, 'Oh, I'm sorry.' We're trying to change that so that people associate Kibera with creativity."

The Superheroes of Kibera are a far cry from the Bakassi Boys and other African vigilante groups, and even the Guardian Angels in South Africa. They also differ dramatically from their grown-up counterparts in the United States and elsewhere, not just by virtue of their age, but also their comparative innocent purity. When adults dress up in costumes to fight crime or help the homeless, questions about their motivations or even sanity inevitably follow—as we'll see in the next chapter. There are no such doubts when kids do it. For that reason, the Superheroes of Kibera may very well be the best and truest real-life superheroes on the planet—unimpeachable, incorruptible beacons of hope and virtue in a place that sorely needs them.

CHAPTER 9

MESSIAH COMPLEX

AN HOUR EARLIER IT SEEMED LIKE THE DEAD OF NIGHT IN DOWNTOWN
Orlando. A deluge had descended out of nowhere, darkening the
heavens like a biblical apocalypse, pelting the city with heavy torrents
of rain. Now, the tumult is dissipating just as quickly as it arrived. It's
early evening and clear skies are again poking through the clouds hovering over central Florida. Puddles and a lustrous sheen on the streets
are the only evidence of the sudden storm.

Like an elemental spirit who hitchhiked in on the tempest, a
strangely clad figure materializes at the intersection of South Orange
Avenue and East Pine Street. He is ostentatious in his silver costume:
motocross pads on his chest, shoulders and arms, spandex tights
and a cape, a black Stahlhelm atop his head and a mask covering the
upper half of his face. The garish gear does much to distract from his
otherwise unremarkable build—not quite dad bod, but a far cry from
the mighty Thor. He's carrying a tattered black backpack in one hand
and a plastic 7-Eleven cup in the other. He splish-splashes across the
road and announces his presence in a distinctive nasal rasp: "Master
Legend, at your service!"

His attention is diverted before I can muster a response. He spots two men sitting on sleeping bags outside an abandoned storefront nearby. He springs over, carefully sets down his cup and reaches into his backpack. "Do you guys need some clean socks?" he asks, pulling out a pair. The men enthusiastically accept. "Clean, dry socks," he says to no one in particular. "They're the number one item you have to carry with you as a superhero. They're in high demand."

A woman, noticing the transaction, makes a beeline for Master Legend and asks him for change. "I'm sorry, I'm short on funds," he tells her, "but I have socks and snacks." She shakes her head and walks away. Master Legend spies another woman panhandling for change across the street. "Everywhere you look, someone is in despair!" he proclaims, again to no one specifically. Spend time with Master Legend and you can't help but notice that he narrates himself, like a voice-over in an old radio serial. He grabs his 7-Eleven cup, glances quickly at the traffic, then dashes over. You'll also notice he only crosses the street in one manner: manically.

The panhandler says her name is Tammy and yes, she'd love some socks. Master Legend hands her a pair, then another for good measure. "I'm always partial to the ladies," he says. "I guess I'm just chivalrous." This isn't Tammy's first encounter with Orlando's resident real-life superhero. "He's helped me out before," she tells me. She's wearing a green poncho and holding a sign that reads, *Seeking human compassion.* Struck by her message, Master Legend reaches into his fanny pack and pulls out a few dollar bills. He hands them over, then hugs her.

That doesn't sit well with the woman he declined moments ago. She runs across the street and lays into him. "You didn't give me any, what the hell?" she barks. Master Legend tries to think fast. "I owed Tammy money," he says sheepishly, "so I was just paying her back." The woman isn't buying it; she's getting angrier. Unable to come up with a clever escape from this impasse and keen to prevent it from escalating, he produces another few bills and hands them over.

That seems to mollify the woman, so Master Legend says it's time to move on. This burst of charity has made him thirsty. His cup— whatever was in it—is now empty. If you know anything about Master Legend, you know it probably wasn't soda. "A lot of the other super-heroes hate me because I like my beers," he says. "But I don't drink to get drunk. I never get drunk. There's nothing wrong with having some beer if that's the case."[1]

He leads the way to the Woods, a second-storey watering hole on North Orange. Bemused patrons eye the masked, caped stranger quizzically as he waits at the bar for a beer. Minutes later, we sit down and he launches into his biography. Master Legend's origin story, as he tells it, is one of the more colorful—and fanciful—among the real-life superhero community. It begins with Baby Legend being born in the swamps of Louisiana with a so-called "veil" over his face. In some belief systems, the phenomenon presages the newborn having a special destiny or superhuman abilities. Medical science, however, explains the "veil" as a caul, or a thin remnant of the amniotic sac that sometimes covers a baby's face as it emerges from the womb.

Master Legend's parents were horrible people, he says. His mother was a voodoo practitioner and Satan worshipper and his father was a member of the Ku Klux Klan. His father forced him to take part in child fighting rings, where he slugged it out with his friends as adult onlookers bet on the outcomes. When he lost a fight, his father locked him in a closet without dinner. Young Legend found his escape through comic books, which helped him imagine himself as a strong hero like Spider-Man or Superman. The comics inspired him to dress up in a costume as a grade schooler and fight bullies. Of course he always won, he says.

His father killed himself and his mother disappeared when he was in his teens, leaving him alone to panhandle and work odd jobs on the streets of New Orleans. One day, he saw a thief steal someone's purse. He chased the criminal down and recovered it, then decided that he too could be a superhero. He initially dubbed himself Captain Midnight, but changed his name after seeing the "master legend" printed in the corner of a map. By this point, he'd also become a proficient motocross rider and was performing reckless stunts, which earned him the nickname "Legend" among his friends. Combining that with his motocross outfit, it felt like the perfect fit.

Master Legend is also one of the few real-life superheroes who actually believes he has superpowers. He says his birth veil gave him the ability to predict the future, which manifests as limited precognition that lets him sense things before they happen. It doesn't give him omniscience, though. "I wish I could predict the lottery, but it doesn't work like that" he says. "It's rigged! You can't predict what's rigged!" He also believes he's capable of super strength and speed, which are powers he gained from drawing an "X" on the tombstone of famed New Orleans voodoo priestess Marie Laveau. The proof, he says, came shortly after doing so, when he was strolling through the cemetery. He had wandered into an open mausoleum, only to have the door mysteriously slam shut on him. Unable to budge it, he started to panic. He calmed himself down, then backed up and ran at the door with a flying kick. "Bam!" It came open—his powers emerged. "It seems like when I'm in a really desperate spot and I need super strength, it comes to me," he says.[2]

By the time he was in his mid-twenties, he was hard up for a job and looking for a life change. A friend convinced him that Orlando had better opportunities, so he moved to Florida. Along the way, he got married, had a daughter and was widowed. Now in his fifties, he's a journeyman carpenter, electrician and construction worker. By night, he becomes Master Legend and patrols the streets looking for people to help. In between gulps of beer, he tells of how he was recently forced to move out of the storage unit he was squatting in thanks to the man in the next locker over, who inadvertently drew the facility owner's attention. The man had been playing with chemicals, possibly cooking crystal meth, which caused a stench that led to the eviction. "I'm better off now, because I'm in a small house," he says.

Master Legend is a pariah within the real-life superhero community. Many of his colleagues don't approve of his drinking or what they consider to be his penchant for far-fetched stories. They feel it gives the community as a whole a bad name. "Dark Guardian [in New York] didn't like me because he said I tell tall tales, about how I got my powers in that mausoleum," he says. "But that really happened! I really did open that door." Geist from Minnesota, meanwhile, was hostile to him at a photo shoot in Los Angeles for the Real Life Superhero Project in 2010. "He told me, 'You better not drink any beer during this shoot,' and I said, 'You're not my babysitter!'" The friction notwithstanding, he believes he's earned respect from his fellow veterans by virtue of his longevity. Media reports have documented his charitable activities since at least the early aughts. Despite his idiosyncrasies, there's little dispute that he's helped many people, like Tammy.

Back outside, the rain has stopped. The bar crowds and homeless people are now out in force. Master Legend heads south down Orange Avenue, stopping to give socks and packs of peanut-butter crackers to a few individuals along the way. He ducks into Gitto's, a hole-in-the-wall pizza joint, but not for food. The place also serves beer, including Bud Light, his favorite. He leads me upstairs to a table overlooking the street, where he continues his biography. "I sat at this very table with a cop and had a beer not too long ago," he says. Florida law prohibits anyone over the age of sixteen from concealing their identity in public, but Master Legend says he has a special exemption from the police. He pulls out his phone and proudly shows a photo where he's receiving a certification of commendation from the Orange County Sheriff's Department. He got it for helping to clean up in the aftermath of Hurricane Charley in 2004. "People laugh at me, but I go, 'You got one of these?'" he says, referring to the award. "'You say you're a real-life superhero? This says I am!'"

His thirst quenched (for now), Master Legend leads us back onto the streets. Steps away from Gitto's, he encounters an older African-American homeless man who says his name is Melvin. It's late and Melvin is tired; he wants a coffee. With nowhere nearby to get one, Master Legend offers him a beer from his backpack instead, which is starting to resemble Batman's utility belt for its actual utility, except of course for the one key difference (the Dark Knight doesn't necessarily carry Bat Ale). Melvin declines, so Master Legend puts an arm around him and points skyward. "Good Lord, please make this man rich, or at least get him a coffee." Melvin smiles and Master Legend moves on. Minutes later, he chats with a young African-American man wearing a sandwich board that reads, *Spoken word*. The man asks us if we'd like to hear some poetry, then launches into a rap about how the rainy weather isn't bringing down his spirits because living on the streets is hard enough. Master Legend again offers a beer. This time, the man accepts and once again, it's time to move on. "Have you ever seen Lake Eola?" Master Legend asks me. "It's one of the nicest parts of Orlando." I haven't, so we head eastward.

A ten-minute walk, punctuated by Master Legend's mad dashes across the streets, takes us to the twenty-three-acre downtown oasis. Lake Eola is surrounded by a multi-use path. It's nearly eleven, but well lit, so the park is still busy with joggers, dog walkers and cyclists. Benches ring the path. We sit down and Master Legend pulls another can from his backpack. A pair of young men walk by and eye him with amusement. "Are you RoboCop?" asks one. "No, he's a Stormtrooper," says the other. A group of young women stroll by, likely aware that

Master Legend is ogling them. "I can still drink my beer and look at the pretty girls," he says.

We had spoken previously about *The Legend of Master Legend*, the fictionalized television pilot commissioned and aired by Amazon Prime Video in 2017, so I ask him to expand on why he didn't like it. His biggest issue was with how his daughter was portrayed as a habitual shoplifter. He says he had a good deal of input with the writers, so the characterization was surprising. "She's never stolen a thing in her life," he says. "I raised her better than that." The show was also set in Las Vegas, rather than Orlando—"I've never even been to Vegas!" The pilot was a windfall, though, with likeness rights garnering Master Legend an eighty-thousand-dollar payday. He says he also earned five hundred dollars per page for drawing his exploits in comic-book format for the show, as storyboards of sorts.

Despite his complaints, he seems disappointed about the show not going ahead as a full series. It was, after all, a chance to grow the legend of Master Legend, as well as a potential ongoing paycheck. He grows quiet and stares at the lake as he finishes his beer. "I always wanted to help people," he says. He relates a story about how he tried to give a homeless man a few dollars when he was still a teenager back in New Orleans, just as he did with Tammy earlier this evening. His father, however, slapped him, took the money away and pepper-sprayed the man. The memory of the constant cruelty still burns. "Anything to be the opposite of my mean old daddy has led me to be this way," he says. "Every bully and mean person out there reminds me of my daddy." Master Legend, the character, has been his escape for years now—a different identity that has separated him from that troubling past. Despite the many years since, it's not clear if the escape is working. He's alone, his relationship with his now-adult daughter is on again, off again. "I don't have much else going on," Master Legend says. "I've almost forgotten my own name."

THE ALLURE OF TOSCHE STATION

CLAIMS OF WANTING TO HELP THE HELPLESS OR MAINTAIN LAW AND order aside, many real-life superheroes take up their capes as a form of personal therapy. Assuming a different identity is, for some, an escape from who they are or have been, an attempt to become someone else entirely. It represents the conscious creation of an idealized, better self who embodies the symbolic virtues of the superhero, as well as the separation from a more mundane and likely negative reality. Whether they admit it or not, many individuals become real-life superheroes to help themselves almost as much as to help others.

The concept of the monomyth, also known as the hero's journey, is well trodden in fiction and especially superhero stories. It begins with an unassuming individual, often hailing from humble beginnings, going on an adventure and finding themselves transformed for the better in the process. The protagonist generally leaves their known, comfortable world behind, sometimes reluctantly, and heads into the unknown to face conflict—either personal or external—resulting in some form of victory. Mythology professor Joseph Campbell summarizes it thusly in *The Hero with a Thousand Faces*: "A hero ventures forth from the world of common day into a region of supernatural wonder: fabulous forces are there encountered and a decisive victory is won: the hero comes back from this mysterious adventure with the power to bestow boons on his fellow man."[3]

Examples abound in folklore and mythology. *Beowulf*, the Old English epic poem, relates a tale in which the titular hero becomes king after slaying the monster Grendel. Jesus's story in the New Testament, in which he deals with doubters, heretics and soldiers on the way to taking his place as the risen son of God is another archetypical monomyth. In modern fiction, *The Lord of the Rings* tells the story of Frodo Baggins as he saves the world by disposing of an evil artifact, discovering his own strength along the way; *The Matrix* sees Neo learn the true nature of his virtual world while assuming his destined savior role within it (and whoa, he also learns kung fu). Perhaps the best-known pop culture monomyth is the original Star Wars trilogy, where a humble farm boy named Luke Skywalker discovers he is part of a powerful legacy as he defeats the evil Empire and becomes a Jedi master. None of it would have happened if he had been able to stick with his original plan of going to Tosche Station to pick up some power converters.

Monomyths are prevalent in comic books too, though with their ongoing and episodic nature—and continuing commercial value— the protagonists' stories are usually never-ending. Bruce Wayne, for example, was shaken from his world of normalcy by the murder of his parents; his crusade against crime as Batman is his effort to overcome that personal trauma. The X-Men, meanwhile, are torn from their realities by genetic mutations and forced into fighting for acceptance in a world that fears and hates them. Spider-Man, perhaps the best example of the superhero monomyth, endeavors to use his accidentally gained powers for good as atonement for his pre-hero hubris, which indirectly resulted in the death of his uncle. He learns the ultimate monomythic lesson—that with great power comes great responsibility.

With superheroes dominating mainstream entertainment now, the monomyth is at the center of much of modern pop culture. It is the engine that drives a huge number of the movies and TV shows we watch. It's no wonder, then, that some people actively seek out their own heroes' journeys in the real world.

The unimaginatively named real-life superhero "Superhero" (Dale Pople)—resident of Clearwater, Florida—is a prime example. Active between 2005 and 2010 and now in his fifties, Pople has reached a point of self-awareness where he understands that he had subconsciously sought out his own monomyth. "My life had a story arc, like a comic book," he says.[4] Like many real-life superheroes, Pople was a skinny kid who was picked on by bullies at school. His mother was abusive physically, verbally and sexually; his father was inattentive and unavailable. It messed him up. "She got away with whatever she wanted," he says. "I've told therapists over the years that if I watch serial killer documentaries, I can go down the checklist: 'Okay, they did this to Henry Lee Lucas, that was done to me; they did this to John Wayne Gacy, that was done to me.'" Like many kids in similarly abusive situations, he found escape in comic books and movies. "Godzilla was probably my first real friend," he says. "I was always fascinated by the big, can-take-care-of-themselves, don't-have-to-take-any-shit guys like Adam West and William Shatner, monsters like Godzilla and superheroes with powers because they were in the exact opposite boat that I was in."

Pople was jaded and angry by the time he hit adulthood—"a fucking asshole would be a better description," he says—but he had bulked up by spending time in the gym. He became smitten with professional wrestling and was determined to become a star of the quasi-sport. Comic books served as the inspiration for his persona, or *gimmick* in the parlance of the wrestling industry. He fashioned a red-and-blue Superman-like spandex costume and decided to call himself, simply, Superhero—a not unusual choice in a business where characters are often named after supposed real-world occupations, like the Undertaker, the Mountie and the Repo Man. Pople enjoyed some success wrestling around Florida, but his ring career was cut short by a torn knee ligament. Since he was already a figurative superhero, he considered taking the next step. "When I was done wrestling, the character didn't go away," he says. "He just kind of stuck around until I eventually said, 'What would happen if I went out to actually do this?'"

His first few patrols in Clearwater went like they usually do for real-life superheroes. He reported an abandoned car to police and nearly got into fight with a drunk. Otherwise, it was total boredom.

Like others would later learn, he discovered over subsequent patrols that helping homeless people was more rewarding because they—unlike crime—weren't hard to find.

The encounters affected him deeply. Pople knew he wasn't doing much to solve the larger problem of homelessness, but his supply handouts and the conversations he had were indeed making small differences with the people he met. It made him feel better about himself and his place in the world. He also started doing voice work for television and met, then married his wife, Karen. His life was slowly coming together. He learned of the existence of other central Florida real-life superheroes, including Master Legend, Aristeroi and Symbiote. They banded together as Team Justice and collectively handed out supplies to homeless people, keeping watch over their communities while doing so. For Pople, the camaraderie and association with like-minded people from similar backgrounds was like group therapy. "When I first started doing it, I was damaged goods. I didn't care what happened to me," he says. "But I have done nothing but gain from being a superhero. I grew as a person, I grew as a husband, as everything. I became a lot more humble.... That's the greatest lesson I ever learned in my life. Be humble or be humbled."

Pople speaks earnestly, intelligently. He has given his personal monomyth a great deal of thought. "Being a superhero really shaped me and made me better than any amount of therapy could," he says. "I'm not telling anyone, 'Blow off therapy and put some tights on,' but actual hands-on experience like that was way better than any therapy could be. You're out there doing good, helping your fellow man. You're preventing if not evil, then bad from happening. You're making a difference. You can't change the world, but you can change a little part of it."

Pople wishes more of his colleagues were honest about their personal motivations, though he understands that such wisdom may only come with experience, as it did for him. With the benefit of hind-sight, he thinks there's a clear division in what drives real-life super-heroes. As with everything in life, comic books can explain it. "Batman does what he does because he's a mess emotionally. Superman does it because he was raised properly and is a nice person. That's a good way to lump the two categories of them," he says of his colleagues. "Sadly, you probably get a lot less Supermans than you do Batmans."

Some real-life superheroes are indeed aware of their own con-scious or subconscious selfish motivations, though again, that reali-zation often comes after the fact. Zero, who co-founded the New York Initiative in 2009, is among those who admit to suiting up for selfish reasons. "None of this was altruistic for me. I started out because I wanted to die," he says. "When I was younger I had a lot of chemical issues and stuff that happened to me that… I don't want to get into. I started to wander the streets because I wanted to die." He continues: "I was an artist and I got high a lot. I did a lot of dumb shit and it got me into a place where I didn't want to live anymore. I was daring the universe to take me out."

Like Pople, Zero says he was abused and molested as a child: "I'm made, bred and nurtured to go out in the world and track down the people who did the same shit to me when I was a kid, and end what they're doing."[5] His former teammate Lucid admitted to the same in the HBO documentary *Superheroes*: "I've always had a fairly abnormal aptitude towards violence. I'm not sure if it was my upbringing or what, but adrenaline and rage have been a very vital part of my life," he said. "For me it's not that hard to get into the mind of a criminal because I used to be a criminal. I used to sell drugs, I used to womanize, I used to be a borderline alcoholic. You name it. I've learned to funnel my rage in a way that is productive."[6]

Zero dropped out of the real-life superhero scene in 2014, when he moved to Mississippi with his girlfriend at the time. He has since found a new partner, whom he married, and says he has achieved some level of happiness. Still, he itches to get back onto the streets where he can make a difference. His monomyth, like Bruce Wayne's, isn't finished yet. "I still want to try and find a way to be that," he says.

Bipolar disorder led Skyler James Minor Nichols to become Skyman in 2010. He learned of the existence of real-life superheroes from the *Watchmen* DVD, which included a featurette on the phenomenon. That inspired him to craft a red, white and green costume and patrol Seattle's streets with other like-minded individuals. That was the beginning of his hero's journey. "I was drunk and depressed and wanted to kill myself and relying on a manic personality called 'Skyman' to protect me from suicide," he says. "I want to save my own life first before I endeavor to help other people, but I truly believe that while I help myself I'm also helping others."

Like Pople, Nichols's experiences have helped him come to terms with his own issues: "I was once that homeless drug addict who held up that cardboard sign... and I figured that was not a life, so I went back home and repaired things with my father and got a stable roof over my head," he says. "The costume gives me hope and inspires me to be a better person. I'm no longer drunk and depressed and I've been able to keep off about a hundred pounds. I'm in it for the long haul—you're not getting rid of Skyman that easily. I'm a lifer."[7]

LIVING ON THE EDGE

THE TRANSFORMATIVE POWER OF WEARING MASKS DURING RITUALS IS well understood, which is why people have been doing it for millennia. But for some real-life superheroes, slipping into a different persona doesn't necessarily have to be part of a therapeutic monomyth to overcome past trauma. It can also be a way to deal with more mundane issues.

Dark Defender, who patrols Harrisonburg, Virginia, says he stut-
ters less when suited up. "When I put on my uniform, I feel a sense of
confidence, a feeling of authority," he says. "It can change you, especially if you're really dedicated to it."[8] The same goes for Impact in St.
Petersburg, Florida, who has palilalia, a language disorder that causes
him to repeat words. He has interviewed for jobs over the phone while
wearing his costume. "It really works," he says. "Being able to don a
different persona, it gives you a boost of confidence you didn't have
before. You're not Bob Smith, you're Wonder Man. You can be whoever you want."[9] Knight Warrior, in the United Kingdom, says he
stands up straighter and walks with more authority when suited up.
The attention he draws in public also forces him to interact with people, which has helped him overcome his shyness. "You're putting yourself in an uncomfortable situation, you've got strangers coming up and
talking to you," he says. "It boosts your confidence."[10]

These more mundane effects—not necessarily the healing of
internal wounds—are indeed the primary reason the majority of
individuals become real-life superheroes, according to a 2015 study.
Dressing up and patrolling the streets is a break from the everyday
grind, not unlike bungee jumping or hang gliding—which might
explain why many ex-soldiers and marines do it. The study refers to
this pursuit of the unordinary as "edgework":

> Both work and entertainment have become boring and
> only serve to deny people the opportunity to exercise their
> skills and creativity. Consequently, people manufacture
> unplanned and sporadic moments of "edgework"; episodes
> of transient excitement, which are adrenaline filled and pro-
> vide emotional enjoyment where individuals can be both
> skilful and creative.... Patrolling, occasionally fighting crime,
> dealing with potentially dangerous situations and helping

people in distress provides emotional highs and a sense of purpose. In addition, for some, being a RLSH [real-life super-hero] also brings a level of celebrity status. Being a visible hero sets the RLSH performance apart from the everyday."[11]

Elaine Fishwick, an education and social work professor at the University of Sydney and the main author of the study, found this desire for edgework to be a common trait among the real-life super-heroes she interviewed. While past trauma was a motivator for some, alleviating mundanity was the bigger driver for the majority: "Contemporary life is so controlled. This provides them with some avenues to challenge that," she says. "They're allowing another element of their persona to emerge. Even if what they're doing is boring, there's the potential of something exciting happening."[12]

This has been the case for Raymond Fagnon, a double-duty edge-worker who has patrolled as "Ikon" with both the Guardian Angels in Tampa and Bay Coast Guardians in St. Petersburg. By day, he's a data center engineer, which generally isn't high on the list of most exciting occupations. "I love the kind of work I do, but I hate working. There's always tons of paperwork. It's not as fun as when I first started doing computing," he says. "When I first started, people saw me as the greatest thing. Now, people just see me as a commodity. I'm not the top dog anymore. As you get older, people get tired of working because their life isn't as fulfilling as when they first started working. I do [patrols] to spice up my life and to give back. My job pays me very well, which allows me to do those things."[13]

Good Samaritan, another of the Bay Coast Guardians, agrees. "The real reason we do what we do is because we want to live out that childhood fantasy of being the hero, the person who saves the day or makes the difference in their community. We want to feel good about ourselves and we want to have fun," he says. "A lot of us, maybe we're not satisfied with our home lives or our jobs, or the way life has stacked the cards against us. We want a sort of out, something to take pride in."[14] Real-life superheroism is thus a hobby for some—a way to spend free time that is more gratifying than stamp collecting or model-airplane building. As the edgework theory suggests, it's also a way to spice up an unassuming existence, which makes it a middle-class luxury of sorts for some. The theory does much to explain why many real-life superheroes—from the California Initiative in San Francisco and the Bay Coast Guardians in St. Petersburg to the Trillium Guard in Canada and individuals in England or New Zealand—go out of their way to avoid real danger. A bit of danger is enough to spice up one's life, but getting involved with real threats is outside the purview. Those real-life superheroes who take crime fighting seriously don't tend to hail from the middle class.

According to Pople's dichotomy, these middle-class edgeworkers don't necessarily qualify as the archetypal Batman, the tortured soul seeking redemption through heroic acts. But they aren't necessary Superman either, where they perform good deeds simply because they are virtuous. Instead, they're bored. Critics suggest this is where such real-life superheroes can fall under a third archetype: Booster Gold.

Considerably less well known than his movie-star DC Comics stablemates, Booster Gold is a pariah among comic-book superheroes, or at least he was in his early days. First introduced in 1986, Booster Gold is the alter ego of Michael Jon Carter, a fame-seeking, football-playing narcissist from the future. Born in twenty-fifth-century Gotham City to a deadbeat father, he becomes a security guard at the Metropolis Space Museum, where he steals a number of superpowered gizmos including a ring that confers the ability to fly, a force field–generating belt and a sphere that allows him to travel back in time. He heads back to the twentieth century with a plan to become rich and famous by performing heroic deeds. Although he often does help save the world as part of the Justice League, Booster Gold has often been depicted as a self-centered, self-aggrandizing narcissist whose main mission is to improve his own standing.

Calling a real-life superhero "Booster Gold" is thus an insult. "It's not the Batman or Superman you have to watch out for," says Zero. "Eighty per cent at least of these guys are in it for the attention." It's not hard to discern who they are, he adds, since the Booster Gold types usually don't wear protective armor or have self-defense training. "You can tell right off they're not thinking straight or they're not doing anything [of substance]. It's one of the two. They're not actually planning to do anything besides be seen." He gets particularly agitated by those real-life superheroes who post pictures online from charity handout missions. "You'll never see my group bring a camera to go feed a homeless person. That's just gross. This person is at the worst part of their life, they certainly don't want to be seen. There's no dignity," he says. "Who is that helping besides themselves?"

Media attention is indeed often likely, especially for real-life superheroes who suit up in small towns, where newspapers and television stations are more likely to notice them. The *Keizertimes*, in Keizer, Oregon—population thirty-nine thousand—is a case in point: "Heroes or Menace?" asked the paper's front page on October 6, 2017, above a full-page photo of Arachnight and Guardian Shield, two resident heroes. Do the gig long enough and more press is bound to happen. Maybe Amazon will shoot a TV show, maybe someone will even write a book about it (!). Aside from that, there are also the local bar-goers who will inevitably want photos with the strangely garbed characters they encounter to post on their social media feeds. Put on some spandex and go viral.

Carl Potts, a longtime editor at Marvel in the eighties and nineties who oversaw the development of the company's foremost vigilante character, the Punisher, isn't a fan of the real-life superhero phenomenon. "If you're going around looking for trouble, is that right? You're looking for something to happen so you can go into action. Is that the right motivation?" he asks. "I don't know if enough of these people have the self-realization to know what their real motivations are." Real-life superheroes may in fact be doing more harm than good. "The best villains don't think of themselves as villains. Doctor Doom doesn't think he's the bad guy," he says. "They're looking to justify their need for that sort of thing."[15]

Ty Templeton, a long-time Batman comic book writer and artist, also worries about the Booster Gold types. He occasionally gets emails from real-life superheroes asking for advice, but he refuses to encourage them. "The guys who dress up as the 'Green Dingo,' I don't know what they're doing it for other than they need an identity that they don't have in real life. They make believe they're doing good by handing sandwiches out," he says. "It starts to become a narcissistic delusion. They may be doing good, but they're doing it under worrying circumstances. Once you get into that level of narcissistic delusion, who knows what's going to happen?" Pople's Superman archetype doesn't enter the picture. "You're not really doing it for the public good," Templeton says, "you're doing it because, 'I hope I get my picture in the paper.' That's not what Pa Kent was teaching you. If you're really there to do good, do good and be quiet about it. It's not about duty to that dude who needs food. There's a narcissistic splash back here."[16]

There is no Superman archetype, critics say. No matter their professed motivations, real-life superheroes always get something in return for their supposedly selfless actions. This raises significant questions about altruism itself—does it even exist? For the answer, we return to where everything related to superheroes seems to inevitably end up: New York.

CORPORATE SUPERHEROES

IN THE EARLY 1980S, IT WAS OBVIOUS TO ANYONE LOOKING AT THE Statue of Liberty—arguably the original American superhero—that Lady Liberty was in dire need of repairs. Her copper skin had holes in it, her torch was ragged and the iron grid that held her insides together was badly corroded. The problem, as her centennial approached in 1986, was that no city, state or federal government was eager to fund the expensive restoration needed. But not to worry, this was America after all. Entrepreneurial gumption to the rescue!

Jerry Welsh, vice president of marketing at credit card purveyor American Express, was casting about for a big target with which he could test an idea he had been developing. Welsh had recently had some small-scale success with a new promotional concept he'd dubbed "cause-related marketing," which involved attaching a marketing campaign to a social need. The company had donated two cents to a San Francisco arts festival for every purchase made locally by cardholders. Festival organizers were grateful for the infusion of funds and the company saw increased card usage thanks to the positive press it received. Welsh took one look at Lady Liberty's decrepit state and knew he had found the jackpot he was looking for.

In September 1983, American Express launched a national campaign that promised to donate to the Statue of Liberty–Ellis Island Foundation one cent for every card transaction, a dollar for each new account opened and for each five-hundred-dollar travel package purchased, and a penny for every traveler's check purchased. The campaign was bolstered by patriotic magazine ads. "In addition to all the logical reasons for using the American Express card, there is now one that is unabashedly sentimental," read one, followed by a modified version of the company's tagline: "The American Express Card: for the sake of the Statue of Liberty, don't leave home without it"—a worthy superhero catchphrase if ever there was one.

Newspaper and television coverage helped make the three-month campaign a success, bringing the company's donation to nearly two million dollars. Welsh estimated the overall effort totaled ten times that amount thanks to the awareness generated, which inspired many direct donations by non-cardholders. The campaign also kicked off a veritable gold rush of other businesses getting involved. More than twenty other companies added almost seventy million dollars to the restoration pot over the next few years in exchange for the rights to use the statue's image in their respective promotions. The contributions helped restore the Statue of Liberty to her proper glory. More importantly for American Express, new card applications shot up by 45 per cent and usage increased by almost 30 per cent.[17] The results were better than Welsh had dreamed, which is why he proclaimed cause-related marketing, or cause marketing for short, as *the* new best way to promote a product or service. "The wave of the future isn't checkbook philanthropy," he told the *New York Times* in 1987. "It's a marriage of corporate marketing and social responsibility."[18]

He was right. Corporations quickly realized they could benefit from associating with good causes and that consumers were more likely to do business with brands that gave them warm feelings, rather than cold, faceless entities that were concerned only with generating profits. Examples of cause marketing since are countless: Yoplait has raised millions for the Susan G. Komen Breast Cancer Foundation by having customers send in specially marked yogurt container lids; Starbucks has donated ten cents from every beverage made on World AIDS Day to help disease treatment and prevention for coffee farmers in Africa; Dove soap has funded self-esteem workshops for women; and so on. By the turn of the millennium, cause marketing had become global and ubiquitous, with virtually every major corporation engaged in some level of social charity attachment—another American product exported to the world. Spending has ballooned since, with corporate sponsorship of causes hitting almost two billion dollars in 2015, nearly double from a decade earlier.[19] Companies even get together once a year to hand out Halo Awards for the best cause-marketing efforts, with past winners including Microsoft, Disney and Viacom.

The reason for the explosion is clear: it works. In a 2013 survey of consumers, nearly three-quarters of respondents said they chose a business over another because of its attachment to a cause of personal relevance. Three-quarters also said it was okay for brands to promote causes while making money at the same time.[20] The benefits of these campaigns are also clear: they're win-win-win scenarios, where the cause in question benefits from an infusion of funding and awareness, the sponsoring company gets a sales bump from the buff to its public image and the consumer feels good about contributing to a worthwhile effort.

But there are also downsides, such as the potential for sponsors to stumble into gaffes and contradictions. A great example was when Pepsi tried to get in on the Black Lives Matter movement in 2017, only to have the effort go awry with a TV spot in which Kendall Jenner—considered by many to be a vapid celebrity (who also happens to be white)—was seen to be trivializing the protest movement by sharing a soda with riot police. Public backlash forced the soft drink company to quickly pull the ad and apologize for its tone-deafness. Bell Canada, meanwhile, came under fire the same year for its annual Let's Talk campaign, which raises money for mental health awareness and funding in Canada. Hundreds of employees complained to the press that aggressive sales targets imposed by the company were causing internal mental health breakdowns, which succeeded in raising the wrong kind of awareness.[21] Soon after, regulators began investigating the company's sales tactics. As both cases illustrate, cause marketing inevitably invites the danger of companies coming off as insensitive or hypocritical.

The bigger problem with cause marketing is the example it sets for the broader population. With most consumers accepting that companies can and should receive benefits in exchange for charitable acts, they're likelier to internalize that attitude when it comes to their own behavior, either consciously or not. When we are surrounded by product and service providers that are boosting their revenues for doing the good and moral things that we are otherwise taught from birth to do anyway, the questions "What's in it for me?" and "Why can't I do that?" become easier to ask. This raises doubts about the nature of altruism, suggests a possible degrading of it and fuels general cynicism. This has particular relevance when it comes to superheroes, both the fictional kind and the real-life kind.

SUPEREGO

IS SUPERMAN AN ALTRUIST? THE GENERAL CONSENSUS IS, YES, HE IS. Marooned on Earth as a baby after the destruction of his home world, Krypton, young Kal-El is taken in and raised by Jonathan and Martha Kent, two salt-of-the-earth farmers living in Smallville, Kansas, a fictional town representing the archetypal American heartland. The Kents are the epitome of simple morality and raise their son to use his powers for the betterment of humanity. They teach him that no act of kindness is too small and no reward is necessary for any good deed. His godlike powers are a gift, which means he has a responsibility to use them benevolently.

With that kind of a moral compass, it's no wonder the character has become a paragon of pop culture virtue. "Superman is precisely what we should be teaching our children," comics creator Greg Rucka wrote in a 2013 opinion piece for the *Hollywood Reporter*. "Superman inspires us to our best."[22] Even some Christians envy his pure morality, comparing him to Jesus. "In Christ and Superman, we find morals backed up by muscles, powers rested on principles—a combination that makes the ethical behavior of either all the more admirable because it comes from a strength of character rather than a position of weakness," writes Stephen Skelton in *The Gospel According to the World's Greatest Superhero*.[23]

Yet, over Superman's eighty years of publishing history, writers have tried to wring more complex motivations out of the Man of Steel. Simple virtue doesn't seem enough—doesn't seem believable—as times change. Some have plumbed Superman's creators' own origins for material, playing heavily on their—and his—alien status. As we saw in Chapter 2, Jerry Siegel and Joe Shuster were the sons of Jewish immigrants living in the United States at a time of virulent anti-Semitism. Superman was their escapist fantasy creation, representing everything they wished they could do, from flying through the air and picking up cars to getting the girl and punching out Nazis. But he was also a realization of how they thought an outsider might go about fitting into his adopted society. Superman would be accepted by subscribing to and espousing American values, which Siegel and Shuster boiled down to the essentials: truth and justice.[24] Out of practicality, the people of Earth would overlook Superman's alienness and accept him as one of their own because of his good deeds.

That certainly was the prevailing attitude of many immigrants to the United States at the time; that adopting the ideals of hard work and industriousness was the surest way of being welcomed. "He's always been the ultimate immigrant story," comic book writer Mark Waid told USA *Today* ahead of the *Man of Steel* movie's release in 2013. "What is the hope of the immigrant than at core a promise that it would be better in America? That no matter what your situation is, it will be better here." Jim Lee, the comics writer and artist who immigrated to the United States from South Korea with his family when he was five, shares the sentiment: "It was all about: Can you adapt and fit into a society?"[25]

According to that interpretation, Superman isn't entirely altruistic. He is indeed governed by Ma and Pa Kent's morality, but there's also something in it for him. He wants to be accepted by his adopted planet, a reward for performing righteous deeds and saving the world. There's at least a little bit of cause marketing driving the Man of Steel. This thinking can be applied similarly to many of the other altruistic superheroes, like Captain America. Scrawny Steve Rogers is bullied as a youth, so he signs up for a government experiment that transforms him into the most capable super soldier the world has ever seen. Like Superman, the change lets him do all the things he couldn't do before, like get the girl and punch out Nazis. "I don't like bullies, I don't care where they're from," he says in the film *Captain America: The First Avenger*, speaking to a motivation—revenge—beyond the altruism he's otherwise known for.

The point isn't to cast cynical aspersions on superheroes' motivations, fictional or real, but rather to suggest that pure altruism is in the eye of the beholder, even in entertainment. One of the realities of modern society is that performing a good deed often results in some benefit to the person doing the deed, whether he or she is looking for it or not. For observers, that can make it difficult to determine where altruism ends and self-interest begins. Philosophy and science are indeed divided on this issue.

Adherents to the "I don't do anything unless I gain from it" school of thought are believers in psychological egoism, or the thesis that we are all motivated, deep down, by self-interest. In this paradigm, no one does anything selflessly; we are slaves to biological imperatives that require us to further ourselves. In an example given by the *Internet*

Encyclopedia of Philosophy, if Pam rescues Jim from a burning office building, the psychological egoist believes it is because she "wanted to gain a good feeling from being a hero, or to avoid social reprimand that would follow had she not helped Jim, or something along these lines."[26] Counterarguments revolve around the notion that self-interest can't always be quantified, known or imagined, even by the supposedly self-interested person in question, in which case there is no conscious or subconscious expectation that any reward will ever be gained. The *Stanford Encyclopedia of Philosophy* gives a good example of this:

Suppose, for example, that I want my young children to be prosperous as adults long after I have died, and I take steps that increase to some small degree their chances of achieving that distant goal. What my desire is for is their prosperity far into the future, not my current or future feeling of satisfaction. I don't know and cannot know whether the steps that I take will actually bring about the goal I seek; what I do know is that I will not be alive when they are adults, and so even if they are prosperous, that will give me no pleasure. (Since, by hypothesis I can only hope, and do not feel confident, that the provisions I make for them will actually produce the good results I seek for them, I get little current satisfaction from my act.) It would make no sense, therefore, to suggest that I do not want them to be prosperous for their sake, but only as a means to the achievement of some goal of my own.[27]

The psychological egoist might counter that argument by suggesting the person taking steps to ensure their kids are prosperous later in life is indeed acting in their own self-interest, to the greatest extent that they can. They may take some satisfaction knowing they at least improved their children's *chances* of prosperity, even if they have no way of knowing whether or not those odds will pay off. That sense of satisfaction is the reward. It's a circular argument, which is why philosophers have come up with no firm answer to the question of whether people can be truly altruistic.

Science doesn't provide easy answers either. Ethologist Richard Dawkins came to prominence in 1976 with his book *The Selfish Gene*, in which he argued that altruism is determined biologically; people (and animals) are more likely to act selflessly when it comes to other people (or animals) they're related to. Under this theory, a mother is indeed capable of true altruism for her child, but the situation changes when a total stranger is involved. The less related the person is, the more likely it is that self-interest determines actions. Social psychologist Daniel Batson, meanwhile, has spent a lifetime performing experiments on this subject and has determined that altruism does indeed exist regardless of biological relations. In one of his better-known experiments, performed back in 1981, Batson tested the reactions of subjects watching a fellow study participant receive electric shocks. Observers were placed into two different scenarios: one in which they could leave the room and no longer have to watch the shocks, and another in which they couldn't. The subjects were just as likely to step in and take the remaining shocks themselves regardless of the scenario they were in, which proved to Batson that empathetic altruism exists regardless of social or familial context. These tests formed the basis of his belief that empathy-motivated altruism was a more powerful instinct than psychological egoism. "The research to date convinces us of the legitimacy of suggesting that empathic motivation for helping may be truly altruistic," he wrote. "In doing so, we are left far less confident than we were of reinterpretations of apparently altruistically motivated helping in terms of instrumental egoism."[28] Critics, however, point out that such experiments often take place under strict experimental conditions that aren't necessarily reflective of how people behave in the real world, so they aren't conclusive.[29]

A more recent experiment that used magnetic resonance imaging to map brain responses to altruism, published in 2016 in *Neuroscience and Neuroeconomics*, also delivered mixed results. Researchers found that altruistic giving lights up several parts of the brain, including those associated with emotional processing, perspective taking, self-discernment and reward centers. "Together, activation in these regions is likely if individuals are actively engaged in thinking about not only the emotions and feelings of others, but also about their own thoughts, feelings, and desired outcomes," the report said.[30] As with philosophy, the scientific debate is circular and continues with no firm conclusion in sight.

A DARK MIRROR

REAL-LIFE SUPERHEROES ARE SPLIT ON THE ISSUE TOO. SOME DENY THAT self-interest has any part in what they do. TSAF, a member of the New York Initiative whose name stands for "The Silent and the Forgotten," told the HBO documentary crew that her appellation is meant to remind her that "It's never about me."[31] Miss Fit, meanwhile, working at a soup kitchen, wears a button bearing the same message: *Not about me.*[32]

Others own up to self-interest and recognize there's at least some element of cause marketing in what they do. "There is a sense of gratification from doing good and I don't think that's a negative thing. It's not bad to help people," says Canadian Justice. "It makes charity fun. That's the thing that's missing in charity. People see it as a chore."[33] Jaguar agrees, echoing what consumer surveys find about cause marketing. "It's okay with me if it's a little selfish, if there's a little bit of self-glorification," he says. "It makes it more fun."[34] Dusk Citizen, in New York, embraces the personal gain. "I've always been like, 'Hey look at me, I'm the center of attention.' I'm welcoming of it," he says. "I'm more okay with it being for a good cause. It's a conversation starter. So many people have helped because they like the idea, just because they saw me in a costume that one time."[35]

Such positions make it easy for observers to adopt a cynical view—to picture Booster Gold. There's the obvious criticism: "When I donate money, I do it anonymously. I don't broadcast it and say, 'Hey, I gave two hundred dollars!' I prefer to be more quiet about it," says Andrea Kuszewski, a psychologist who has studied real-life super-heroes. "I don't know if they broadcast it because they want to get other people involved or if there's some narcissism involved. I think it's a mix."[36] With cynicism being the stock-in-trade of real-life super-villains, it's no surprise that they have few kind words for what real-life superheroes do. "In anthropological terms, no primate does anything without some sort of reciprocation expected. That reward can also just come from within," says Tamerlane, a real-life super-villain in Florida. "There's a theory that you give Christmas presents not because you want someone to feel good about that present; you want to make your-self feel better about giving a Christmas present. You're doing it for selfish reasons. This is the human animal, it's one part god, one part devil. It's a horrible, cynical view, isn't it?"[37]

Many real-life superheroes bemoan this attitude, which they say is the product of an overstimulated culture that is making peo-ple increasingly negative and paranoid. It's even reflected in the types of superhero fiction that are popular—movies starring Batman, the darker and more cynical of DC's protagonists, for example, dwarf films with the colorful and virtuous Superman in box-office returns. "It's seen as offensive to not be cynical," says Zimmer, who cofounded the New York Initiative with Zero. "It's this weird cultural thing, but

I think it needs to shift."[38] Rock N Roll, the superhero bakery owner, gets angry when people are reflexively cynical about the concept of real-life superheroes. "They say, 'Why are you doing that? No one does that. What's your motivation? There's always got to be something, no one is so magnanimous,'" she says. "Even if it's a tiny little bit of good that you did, it makes you feel better about anything asshole-ish you might have done earlier in the week. It's self serving, of course, but people also don't want to see that it's this easy to do something good because it holds a mirror up to them and they have to answer the question 'Why am I not doing this?'"[39]

Ultimately, the argument over real-life superhero altruism is as circular as it is with philosophy and science: maybe it exists and maybe it doesn't. To the observer, it often boils down to believing that real-life superheroes are entirely self-interested and are trying to fool themselves or others if they say anything different. Or perhaps their selflessness comes bundled with some amount of selfishness, but that's okay—it's just like cause marketing. The attention they get "gives them a license to do good," says Elaine Fishwick, the human rights researcher in Australia. "But I don't think that's something bad."[40]

ON THE SPECTRUM

BACK IN ORLANDO, MASTER LEGEND TELLS ME ABOUT HOW HE DISLIKED the HBO *Superheroes* documentary almost as much as he disliked the Amazon TV pilot based on him. The HBO documentary made him look bad, he says, because he was depicted as constantly drinking beer. His good deeds with the homeless, meanwhile, didn't make the cut. Still, it wasn't all bad because the film did boost his profile, which likely led to the TV show that almost happened, as well other opportunities. Just the other day, he says, he got to preach superhero virtues to a classroom full of students in Turkey via a Skype video call. "I never thought I'd become world famous because of it, but I sure did."

With the possible exception of Phoenix Jones, there isn't a real-life superhero alive who has drawn more media attention than Master Legend. Does that make him a Booster Gold? Perhaps. But his good deeds are also hard to argue with. He seems genuine in his desire to help people. Does that make him a Superman? That may be a stretch, but it doesn't disqualify him entirely from the archetype. His difficult past also looms heavy. It's difficult if not impossible to verify his story, especially given that Master Legend is secretive about his real identity, but it's hard not to feel the aura of sadness about him—that he's someone haunted by inner demons. Does that make him a Batman?

Figuring out real-life superhero motivations isn't as simple as pigeonholing them into one of two or three categories. Master Legend is proof that the reality is more of a spectrum—these individuals do what they do for a variety of reasons, some that are conscious and others that are not. Some real-life superheroes may indeed break down into the simple Batman, Superman and Booster Gold archetypes, but many more probably qualify as a bit of all three. It is usually the case that real-life superheroism is born out of a desire to help others coupled with a desire to also help oneself. A question remains: How does that measure up against the symbolic paragon of virtue as represented by superheroes in fiction? Superheroes in comic books, movies and television are mythic characters who are supposed to represent unselfish altruism—do their real-world counterparts fall short of that ideal? Until philosophers or scientists arrive at a conclusion on the question of whether altruism truly exists, the answer depends entirely on one's own point of view. To the idealist, real-life superheroes do indeed fall short because of what they gain personally from their actions. To the realist, that's not a factor. Doing good is all that matters.

CHAPTER 10

ENDGAME

MICHAEL BARNETT GREW UP READING COMIC BOOKS AND CONSIDERS
himself a lifelong fan of superheroes, which is why he's disappointed
in their real-life counterparts. In the late aughts, just after the Great
Recession, he became aware of the real-life superhero community
by reading about Mr. Xtreme and Master Legend in a magazine. As
a budding filmmaker, he initially thought their stories—the tip of a
larger phenomenon that stretched around the world—might make a
good script for a fictional movie. Instead, he decided the actual truth
was more interesting and set to work on what became *Superheroes*, the
quintessential documentary on the subject that first aired on HBO in
2011. He couldn't help but be impressed by the individuals he met
while working on the film. He found their do-it-yourself ethos inspiring and their positivity infectious. Science and philosophy may be
undecided, but Barnett was satisfied with their motivations. "It's from
a pure, altruistic and selfless place... They're people who find the good
in things," he says.[1]

Barnett hoped his film would do more than just document a
subculture. He wanted to spur those involved into becoming a real
movement that could effect larger, positive change. Instead, the

community—mirroring society in general—fell to infighting. Rather than coalesce and work together for their common causes, real-life superheroes collectively devolved into name-calling and self-sabotage on social media. "I thought we were creating a platform for extraordinary good to happen, but really, no one got organized," Barnett says. "It didn't evolve. It got stuck in an online battle with a few beacons. I've been consistently disappointed in the aftermath."

This division was noted in a 2016 study of real-life superheroes, which found that many in the community held strongly negative opinions about their colleagues. Criticisms ranged from differences in political views to whether or not certain individuals were "real" or "fake"—as in those who were actually performing good deeds versus those who were only pretending to do so. Some even took issue with their compatriots' physical appearances, claiming that "most of them are out of shape and look ridiculous."[2] This "toxicity," as Barnett calls it, is a big reason why some real-life superheroes end up quitting. Ilya King, who patrolled Portland, Oregon, as Zetaman, was one of those. "The RLSH community as a whole is nothing more than an internet social circle that cares for who is popular and who isn't," he told author Tea Krulos. "I do not want to return to the cesspool that is the RLSH community."[3]

All subcultures have divisions—try popping into an online conversation among video game or heavy metal music fans if you doubt it—but schisms among this particular group are especially acute given the origin of the species, so to speak. The comic-book world gave birth to the fanboy—the person who obsesses over an interest to the point of toxicity to others. Fanboys have been arguing about minutiae, like the supposedly correct fictional interpretations of Batman, Superman and the rest, since well before the internet allowed the rest of us to engage in similarly pointless quarrels over the smallest of things. First it was via letter pages in fan magazines, then it was in person at comic book stores and conventions, and now it's happening—as modern squabbles do—on the internet. As Glen Weldon puts it in *The Caped Crusade*, a book about the rise of fandom, these disagreements essentially boil down to one universally held view: "If you do not love my thing in the same way, to the same degree, and for exactly the same reasons that I do, you are doing it wrong."[4] It should come as no surprise that toxic fanboyism over works of fiction is now bleeding into the real world as comic books become more of a participatory phenomenon. For many real-life superheroes, it isn't enough to argue about whether or not Michael Keaton or Ben Affleck were good casting choices for Batman movies. Now, they fight over whether carrying a broadsword or taking photos on patrol is advisable.

Some examples of real-world disputes include Dark Guardian splitting from the New York Initiative in 2016 on "bad terms" to form his own team, the New York Ronin.[5] In 2019, meanwhile, Raymond "Ikon" Fagnon split with the Bay Coast Guardians as the result of frustration with the team's direction. "When the [Seminole Heights] serial killer was loose in Tampa [in 2017], I approached the BCGs [and said] let's head out there to look for them. They immediately got scared and so forth. I was totally disappointed," he says. "We modeled ourselves after the comic and movie characters, so let's act more like them."[6] The other team members have their own version of events. "He stopped coming to patrols because he didn't like the routes we chose and never actually brought it up," says Impact. "He got pissy because none of us wanted to try and stake out a possible prostitute motel because we don't want to get these girls arrested."[7]

Many agree that the internet has only helped to worsen such disagreements. Conversations used to be more private and differences in opinion were smaller in scale, which meant they could be glossed over and forgotten more easily. Now, debates are often public, which adds elements of performance and competition to the arguments, which leads to the entrenchment of views. That point also extrapolates to society at large. "Every post now has to be okay with every single person you know and you can't really have a private group experience or conversation," says Zimmer, who cofounded the New York Initiative with Zero in 2009. "That has changed the direction." The internet, he adds, has indeed derailed the movement's evolution. "I don't want to blame Facebook for everything, but I think it's definitely dampened a momentum that could have been there if we'd stuck to message boards."[8] Minnesota's Geist says the internet has harmed the community by magnifying its members' worst traits, which again reflects the general populace. "It takes a pretty strong personality, and ego probably, to do something this stupid. It's not your average person... that's going to do it," he says. "We're all leaders, no one wants to follow."[9] Ultimately, many are as disappointed as Barnett in the lack of progress, which highlights a contradiction in what real-life superheroes are supposedly trying to accomplish. As the Bay Coast Guardians' Good Samaritan puts it, "How can we promote community if we can't be a community?"[10]

In this way, real-life superheroes mirror their fictional counterparts. Despite their supposedly symbolic positions as paragons of virtue, superheroes don't always get along in the comic books or movies. Far from it—they've been fighting amongst each other for much of their history. Batman and Superman first duked it out in the comic books in 1964, three years after the Thing and the Human Torch started making a habit of it as of *Fantastic Four #1*. One of Marvel's most successful comic-book storylines in recent history, *Civil War* in 2006, featured the publisher's most prominent good guys choosing sides between Iron Man, who wanted them to register their secret identities and act as government agents, and Captain America, who espoused continued liberty from third-party oversight and control. The clash was brought to the big screen in 2016 as *Captain America:*

Civil War, and in both cases the supposedly virtuous heroes beat the hell out of each other, doing untold property damage and endangering civilians in the process. Fortunately, real-life superhero squabbles are limited mostly to hurt feelings on Facebook, rather than carnage in Times Square or airports in Germany.

There is a feeling in some corners of the community that a leader is needed—someone who can perform all the heroic acts, from fighting crime and helping the helpless to rescuing cats in trees and holding Granny's arm while she crosses the street, who can marshal the resources, brains and physical abilities needed to inspire others to rise above their disagreements and unify behind shared goals. In DC comic books, this role is often filled by Superman, the community's de facto leader whose truest superpower is his ability to inspire people to be better than they are, his fellow heroes included. When Superman isn't available, the job of leadership often falls to Batman, who is similarly respected for his smarts, longevity and results. In the context of a real-world leader, Batman is the more likely archetypal model because, well, Superman is impossible.[11]

"One day, some kid in some basement is going to build himself a really cool suit that lifts off the ground or shoots something from its hands," says Florida's Purple Lotus. "As long as there's one real-life superhero in the world, there's a chance for something wonderful and stupendous to happen because that one motherfucker might get his wish fulfillment."[12] Zero furthers that thought. "I've always wanted to see that guy come out of nowhere who has all the cool gear; he's put time and thought into this," he says. "He or she knows how to plan, how to set up and execute a good plan, when to knock someone out or let them talk. I want to see a fucking Batman in the world."[13]

THE BAT CAVE

T.J. CUENCA WANTS TO SEE A REAL-WORLD BATMAN UNITE THE COMMU-
nity too, but he understands it isn't just going to happen on its own.
After all, Bruce Wayne put in years of training to become the Dark
Knight. That's why Cuenca opened the Superhero Foundry in Las
Vegas in 2016. For a few years before it closed in 2019, the Superhero
Foundry welcomed everyone who wanted to become something akin
to Batman. A short car trip south of the main casino strip and a few
doors down from a gun range and the Hustler strip club, a sign on
the front door read: *The world's first superhero training center.* A sign
just inside told visitors, *We are not the comic book store*, a reference to
MaximuM Comics, which was in fact next door.[14]

On the Sunday afternoon of my visit, the Superhero Foundry
was quiet. The main lights were off, but small track lights ringed the
spacious, three-thousand-square-foot converted warehouse. On the
north wall they highlighted a collection of weapon displays, which
held everything from swords and axes to whips and six-shooter pis-
tols. There was even a *bat'leth*, the large curved blade weapon used
by Klingons on *Star Trek*. And of course, there were batarangs. The
displays hung above a set of aluminum bleachers, similar to the kind
found in a high school gymnasium. An array of targets, like those at
an archery or axe-throwing range, lined the south wall. Tucked into
the corners of the space were a classroom and a pocket-sized obstacle
course, complete with a climbing wall and ropes.

Cuenca's résumé is as colorful as it is distinguished. Born
into a military family in the Philippines, he served in the country's
Marine Corps before moving to Las Vegas in 1993. He met his even-
tual wife, Melody, after getting into competitive knife throwing and
fighting. The duo has won multiple knife-throwing championships;
Melody has performed on *America's Got Talent* and is a member of the

International Knife Throwers Hall of Fame.[15] Cuenca was a dentist until he shattered his wrist while sparring with bō staffs. Losing fine motor movements in his hand, he was forced to retire from dentistry and move into the entertainment and training fields. He has since performed with Cirque du Soleil and taught self-defense courses for film and television productions and government agencies, including the Transportation Security Administration and the secret service. Much of this was evidenced by a slew of plaques and photos that hung on the walls next to the weapon displays in the Superhero Foundry.

Just to be sure of his bona fides, I asked Cuenca to demonstrate his throwing skills. He started off a few feet away from one of the targets and sure enough, he hit the bullseye. That's not that impressive, I thought, but my eyes grew wider as he moved back. Before I knew it, he was hitting his mark from a full forty feet away. He saw my surprise and acknowledged that people sometimes have difficulty believing his colorful past. "I Bruce Wayned my way through life," he joked.

Cuenca wanted the Superhero Foundry to be more than just a knife-throwing and self-defense academy. In the classroom adjacent to the throwing range, he taught students Nevada state laws on self-defense, property rights and concealed weapons. He also stressed nonlethal disarming and restraint techniques, part of what he called "the Batman Code," which forbids killing and emphasizes protecting civilians. "If we're going to become superheroes, we need to think like superheroes," he said. "We need to think super, to think ahead. Plan, don't just jump in there. I mean Batman plans everything, for heaven's sake." He also encouraged students to create their own costumes and personas, which could help them visualize and strive toward the superhero ideal, like real-life superheroes do. Cuenca himself frequently dressed up for classes as Bladepool, a character closely resembling Marvel's Deadpool. His costume incorporated stab-proof Kevlar and flame-resistant Nomex, because you never know when you might have to run into a burning building to save someone's puppy.

Like other critics, Cuenca doesn't believe many real-life superheroes are doing it correctly. Few have any training or proper preparation, he said, which could be why so many of them actively avoid danger and go the less perilous route with homeless outreach. "They don't pass muster. They're not as great as they say," he said. "I would really love to have them come out here and train because then they'd see the big picture. They'd see how difficult and dangerous it is. A lot of these people will jump into this like Kick-Ass. That's not how you do it. I understand courage, but you have to have some training." He continued, echoing the concerns others have about real-life superhero motivations: "Their hearts are in the right place, but if they're not trained properly it gives a bad impression of someone who's out there for revenge or for personal gratification. That does not wash well."

I couldn't help but wonder how training people to throw knives was teaching them to be heroic, so I asked Cuenca to explain. His initial response was defensive: "Lots of superheroes carry weapons! Thor has a hammer and Captain America throws his shield!" That's true, but I pointed out that those characters have the luxury of operating in fictional worlds, where writers can easily have them avoid inflicting serious wounds or death. His response was more measured. The point isn't to teach lethality with weapons, but rather how to incapacitate bad guys. That can be accomplished in simple hand-to-hand fashion, but it's also easier, more effective and safer to do with a weapon, he said. Cuenca taught students to aim for their opponent's hands— ironic, given his *bō* injury—as the best way to defuse a threat. "There's no way you can kill a human being by breaking their hand," he said. "It then becomes very difficult for them to attack you."

The problem for the Superhero Foundry, which closed in May 2019, wasn't its techniques, Cuenca said, but its location.

Sequestered in a relatively uninhabited part of Las Vegas, the school lacked foot traffic, resulting in few students. Without many paying customers, there wasn't much money for marketing. There was also the whole thing about how it takes an odd kind of person to become a real-life superhero, and those individuals aren't exactly common. "Very few people want to step up and do something that's scary," he said. Despite the closure, Cuenca continues to believe that the Superhero Foundry could be viable, perhaps in another location or city. Ultimately he would like to train and launch a fully capable and equipped unit of real-life superheroes—a veritable team of Batmen and Batwomen—to help make some small corner of the world safer. He even has a name picked out for this team: the Guardians of Tomorrow.

FALSE STARTS

THERE ISN'T NECESSARILY A NEED TO WAIT TILL TOMORROW FOR Batman because he's already here, in a sense. I had the chance to sit down and chat with him in a bookstore in Brampton, a suburb of Toronto. Brampton Batman, as he's known, is actually Stephen Lawrence, a black man in his forties who works at a beverage plant during the day. At night, he dons an impressively authentic Dark Knight costume and hops in his Batmobile replica—a modified Chevrolet Caprice modeled on the car Michael Keaton used in the 1989 movie—and patrols the streets. Lawrence—who bristles at the fact that local press have published his real name—doesn't consider himself a real-life superhero, but he says he does perform good deeds such as helping motorists and appearing at charity event photo opportunities. He's a veritable celebrity in these parts—our conversation is interrupted several times by gawking bookstore shoppers and staff wanting selfies.

Lawrence believes he has been Batman in spirit since the age of fourteen, when his father died at the hands of one of his other sons. Since then, he has been trying to forget the trauma by being the best person he can be. "The synchronicity between Bruce Wayne and myself is eerily similar," he says, his voice reminiscent of actor Kevin Conroy's robotic delivery from *Batman: The Animated Series*. "I've been Batman for over twenty years now."[16]

Brampton Batman says he is true to his namesake—that he is constantly patrolling his city looking for evil-doers to thwart. "I am not Bruce Wayne. It [is] also not known how much money I have or have not," he tells me in his formal tone during a follow-up conversation on Facebook. "[What is documented is] that I do fight crime. I have done it, and will continue." Given the paucity of media reports or other evidence pointing to his involvement in foiling crimes, it's likely that he is simply committing to the bit. Or, depending on how much one wants to believe in such a thing, it's possible he's actually very good at being a secret crime fighter.

Perhaps what the world needs more than a real-life Batman is a real-life Bruce Wayne—a wealthy individual who doesn't think twice about using his fortune to stop bad guys and otherwise help the helpless. According to the departed Stan Lee, that person may also exist in the form of Ivan Wilzig, otherwise known as Peaceman, a well-to-do philanthropist and erstwhile real-life superhero who lives in a castle in the Hamptons. Wilzig's father, Siggi, immigrated to the United States in 1947 as a Holocaust survivor from Germany and worked his way up to become chief executive of the Texas-based Wilshire Oil Company, as well as the Trust Company of New Jersey, a midsize bank. He left his sizeable estate to his son after his death in 2013. Ivan, for his part, chose to become a hippie-cum-entertainer, recording and releasing a dance remake of John Lennon's "Imagine" in 2001. He also adopted a "Peaceman" superhero persona, dressing in colorful costumes and capes, before releasing an album of sixties and seventies peacenik-anthems-as-dance-songs, *I Am Peaceman*, in 2010.

In between, in 2007, he appeared on Stan Lee's reality television show, *Who Wants to Be a Superhero?* albeit under a different nom de guerre. The producers wanted to own the rights to Wilzig's Peaceman persona, but he refused to give up his developing brand. Instead, he appeared as Mr. Mitzvah, billed as the world's first Jewish super-hero. Wilzig lasted just three episodes before being eliminated, but not before the Marvel impresario dubbed him the real-life Bruce Wayne. The experience led to contact with Chaim Lazaros, other-wise known as Life. Despite being in his fifties, Wilzig says he joined Life and other real-life superheroes on street patrols in New York a few times. He also helped bankroll Superheroes Anonymous, the workshop-slash-conference Lazaros had put together as a meeting of the minds for costumed do-gooders. "I became like their under-writer. My superpower is my checkbook. I was underwriting these activities rather than going on them myself," he says. "I'd say, 'What do you need, how much are you short?' I'd supply what he needed. I would come to the rescue. I was like a superhero's superhero. They knew they could count on me."[17]

Wilzig has retreated from the real-life superhero community in recent years, to the chagrin of other costumed individuals who had hoped he would take a leadership role. These days, he appears more interested in his music and television career. "The money would have been wiser spent had I or they gotten our own reality TV show, because then we would have reached millions of people without me having to fund the entire organization, because I have other commitments and projects I'm working on," he says. "In that capacity I felt like I could be a leader... I'm in the entertainment business. Between my natural ability to entertain crowds and because I have an incredible sense of humor, I could capture the imagination of America and the world."

UTILITY BELTS

SOME BLEND OF BRUCE WAYNE AND BATMAN—OR, RATHER, BATMEN—IS also already here, albeit in a less fantastical, less performance art–oriented form. Athena Finger, granddaughter of Dark Knight cocreator Bill Finger, points this out when I speak with her. "Special forces have all kinds of gadgets that are Batman-esque, and detectives are great at solving puzzles," she says. "Maybe if you put four or five people together, you'll have a Batman. I don't think one person can pull it off."[18]

Military and law enforcement agencies do indeed have all manner of modern gadgets and technology at their disposal, from lightweight bulletproof armor and infrared night-vision goggles to tiny surveillance drones, plus sonic and light-burst weapons. To soldiers and police of only a few decades ago, these capabilities would have seemed like something out of a comic book. The same goes for investigators and intelligence agencies, who can now employ artificial intelligence to scour vast databases of information gleaned from ubiquitous communications networks to find criminals and prevent wrongdoings before they happen. Their efforts are obviously imperfect, but law enforcement's current intelligence and surveillance capabilities are superhuman compared to what their predecessors were working with. Heck, even the ordinary citizen has relative superpowers thanks to technology—the smartphones in our pockets give us informational and communication capabilities that were the exclusive domain of X-Men telepaths not so long ago.

These tools are part of the reason why crime—both violent and property-related—has been on the decline in most developed countries since the 1990s. As Patrick Sharkey, a sociology professor at New York University, puts it, police and citizens alike have become much more capable in recent years, resulting in the current era being one of the safest times in US history. "Part of that was the police. Law enforcement became more effective at what they were doing by using data about where police should be stationed, where the problems were arising," he told CityLab in 2018. "Home-owners started to install alarm systems and camera systems. Technology improved that made motor-vehicle theft much less successful. Cities started to install camera systems."[19] The same holds true in Canada, the United Kingdom, Australia and many other countries. Globally, almost 70 per cent of people say they have confidence in their local police and feel secure, according to Gallup's Law and Order Index. Those figures are considerably higher in the developed world, at more than 80 per cent in the United States, Canada, Western Europe and Southeast Asia.[20]

Of course, such feelings are highly relative, dependent on who you happen to be and where you happen to live. A well-to-do family living in a gated community in Florida, for example, has considerably more reason to feel safe and trust the police than their poorer counterparts in, say, inner-city Baltimore. Continuing racial strife and incidents of police brutality in African-American communities highlight the larger concern with arming law enforcement with advanced technologies—that those capabilities can be used against innocent civilians, and particularly against specific civilians. Skepticism about police motivations and effectiveness abounds, despite the overall decline in crime, and continues to act as a prime driver for entrepreneurial law enforcement, which includes everything from private security and vigilantes to a certain subset of real-life superheroes. Until there's total faith in police, which is unlikely to happen anytime soon, some portion of the population will always argue for some form of independent counterbalance. Someone will always be waiting for Batman. To some extent, counting fully on the state to protect you is un-American.

There's also the notion that more can always be done, especially in situations where there is a consensus that not enough is currently being done, as is the case with homelessness. Until officials in developed countries can solve this problem—which also isn't likely in the near term—it will likely continue to be a motivator for real-life superheroes. In this case, it's difficult to argue for the status quo; more can indeed always be done.

Few real-life superheroes are under any delusions that their activities are resulting in significant changes in the meantime, either in law enforcement or homelessness, but many are quick to say that isn't the point. Their mission, if it isn't clear by now, is to effect positive change on a smaller, more individual level. They're trying to corral that truest, most Supermanly of superpowers—the ability to inspire—in the hopes of seeding and nourishing grassroots change. Their success is thus measured in the smiles they put on the faces of destitute people living on the streets of New York, Toronto or Liverpool, or in Chicago's Lower Wacker, or the curiosity they provoke in the otherwise unengaged civilians who happen to witness their charitable acts. It's also measured in the thanks they get from revelers in San Diego or Seattle for breaking up a bar fight or escorting a drunken tourist to safety, or even in silly selfie shots with tourists. Some of those encounters inevitably spur strangers into doing something good, or even into suiting up and joining the movement themselves. The community's success can also be quantified by its growth, going from a single individual in the late 1960s who fought environmental crime under a secret identity, to the hundreds of armor- and spandex-clad individuals who now patrol streets around the world.

Their success can also be measured in the effect they have on the people who take the time to understand them. Although he's cynical about how the movement has evolved, Barnett the filmmaker is no less idealistic about the real-life superhero concept. Since he made *Superheroes*, he has gone on to produce other socially progressive documentaries, including *Becoming Bulletproof*, about filmmakers living with disabilities, and *Changing the Game*, about transgender high school athletes. He credits some of the individuals he met during the making of *Superheroes*, such as Mr. Xtreme in San Diego, with steering him down a more righteous path. "I was really inspired by it and continue to take some of the more positive aspects of what I learned and put it to use in context of my life and work," he says. "It really has informed my entire career."

Peter Tangen, the photographer who organized the Real Life Superhero Project, continues to get hundreds of emails from people who read about the various characters on his website. Their communiqués also inspire him to be a better person. "I got something from a girl who was profoundly moved by what she read on the site who had found strength in combating the challenges in her life based on the good she saw in people," he says. "There's a great deal of power in the costume."[21] Denise Masino was skeptical about real-life superheroes when she started filming a documentary about them, but they won her over as the project continued, to the point where she joined the community by becoming the titular real-life character in her 2016 film, *The Adventures of Miss Fit.* "What's not to like? It's a group of people who are thinking about other people," she says. "When they have extra, they share it with a complete stranger. I was inspired by what I saw from different people at different times on different levels. It made me think." Masino now regularly takes part in the annual charity warrior dash for St. Jude Children's Research Hospital. By 2019, her team of real-life superheroes had raised more than 140,000 dollars for the cause. "The real-life superheroes I've met have made me a better person because it's made me question my own motives and actions," she says.[22]

There is something infectious about their attitude. For my part, I've been as guilty as anyone of apathy toward homelessness. Like so many people, I've seen so much of it that I had tuned it out, ignoring homeless people I'd pass on the street like they were invisible. Patrolling with real-life superheroes changed that. I too learned to start seeing the world more fully, which includes *all* the people in it. Whatever their individual motivations may be and whatever their presence may say about society, government, law enforcement and culture, this particular effect of real-life superheroes—of spurring people to be better—can't possibly be a bad thing.

Some recognize this as the ultimate internal goal of what they do. It is indeed about the realization of the monomyth, the transformation of the self into something better. The costume is just a means to an end, a stepping stone that helps one figure out how to improve as a person in real life. "Once you get in the habit of doing that in costume you find that it bleeds back into your real life," Geist says. "You're not a person who carelessly walks by a situation anymore. You're the person who is attendant to it, who feels the need to address problems and help people." Some, like James Marx, who used to patrol the Seattle streets alongside Phoenix Jones as Evocatus, graduate from wearing the mask. Marx now works with fellow veterans, helping them cope with their own post-traumatic stress disorders. "It was exactly what I needed, when I needed it," he says of his adventuring days. "But now, some of us are finding other, perhaps less scandalous ways of serving our community."[23] Zimmer, post-retirement, has worked on scientific and technological projects that he hopes will improve the world, such as hydroponic systems that filter air pollutants and even brain-enhancing chewing gum. "It was caterpillar-to-butterfly," he says of his real-life superhero career. "My hope is that it plants that seed of philosophy in people's minds that they have more power than they think they do, that if they feel trapped by societal expectations and their normal routine and feel like they're not addressing things that are important to them, they can change that and rebel and they can do this thing that feels kind of mischievous at times, but do it for a good purpose. My hope is that people see this idea of becoming a superhero in that larger context, that there are a lot of opportunities to do good."

SAVING THROUGH INSPIRATION

IN THEIR FORMATIVE YEARS, COMIC-BOOK SUPERHEROES WERE PUR-posely designed as tableaux onto which readers could project their own thoughts, views and beliefs, to imagine themselves under the mask. Superheroes have throughout their history dared the reader or viewer to ask, What would I do if I were under there? Would I kill the Joker or would I let him live? Would I stop the Green Goblin or save Gwen Stacy from falling to her death? Would I join Iron Man in working for the government or rebel alongside Captain America?

Critics who bemoan the superheroization of culture because it has conditioned a populace to wait for a hero to save them have it wrong. For every person who reads a comic book or watches a movie and transposes that fictional experience into a belief or expectation that a real-life hero will someday swoop in to save the day, there may be at least an equal number of people—and possibly a great deal more—who understand the truer value of superheroes. Their purpose is not necessarily to save, but rather to inspire. They are meant to make us want to be better people, to strive closer toward the heroic ideal ourselves. Despite their internecine squabbling, they are archetypes whose job is to remind us of the so-called better angels of our nature.

There is at least some science that shows this to be the case. A 2018 study published in *Frontiers in Psychology* found that people who were exposed to images of superheroes were more likely to engage in helpful behavior than those who weren't. In the first experiment, researchers had participants describe images of four everyday scenes. For half of them, the images were edited to include an easily recognizable superhero logo or image, such as that of Spider-Man or Superman. Researchers had participants self report their own levels of virtue and altruism, then had them read through a series of scenarios that involved benevolent actions such as returning lost money or shoveling snow from an elderly neighbor's driveway. Participants were then asked to indicate how likely they would be to help. Those who had seen the superhero images were far more likely to get involved, a result that held true regardless of whether they saw themselves as particularly virtuous or not. In a second experiment, subjects were ushered into a room that contained a small poster of either Superman or a bicycle on the wall, then asked to complete the first experiment above. Afterward, they were asked if they would like to remain for an additional twenty-minute pilot project that involved "a boring task of rating up to sixty geometric shapes." More than 90 per cent of those who saw the Superman poster agreed to stay, versus only 75 per cent of those who saw the bicycle. The researchers cautiously said their results show that "even the subtle activation of heroic constructs through virtual images of superheroes may influence intentions to help, as well as actual helping behavior."[24]

There is at least some evidence, anecdotal as it is, that seeing the same in the real world and outside a lab setting has a similar effect. I believe that most people who appreciate superheroes in any form understand this and that's why we like them. Superheroes remind us of the good that we're capable of.

Grant Morrison, who achieved cult status during the 1980s and 1990s with his thought-provoking runs writing Doom Patrol and Batman comics, thinks the likes of the Xtreme Justice League, the Rain City Superhero Movement, the Trillium Guard, the Hope mission participants, the socially conscious *luchadores* of Mexico, the Superheroes of Kibera and everyone in between could be the shape of things to come, as the culture started in comic books nearly a century ago becomes ever more participatory. Rather than this being a negative or questionable development, it's a sign of hope for a better tomorrow. "These real-life superheroes are waiting for a world that's not quite here, but one day soon they might be recognized as pioneering neonauts, part human, part story," Morrison writes in his book *Supergods*. "It should give us hope that superhero stories are flourishing everywhere because they are a bright flickering sign of our need to move on, to imagine the better, more just, and more proactive people we can be."[25]

Whatever your view may be of real-life superheroes, it's hard to dispute the purity of the message they espouse. As the members of the Xtreme Justice League are fond of saying, it's about being the change you want to see. Anyone who wants to change the world must first start by changing themselves. It's the most superheroic thing anyone can do.

ACKNOWLEDGMENTS

NOT ALL HEROES WEAR CAPES, AS THE SAYING GOES. THERE ARE A GREAT many individuals without whom this work would not have been possible. I'm grateful to them for inspiring it, saving it or both.

Canadian Justice, Night Bug and Impact are real-life superheroes who were instrumental in connecting me to the community at large. Without these three do-gooders I doubt the many RLSH out there, distrustful of the media as they are, would have replied to my requests for interviews, meetings and tagalongs.

Mark Askwith is also a special kind of hero who read and critiqued an early version of the manuscript. He provided invaluable insights, especially when it came to the history of comic books and how they came to dominate pop culture. There are few people more knowledgeable when it comes to this stuff and I was fortunate he took the time to help.

Derek Fairbridge, Emma Skagen, Nicola Goshulak, Blaine Willick and Anna Comfort O'Keeffe at Douglas & McIntyre did an excellent job shepherding this project through from beginning to end. Their suggestions, comments, edits and questions helped rein it in when it threatened to run off the rails. Chris Casuccio and John

Pearce at Westwood Creative Artists maintained faith even when mine was running low.

My wife, Claudette, also deserves much gratitude as a tireless sounding board. Her support through the inevitable ups and downs of the process was simply superheroic.

Lastly, everything is due to the people who started it all: Jerry Siegel, Joe Shuster, Bob Kane, Bill Finger, Stan Lee, Jack Kirby, Steve Ditko and many more; those writers, artists and dreamers whose fantasies of a better world filled with more virtuous people have become a pillar of our culture and an inspiration to imaginations everywhere, mine included.

I'm especially grateful to Chris Claremont, the X-Men writer who originally hooked me on comics by taking fantastical beings and making them real. The world his superheroes dreamed of—a more tolerant, enlightened and virtuous one—is the reality we should all strive for.

ENDNOTES

CHAPTER 1

1   *An Unlikely Prophet* by Alvin Schwartz, publushed by Inner Traditions International and Bear & Company © 2006. All rights reserved. http://www.innertraditions.com. Reprinted with permission of publisher.

2   Ibid., 16.

3   Ibid., 17–18.

4   Ibid., 193–94.

5   Ibid., 216.

6   "Mutie" being the comics' slur for "mutant."

7   Honorable mention goes to *Blade*, released in 1998, which was a success as well. The only strike against considering the film—which starred Wesley Snipes as a half-vampire vampire hunter—a landmark in the genre is that traditional audiences didn't necessarily recognize the character as a proper superhero.

8   Some say they've never read a comic book in their lives. They just like dressing up anyway.

9   The consensus is: it isn't very.

10   Bronies are adult male fans of the My Little Pony toys and TV show. My instinct is to mock them, but a good friend considers himself one.

11   Bill Maher, "Adulting," *Real Time with Bill Maher Blog*, November 17, 2018, http://www.real-time-with-bill-maher-blog.com/index/2018/11/16/adulting.

12   Daniel White et al., "Look Up in the Sky: Latent Content Analysis of the Real Life Superhero Community," *The Qualitative Report*, 21(2), 2016, 178–95.

13   Author interview with Peter Tangen, March 1, 2017.

14   Author interview with James Marx, November 9, 2018.

15 Author interview with Nyght, April 23, 2018.

16 Author interview with Life, March 6, 2018.

17 Author interview with El Caballero, September 12, 2018.

18 Author interview with Blackhat, May 9, 2017.

19 Author interview with Grim, March 1, 2018.

20 Author interview with Nyghtingale, April 19, 2018.

21 Author interview with Crimson Canuck, April 17, 2017.

22 Author interview with Urban Avenger, November 6, 2017.

23 Author interview with Rock N Roll, August 15, 2018.

24 Author interview with Skyman, March 6, 2018.

25 Elaine Fishwick and Heusen Mak, "Fighting Crime, Battling Injustice: The World of Real-Life Superheroes," *Crime, Media, Culture*, 11(3), 2015, 335–56.

CHAPTER 2

1 Author interview with Phil Hui, October 4, 2018.

2 Milton Griepp, "Number of Comic Stores Up in 2016," ICV2, July 28, 2016, https://icv2.com/articles/markets/view/35123/number-comic-stores-up-2016.

3 Travis M. Andrews, "The Resurgence of Comic Books: The Industry Has Its Best-Selling Month in Nearly Two Decades," *The Washington Post*, July 12, 2016, https://www.washingtonpost.com/news/morning-mix/wp/2016/07/12/the-resurgence-of-comic-books-the-industry-has-its-best-selling-month-in-nearly-two-decades.

4 His thought process sounds familiar.

5 Jim Steranko, *The Steranko History of Comics, Volume One* (Reading, PA: Supergraphics, 1970), 35.

6 Ibid., 39.

7 Mike Benton, *The Comic Book in America: An Illustrated History* (Dallas, TX: Taylor Publishing Company, 1989), 23.

8 Steranko, *The Steranko History of Comics*, 39–40.

9 Grant Morrison, *Supergods: What Masked Vigilantes, Miraculous Mutants, and a Sun God from Smallville Can Teach Us about Being Human* (New York: Spiegel & Grau, 2012), 9.

10 Marc Tyler Nobleman, *Bill the Boy Wonder: The Secret Co-Creator of Batman* (Waterton, MA: Charlesbridge, 2012), 12.

11 Benton, *The Comic Book in America*, 32.

12 Nirit Anderman, "Supermensches: Comic Books' Secret Jewish History," *Haaretz*, January 24, 2016, https://www.haaretz.com/israel-news/culture/MAGAZINE-supermensches-comic-books-jewish-history-1.5393475.

13 Ibid.

14 Ibid.

15 Steranko, *The Steranko History of Comics*, 51–52.

16 Benton, *The Comic Book in America*, 35.

17 Ibid., 51.

18 Glen Weldon, *The Caped Crusade: Batman and the Rise of Nerd Culture* (New York: Simon & Schuster, 2016), 56.

19 Benton, *The Comic Book in America*, 71.

20 Weldon, *The Caped Crusade*, 72.

21 It's worth noting that DC Comics is a redundant name because it technically stands for "Detective Comics Comics."

22 *Superman* movie review, *rogerebert.com*, November 4, 2010, https://www.rogerebert .com/reviews/great-movie-superman-1978.

23 "Box Office History for Batman Movies," *The Numbers*, accessed January 29, 2020, http://the-numbers.com/movies/franchise/Batman#tab-summary.

24 Weldon, *The Caped Crusade*, 171.

25 Ibid, 194.

26 "Movie Franchises," *The Numbers*, accessed January 29, 2020, http://the-numbers .com/movies/franchises.

27 Weldon, *The Caped Crusade*, 199.

28 Colin Bertram, "Comic-Con: the Power and Politics of Cosplay," NBC *San Diego*, July 25, 2014, https://www.nbcsandiego.com/entertainment/entertainment-news /Comic-Con-Cosplay-the-Power-and-Politics--268627532.html.

29 James Pethokoukis, "Why the Rise of Cosplay Is a Bad Sign for the U.S. Economy," *The Week*, October 9, 2014, https://theweek.com/articles/443181/why-rise-cosplay -bad-sign-economy. (Pethokoukis obviously meant "the Doctor" rather than "Doctor Who.")

30 Adam Ozimek, "No, the Rise of Cosplay Is Not a Bad Sign for the U.S. Economy," *Forbes*, October 14, 2014, https://www.forbes.com/sites/modeledbehavior /2014/10/14/no-the-rise-of-cosplay-is-not-a-bad-sign-for-the-u-s-economy.

CHAPTER 3

1 Kevin Baker, "'Welcome to Fear City'—the Inside Story of New York's Civil War, 40 Years On," *The Guardian*, May 18, 2015, https://www.theguardian.com/cities /2015/may/18/welcome-to-fear-city-the-inside-story-of-new-yorks-civil-war -40-years-on.

2 Nicholas Pileggi, "The Guardian Angels: Help—or Hype?," *New York*, November 24, 1980.

3 Jere Hester, "The Early History of the Guardian Angels and Their Controversial New York City Subway Patrols," *New York Daily News*, August 14, 2017, https:// www.nydailynews.com/new-york/guardian-angels-started-protecting-nyc-subways -article-1.804336.

4 Pileggi, "The Guardian Angels."

5   Ibid.

6   US numbers are from the Bureau of Labor Statistics, https://www.bls.gov/ooh /protective-service/private-detectives-and-investigators.htm; UK numbers are from Quality Investigators, https://www.findadetective.co.uk/articles/how-many -investigators.html.

7   "What You Need to Know When an Investigation Leads You to France," *Pursuit Magazine*, April 16, 2012, http://pursuitmag.com/what-you-need-to-know-when -an-investigation-leads-you-to-france/.

8   Claire Provost, "The Industry of Inequality: Why the World Is Obsessed with Private Security," *The Guardian*, May 12, 2017, https://www.theguardian.com /inequality/2017/may/12/industry-of-inequality-why-world-is-obsessed-with -private-security.

9   "Bodyguards Aren't Just for Celebrities Anymore," *Town & Country*, November 9, 2016, https://www.townandcountrymag.com/society/money-and-power/a8518 /bodyguards-wealthy-people/.

10   Ray Abrahams, *Vigilant Citizens: Vigilantism and the State* (Cambridge: Polity, 1998), 7–9.

11   Ibid., 55.

12   Albert C. Stevens, *The Cyclopædia of Fraternities* (New York: Hamilton Printing and Publishing Co., 1907).

13   "Ku Klux Klan in the Twentieth Century," *New Georgia Encyclopedia*, July 7, 2005, http://www.georgiaencyclopedia.org/articles/history-archaeology/ku-klux-klan -twentieth-century.

14   Eric Markowitz, "The Most Dangerous Gay Man in America Fought Violence with Violence," *Newsweek*, January 25, 2018, https://www.newsweek.com /2018/02/02/most-dangerous-gay-man-america-789402.html.

15   Abrahams, *Vigilant Citizens*, 105.

16   Ibid., 160.

17   *Vigilante: The Incredible True Story of Curtis Sliwa and the Guardian Angels*, Journeyman Pictures Ltd., 2017.

18   Author interview with Curtis Sliwa, July 18, 2018.

19   "Guardian Angels Return to Central Park as Crime Rises," *BBC News*, October 27, 2015, https://www.bbc.com/news/av/world-us-canada-34650712/guardian-angels -return-to-central-park-as-crime-rises.

CHAPTER 4

1   Ray Fox, *Raising Kane: The Fox Chronicles* (Montgomery, IL: Kindred Spirits Press, 1999), 19.

2   Ibid., 22–23.

3   From his diary, now kept in the Little White School Museum in Oswego, Illinois.

4   Fox, *Raising Kane*, 148.

5   Author interview with Nellie Bly Workman, April 4, 2018.

6   Author interview with Roger Matile, April 6, 2018.

7   Bryan Thomas, "Captain Sticky: America's Only Practicing Caped Crusader," *Night Flight*, March 4, 2015, http://nightflight.com/meet-captain-sticky/.

8   Mark Evanier, "Captain Sticky, R.I.P.," *News from Me*, January 29, 2005, https://www.newsfromme.com/2005/01/29/captain-sticky-r-i-p/.

9   Thomas, "Captain Sticky."

10 "Richard Pesta; 'Captain Sticky' Championed Consumer Causes," *San Diego Union-Tribune*, February 18, 2004.

11 Jon Reed, "It's Willie Perry Day: Remembering Birmingham's Batman," *al.com*, August 3, 2015, https://www.al.com/news/birmingham/index.ssf/2015/08/its _willie_perry_day_rememberi.html.

12 Solomon Crenshaw Jr., "Birmingham's Batman Legacy Lives on through Daughter's Efforts," *Alabama Newscenter*, June 23, 2016, https://alabamanewscenter .com/2016/06/23/birminghams-batman-legacy-lives-daughters-efforts/.

13 Reed, "It's Willie Perry Day."

14 Tea Krulos, *Heroes in the Night: Inside the Real Life Superhero Movement* (Chicago: Chicago Review Press, 2013), ebook location 751.

15 Author interview with Dark Guardian, December 18, 2017.

16 Cameron Reilly, "GDay World 376—Kevlex, a Real-Life Superhero," *Cameron Reilly*, May 13, 2009, http://cameronreilly.com/gday-world-376-kevlex-a-real-life -superhero/.

17 Author interview with Urban Avenger, November 6, 2017.

18 Author interview with Geist, November 6, 2017.

19 Author interview with Life, March 6, 2018.

20 Author interview with Nameless Crusader, February 27, 2018.

21 Author interview with Michael Barnett, December 13, 2018.

22 Author interview with Canadian Justice, April 13, 2017.

23 Jenny Kuglin, "Phoenix Jones: Real Life Superhero," KOMO *News*, March 7, 2013, https://komonews.com/archive/phoenix-jones-real-life-superhero-11-21-2015.

24 Casey McNerthney, "Police Alerted to 'Superheroes' Patrolling Seattle," *Seattle Post-Intelligencer*, November 18, 2010, https://www.seattlepi.com/local/article /Police-alerted-to-superheroes-patrolling-Seattle-821425.php.

25 Nick Allen, "Phoenix Jones: The Masked Vigilante Protecting Lynnwood, Washington," *The Telegraph*, January 6, 2011, https://www.telegraph.co.uk/news /worldnews/northamerica/usa/8244078/Phoenix-Jones-the-masked-vigilante -protecting-Lynnwood-Washington.html.

26   Lanford Beard, "Phoenix Jones, Seattle's Real-Life 'Superhero,' Is Unmasked,"
      Entertainment Weekly, October 14, 2011, https://ew.com/article/2011/10/14
      /phoenix-jones-seattle-superhero-unmasked/.

27   According to photographer Peter Tangen.

28   McNerthney, "Police Alerted."

29   "Wannabe Superhero Won't Face Charges," WIBW, November 23, 2011,
      https://www.wibw.com/home/headlines/Wannabe_Superhero_Wont_Face
      _Charges__134433358.html.

30   "Batman Look-Alike Wanted to 'Inspire Hope' Before Arrest Outside Home
      Depot," *Lehigh Valley Live*, August 2, 2012, https://www.lehighvalleylive.com/
      warren-county/express-times/index.ssf/2012/08/batman-like_mask-clad_man
      _says.html.

31   Krulos, *Heroes in the Night*, location 1595.

32   Ibid., location 1704.

33   Author interview with Purple Lotus, December 6, 2018.

34   Author interview with Lord Mole, December 8, 2018.

35   Author interview with Zero, December 5, 2018.

36   Author interview with Skyman, March 6, 2018.

37   Author interview with El Caballero, September 12, 2018.

38   Jon Ronson, "It's a Bird! It's a Plane! It's... Some Dude?!" GQ, August 4, 2011,
      https://www.gq.com/story/real-life-superheroes-phoenix-jones.

39   Author interview with Evocatus, November 9, 2018.

40   Sara Jean Green, *Seattle Times*, January 28, 2020, https://www.seattletimes.com
      /seattle-news/crime/seattle-superhero-phoenix-jones-charged-after-undercover
      -drug-bust/.

41   Dark Guardian Twitter post, January 28, 2020.

CHAPTER 5

1   "Military Population in San Diego," *Partners at Learning*, accessed on July 12, 2018.
      http://palmilitaryresources.weebly.com/military-demographics.html.

2   "The Most Visited Cities in the US," *World Atlas*, accessed on July 12, 2018,
      https://www.worldatlas.com/articles/the-most-visited-cities-in-the-us.html.

3   "San Diego Colleges, Universities, Trade and Vocational Schools," *CityTownInfo*,
      accessed on July 12, 2018, https://www.citytowninfo.com/places
      /california/san-diego/colleges.

4   Megan Burks, "The Scope of San Diego's Gang Problem," *Voice of San Diego*,
      April 2, 2014, https://www.voiceofsandiego.org/topics/news/the-scope-of-san
      -diegos-gang-problem/.

5   "Gaslamp Quarter Showcasing a Pulsating Night Life," *Stipp Law Firm*, accessed
     on July 12, 2018, https://www.sd-personalinjury.com/gaslamp-district-dangerous
     -weekends-look-high-rate-bar-fights-downtown-san-diego/.

6   Steven Luke, "San Diego Police Getting Creative to Address Staffing Shortage,"
     NBC *San Diego*, September 13, 2018, https://www.nbcsandiego.com/news
     /local/San-Diego-Police-Getting-Creative-to-Address-Staffing-Shortage
     -493215401.html.

7   Author interview with Nyghtingale, April 19, 2018.

8   Author patrol with Xtreme Justice League, May 25, 2018.

9   *Superheroes*, Superfilms!, 2011.

10   Author interview with Mr. Xtreme, February 19, 2018.

11   Ibid.

12   Author interview with Curtis Sliwa, July 18, 2018.

13   Author interview with Grim, March 1, 2018.

14   Author interview with Nyght, April 23, 2018.

15   Author interview with Fallen Boy, December 22, 2018.

16   Author patrol with Xtreme Justice League, May 25, 2018.

17   Author interview with Rock N Roll, August 15, 2018.

18   Author interview with Gavin Weston, June 25, 2018.

19   Nicole E. Haas et al., "Public Support for Vigilantism, Confidence in Police and
     Police Responsiveness," *Policing and Society: An International Journal of Research and
     Policy*, 2014, 224–41.

20   Kareem Abdul-Jabbar, "Kareem Abdul-Jabbar: America's Dark Obsession with
     Vigilante Justice," *Time*, August 28, 2014, http://time.com/3184586/kareem-abdul
     -jabbar-americas-dark-obsession-with-vigilante-justice/.

21   Julie Ray, "Peace, Security Still Out of Reach for Many Worldwide," *Gallup*, June 7,
     2018, https://news.gallup.com/poll/235391/peace-security-reach-worldwide
     .aspx?g_source=link_NEWSV9&g_medium=LEAD&g_campaign=item_&g
     _content=Peace%2c%2520security%2520still%2520out%2520of%2520Reach%2520for
     %2520many%2520worldwide-.

22   James Daily and Ryan Davidson, *The Law of Superheroes* (New York: Gotham
     Books, 2013), 3–4.

23   Abrahams, *Vigilant Citizens*, 4.

24   Glen Weldon, "Superheroes and The F-Word: Grappling with the Ugly Truth
     Under the Capes," NPR, November 16, 2016, https://www.npr.org/2016/11/16
     /502161587/superheroes-and-the-f-word-grappling-with-the-ugly-truth-under
     -the-capes.

25   Damien Walter, "Frank Miller's Fascist Dark Knight Is a Very Modern Archetype,"
     The Guardian, April 1, 2016, https://www.theguardian.com/books/booksblog/2016
     /apr/01/frank-miller-fascist-dark-knight-modern-archetype-donald-trump.

26   Mark Fisher, "Batman's Political Right Turn," *The Guardian*, July 22, 2012, https://
www.theguardian.com/commentisfree/2012/jul/22/batman-political-right-turn.

27   Jared Keller, "Anti-Government Unrest and American Vigilantism," *The Atlantic*,
March 30, 2010, https://www.theatlantic.com/politics/archive/2010/03/anti
-government-unrest-and-american-vigilantism/38229/.

CHAPTER 6

1   Gregory Pratt and Quinn Ford, "Driving, Skidding and Drifting on Chicago's
Underground Lower Wacker Track," *Chicago Tribune*, July 17, 2015,
http://www.chicagotribune.com/news/ct-lower-wacker-drag-racing-met-20150717
-story.html.

2   Bill Zwecker, "'Batman' Director Christopher Nolan Re-creates History with
'Dunkirk,'" *Chicago Sun-Times*, July 19, 2017, https://chicago.suntimes.com
/2017/7/19/18357795/batman-director-christopher-nolan-re-creates-history-with
-dunkirk.

3   Cindy Richards and Diane Struzzi, "1999 Look Back: Chicago Tribune, 'Lower
Wacker to Shut Its Gates on Homeless, Fences to Be Locked,'" *Chicago Coalition
for the Homeless*, January 7, 2018, http://www.chicagohomeless.org/1999-look
-back-chicago-tribune-lower-wacker-to-shut-its-gates-on-homeless-fences-to-be
-locked/.

4   Michael Lansu, "Chicago's Homeless Population Stretches Beyond Those on
Streets, in Shelters," *Chicago Tribune*, November 9, 2015,
http://www.chicagotribune.com/redeye/redeye-couch-surfing-to-shelters-defining
-homeless-chicago-20151109-story.html.

5   Mina Bloom and Ariel Cheung, "With More than Half of Its Tenants Burdened by
Soaring Rents, Chicago Considers Rent Control," *Belt Magazine*, March 8, 2018,
http://beltmag.com/chicago-rent-control/.

6   Author interview with Paul Hamann, July 2, 2018.

7   Author patrol on April 7, 2018.

8   Scott Greenstone, "Is Seattle's Homeless Crisis the Worst in the Country?" *The
Seattle Times*, January 16, 2018, https://www.seattletimes.com/seattle-news
/homeless/is-seattles-homeless-crisis-the-worst-in-the-country/.

9   Soo Youn, "Battling Homelessness and Hepatitis A, San Diego Employs Tent
Structures to Help," nbc *News*, February 4, 2018, https://www.nbcnews.com/news
/us-news/battling-homelessness-hepatitis-san-diego-employs-tent-structures
-help-n844556.

10   "Hawaii Governor Declares State of Emergency Amid Homelessness Crisis," *The
Guardian*, October 17, 2015, https://www.theguardian.com/us-news/2015/oct/17
/hawaii-homelessness-state-of-emergency.

11   OECD homelessness report, accessed July 24, 2017, https://www.oecd.org/els
      /family/HC3-1-Homeless-population.pdf.

12   Erik Sherman, "America Is the Richest, and Most Unequal, Country," *Fortune*,
      September 30, 2015, http://fortune.com/2015/09/30/america-wealth-inequality/.

13   Jon Ronson, "Book Excerpt: Narcissistic Superheroes in *Amazing Adventures of
      Phoenix Jones*," *Wired*, November 22, 2011, https://www.wired.com/2011/11
      /amazing-adventures-of-phoenix-jones/.

14   Author interview with Life, March 6, 2018.

15   "CAF World Giving Index 2017," *Charities Aid Foundation*, September 2017,
      https://www.cafonline.org/docs/default-source/about-us-publications
      /cafworldgivingindex2017_2167a_web_210917.pdf?sfvrsn=ed1dac40_10.

16   Author interview with Geist, November 6, 2017.

CHAPTER 7

1   Author interview with Flat Man, May 28, 2018.

2   The prank is known by various names around the world, including Nicky Nicky
      Nine Doors in Canada and the United States, Cherry Knocking in the United
      Kingdom and Tok-Tokkie in South Africa.

3   "New Zealand to House Country's Entire Homeless Population Before Winter
      Hits Next Month," CBC, May 4, 2018, https://www.cbc.ca/radio/asithappens
      /as-it-happens-friday-edition-1.4648602/new-zealand-to-house-country-s-entire
      -homeless-population-before-winter-hits-next-month-1.4649023.

4   Henry Cooke, "New Zealand Has Worst Level of Homelessness in the World,
      Labour Says," *stuff*, July 21, 2017, https://www.stuff.co.nz/national/politics
      /94983470/new-zealand-has-worst-level-of-homelessness-in-the-world-labour-say.

5   Author interview with Knight Warrior, June 24, 2018.

6   "'Superhero' Takes On Clampers," BBC *News*, September 16, 2003,
      http://news.bbc.co.uk/2/hi/3112670.stm.

7   Author interview with Gavin Weston, June 25, 2018.

8   Author interview with Lord Mole, December 8, 2018.

9   Author interview with Black Mercer, December 4, 2018.

10   Benjamin Franklin Fairless testimony, April 26, 1950, *Study of Monopoly Power*,
      hearings before the Subcommittee on Study of Monopoly Power of the Committee
      on the Judiciary, House of Representatives, https://www.bartleby.com/73
      /142.html.

11   Abrahams, *Vigilant Citizens*, 101.

12   Author interview with Curtis Sliwa, July 18, 2018.

13   The two cities are very close in population, with London having 8.9 million people
      and New York 8.6 million as of mid-2017.

14   "The Guardian Angels' History in Toronto," *CityNews*, July 13, 2006,
      https://toronto.citynews.ca/2006/07/13/the-guardian-angels-history-in-toronto/.
15   Author interview with Polar Man, August 8, 2018.
16   Author interview with Ark Guard, November 6, 2017.
17   Author interview with Urban Knight, February 15, 2018.
18   Author interview with T.O. Ronin, March 3, 2018.
19   Robyn Doolittle, "Dundas-Sherbourne Ranks No. 1 in Violence," *Star*,
      September 1, 2009, https://www.thestar.com/news/gta/2009/09/01
      /dundassherbourne_ranks_no_1_in_violence.html.
20   Author interview with Nameless Crusader, February 27, 2018.
21   Heather Levi, *The World of Lucha Libre: Secrets, Revelations, and Mexican National
      Identity* (London: Duke University Press, 2008), 7.
22   Ibid., 78.
23   Ibid., 23.
24   Ibid., 190.
25   Author interview with Luis Coronado Guel, September 17, 2018.
26   Gustavo Martinez Contreras, "Mexico Honors Its Greatest Wrestler, El Santo,
      at Centennial," *Associated Press*, September 24, 2017, https://www.denverpost.com
      /2017/09/24/mexico-honors-greatest-wrestler-el-santo/.
27   Despite his over-the-top portrayal, I personally feel Black deserved an Oscar for
      how firmly he committed to the buffoonish-yet-lovable title character.
28   Tim Vandenack, "Mexican Hero Seeks U.S. Presidency," UPI, March 20, 1996,
      https://www.upi.com/Archives/1996/03/20/Mexican-hero-seeks-us-presidency
      /5380827298000/.
29   Author interview with Marco Rascón, December 13, 2018.
30   Author interview with Peatonito, September 18, 2018.
31   Author interview with Tacubo, November 15, 2018.
32   Author interview with Ian Hodgkinson, February 20, 2019.
33   Both Guardian Angels and professional wrestlers are known for being a bit lib-
      eral with their version of the truth, so their comments should be taken with a
      grain of salt.

CHAPTER 8

1   Johannes Harnischfeger, "State Decline and the Return of Occult Powers: The
      Case of Prophet Eddy in Nigeria," *Magic, Ritual and Witchcraft*, 1, 2006, 56–78.
2   Kate Meagher, "Hijacking Civil Society: The Inside Story of the Bakassi Boys
      Vigilante Group of South-Eastern Nigeria," *The Journal of Modern African Studies*,
      45(1), 2007, 89–115.
3   "The Bakassi Boys: The Legitimization of Murder and Torture," *Human Rights
      Watch*, 14(5) (A), 2002.

4   Meagher, "Hijacking Civil Society."

5   Ade Adesomoju, "Supreme Court Affirms Death Penalty Imposed on Three Bakassi Boys," *Punch*, July 7, 2018, https://punchng.com/supreme-court-affirms -death-penalty-imposed-on-three-bakassi-boys/.

6   "Exposed: Bakassi Boys, the Militia Group Being Bred by Gov Yahaya Bello," *Sahara Reporters*, December 19, 2018, http://saharareporters.com/2018/12/19 /exposed-bakassi-boys-militia-group-being-bred-gov-yahaya-bello.

7   Felix Moses Edoho, "Entrepreneurialism: Africa in Transition," *African Journal of Economic and Management Studies*, 6(2), 2015, https://www.emeraldinsight.com/doi/ full/10.1108/AJEMS-03-2015-0038.

8   Teo Kermeliotis and Milena Veselinovic, "The Numbers That Show Africa Is Buzzing with Entrepreneurial Spirit," CNN, June 10, 2014, http://edition.cnn.com /2014/05/13/business/numbers-showing-africa-entrepreneurial-spirit /index.html.

9   "World's Fastest Growing Economies in 2018 & 2019," *Global Macro Monitor*, October 9, 2018, https://global-macro-monitor.com/2018/10/09/54833/.

10 Yomi Kazeem, "Startup Investment in Africa Jumped to Record Levels in 2018 as Later Stage Rounds Rose," *Quartz Africa*, January 11, 2019, https://qz.com/africa /1520173/african-startups-funding-in-2018-broke-records/.

11 Author interview with Charl Viljoen, December 19, 2018.

12 George L. Kelling and James Q. Wilson, "Broken Windows: The Police and Neighborhood Safety," *The Atlantic*, March 1982, https://www.theatlantic.com /magazine/archive/1982/03/broken-windows/304465/.

13 Ben Kharakh, "Curtis Sliwa, Founder of Guardian Angels and Radio Personality," *Gothamist*, June 5, 2007, http://gothamist.com/2007/06/05/curtis_sliwa_fo.php.

14 "The List: Murder Capitals of the World," *Foreign Policy*, September 29, 2008, https://foreignpolicy.com/2008/09/29/the-list-murder-capitals-of-the-world/ and "Violent Crime Is Soaring in Cape Town," *The Economist*, October 4, 2018, https://www.economist.com/graphic-detail/2018/10/04/violent-crime-is-soaring -in-cape-town.

15 Paul Vecchiatto and Mike Cohen, "South Africa's Murder Rate Climbs as Police 'Drop the Ball,'" *Bloomberg*, September 11, 2018, https://www.bnnbloomberg.ca /south-africa-s-murder-rate-climbs-as-police-drop-the-ball-1.1135855.

16 Zoah Hedges-Stockes, "African Audiences Are Having a Very Emotional Response to Black Panther: 'We Were Humanised, and that Matters,'" *The Telegraph*, February 21, 2018, https://www.telegraph.co.uk/films/2018/02/21 /african-audiences-having-emotional-response-black-panther-humanised/.

17 Author interview with Jide Martin, December 14, 2018.

18 "Internet Users in the World by Geographic Regions," *Internet World Stats*, March 31, 2019, https://www.internetworldstats.com/stats.htm.

19   Alphonce Shiundu, "More Must Happen," *Development and Cooperation*,
     July 2, 2018, https://www.dandc.eu/en/article/literacy-rates-have-risen-sub
     -saharan-africa-reality-probably-worse-official-numbers-suggest.

20   Kazeem Ugbodaga, "Lagos Records 837 Violent Deaths in 2016—Report," PM
     News, December 10, 2017, https://www.pmnewsnigeria.com/2017/12/10/lagos
     -records-837-violent-death-2016-report/.

21   Ibid.

22   Catherine Soi, "'Superheroes of Kibera' Inspiring Kenyan Children to Success,"
     Al Jazeera, March 16, 2018, https://www.aljazeera.com/news/2018/03/superheroes
     -kibera-inspiring-kenyan-children-success-180316143132893.html.

23   Author interview with Steve Kyenze, February 21, 2019.

CHAPTER 9

1   Author patrol with Master Legend, June 8, 2018.

2   Some people might call these powers simple intuition and adrenaline.

3   Campbell, Joseph, *The Hero with a Thousand Faces*. New World Library, 2008.
     pg. 23.

4   Author interview with Superhero, August 7, 2018.

5   Author interview with Zero, December 5, 2018.

6   *Superheroes*, Superfilms!, 2011.

7   Author interview with Skyman, March 6, 2018.

8   Author interview with Dark Defender, September 4, 2018.

9   Author interview with Impact, March 5, 2018.

10   Author interview with Knight Warrior, June 24, 2018.

11   Fishwick, "Fighting Crime, Battling Injustice," 352.

12   Author interview with Elaine Fishwick, December 6, 2018.

13   Author interview with Ikon, May 2, 2018.

14   Author interview with Good Samaritan, March 22, 2018.

15   Author interview with Carl Potts, January 21, 2019.

16   Author interview with Ty Templeton, December 5, 2018.

17   Sue Adkins, "Cause-Related Marketing: Who Cares Wins," from *The Marketing
     Book*, 5th ed., Michael J. Baker, ed. (Oxford: Butterworth Heinemann, 2003), 670.

18   Fritz Jellinghaus, "Business Forum: Doubts About Cause-Related Marketing;
     Profits Have a Place in Philanthropy," *The New York Times*, March 29, 1987,
     https://www.nytimes.com/1987/03/29/business/business-forum-doubts-about
     -cause-related-marketing-profits-have-place.html.

19   "Sponsorship Spending Growth Slows in North America as Marketers Eye Newer
     Media and Marketing Options," *sponsorship.com*, January 7, 2014,
     http://www.sponsorship.com/iegsr/2014/01/07/Sponsorship-Spending-Growth

-Slows-In-North-America.aspx?utm_source=twitter&utm_medium=referral&utm
_content=tweet&utm_campaign=iegsrTweet#.UtBkbmRDscJ.

20   Monaem Ben Lellahom, "Cause-Related Marketing: A Win-Win for Brands,
     Charities and the Consumer," *Entrepreneur*, July 18, 2017, https://www.entrepreneur
     .com/article/297333.

21   Erica Johnson, "Bell's 'Let's Talk' Campaign Rings Hollow for Employees Suffering
     Panic Attacks, Vomiting and Anxiety," CBC *News*, November 25, 2017, https://www
     .cbc.ca/news/health/bell-employees-stressed-by-sales-targets-1.4418876.

22   Greg Rucka, "Keep 'Man of Steel' PG: A Comic Writer's Plea," *The Hollywood
     Reporter*, April 29, 2013, https://www.hollywoodreporter.com/heat-vision/greg
     -rucka-a-pg-man-448386.

23   Stephen Skelton, *The Gospel According to the World's Greatest Superhero*
     (Eugene, OR: Harvest House Publishers, 2006), 89.

24   Other writers later added "and the American way" to that motto.

25   Brian Trutt, "Why Superman Is the Greatest American Hero," USA *Today*, June 13,
     2013, https://www.usatoday.com/story/life/movies/2013/06/13
     /superman-75th-anniversary/2368055/.

26   "Psychological Egoism," *Internet Encyclopedia of Philosophy*, retrieved on
     May 6, 2019, https://www.iep.utm.edu/psychego/.
     Also, did anyone bother to rescue Michael or Dwight?

27   "Altruism," *Stanford Encyclopedia of Philosophy*, August 25, 2016, https://plato
     .stanford.edu/entries/altruism/.

28   Daniel Batson et al., "Is Empathic Emotion a Source of Altruistic Motivation?"
     Journal of Personality and Social Psychology, 40(2), 1981, 290–302.

29   Dieneke Hubbeling, "Altruism in Humans," *Evolutionary Psychology*, 10(2), 2012,
     95–99, https://pdfs.semanticscholar.org/4011/7f15b791482a178fd001ef308d3
     d0e4756eb.pdf.

30   Megan Filkowski et al., "Altruistic Behavior: Mapping Responses in the Brain,"
     Neuroscience and Neuroeconomics, 2016, 65–75.

31   *Superheroes*, Superfilms!, 2011.

32   *The Adventures of Miss Fit*, Llama Pictures, 2016.

33   Author interview with Canadian Justice, April 13, 2017.

34   Author interview with Jaguar, March 24, 2018.

35   Author interview with Dusk Citizen, September 27, 2018.

36   Author interview with Andrea Kuszewski, November 19, 2018.

37   Author interview with Tamerlane, December 6, 2018.

38   Author interview with Zimmer, February 22, 2018.

39   Author interview with Rock N Roll, August 15, 2018.

40   Author interview with Elaine Fishwick, December 6, 2018.

CHAPTER 10

1   Author interview with Michael Barnett, December 13, 2018.

2   Daniel White et al., "Look Up in the Sky: Latent Content Analysis of the Real Life Superhero Community," *The Qualitative Report*, 21(2), 2016, 178–95.

3   Krulos, *Heroes in the Night*, location 3309.

4   Weldon, *The Caped Crusade*, 217.

5   Kelly Weill, "New York City's Real-Life Superhero Civil War," *Daily Beast*, May 16, 2016, https://www.thedailybeast.com/new-york-citys-real-life-superhero-civil-war.

6   Author interview with Ikon, April 1, 2019.

7   Author interview with Impact, April 5, 2019.

8   Author interview with Zimmer, February 22, 2018.

9   Author interview with Geist, November 6, 2017.

10   Author interview with Good Samaritan, March 22, 2018.

11   At least with today's technology. With a few more decades of genetic engineering, all bets are off.

12   Author interview with Purple Lotus, December 6, 2018.

13   Author interview with Zero, December 5, 2018.

14   Visit on January 6, 2019. Interview on October 5, 2018.

15   Yes, this really is a thing.

16   Author interview with Brampton Batman, December 17, 2018.

17   Author interview with Ivan Wilzig, October 10, 2019.

18   Author interview with Athena Finger, December 11, 2018.

19   Richard Florida, "The Great Crime Decline and the Comeback of Cities," *CityLab*, January 16, 2018, https://www.citylab.com/life/2018/01/the-great-crime-decline-and-the-comeback-of-cities/549998/.

20   "2018 Global Law and Order," *Gallup*, 2018.

21   Author interview with Peter Tangen, March 1, 2017.

22   Author interview with Denise Masino, December 10, 2018.

23   Author interview with James Marx, November 9, 2018.

24   Tom Jacobs, "Superman May Inspire Altruistic Behavior," *Pacific Standard*, November 27, 2018, https://psmag.com/economics/why-superman-may-inspire-altruistic-behavior.

25   Morrison, *Supergods*, 399 and 414.

INDEX

The acronym **INS** indicates a photo in the insert after page 132.